LIBRARY OF NEW TESTAMENT STUDIES

560

Formerly the Journal for the Study of the New Testament Supplement Series

Editor
Chris Keith

Editorial Board
Dale C. Allison, John M.G. Barclay, Lynn H. Cohick,
R. Alan Culpepper, Craig A. Evans, Robert Fowler, Simon J. Gathercole,
John S. Kloppenborg, Michael Labahn, Love L. Sechrest,
Robert Wall, Steve Walton, Catrin H. Williams

This book is for E.--
With heartfelt thanks for your unstinting generosity,
and gratitude for your ever-present companionship on life's highway.

HOLY TERROR

Jesus in the Infancy Gospel of Thomas

J.R.C. Cousland

Bloomsbury T&T Clark
An imprint of Bloomsbury Publishing Plc

BLOOMSBURY
LONDON • OXFORD • NEW YORK • NEW DELHI • SYDNEY

Bloomsbury T&T Clark
An imprint of Bloomsbury Publishing Plc
Imprint previously known as T&T Clark

50 Bedford Square	1385 Broadway
London	New York
WC1B 3DP	NY 10018
UK	USA

www.bloomsbury.com

BLOOMSBURY, T&T CLARK and the Diana logo are trademarks of Bloomsbury Publishing Plc

First published 2018

© J.R.C. Cousland, 2018

J.R.C. Cousland has asserted his right under the Copyright, Designs and Patents Act, 1988, to be identified as Author of this work.

All rights reserved. No part of this publication may be reproduced or transmitted in any form or by any means, electronic or mechanical, including photocopying, recording, or any information storage or retrieval system, without prior permission in writing from the publishers.

No responsibility for loss caused to any individual or organization acting on or refraining from action as a result of the material in this publication can be accepted by Bloomsbury or the author.

British Library Cataloguing-in-Publication Data
A catalogue record for this book is available from the British Library

ISBN: HB: 978-0-5676-6816-5
ePDF: 978-0-5676-6817-2
ePub: 978-0-5676-6818-9

Library of Congress Cataloging-in-Publication Data
Names: Cousland, J. R. C., author.
Title: Holy terror: Jesus in the infancy Gospel of Thomas / by J.R.C. Cousland.
Description: New York: Bloomsbury T&T Clark, 2017. | Includes bibliographical references and index.
Identifiers: LCCN 2017032155 (print) | LCCN 2017039276 (ebook) | ISBN 9780567668172 (epdf) | ISBN 9780567668165 (hb : alk. paper)
Subjects: LCSH: Gospel of Thomas (Infancy Gospel)–Criticism, interpretation, etc.
Classification: LCC BS2860.T42 (ebook) | LCC BS2860.T42 C68 2017 (print) | DDC 229/.806–dc23
LC record available at https://lccn.loc.gov/2017032155

Typeset by Deanta Global Publishing Services, Chennai, India
Printed and bound in Great Britain

CONTENTS

Preface	vii
Abbreviations	x

Chapter 1
INTRODUCTION — 1
1.1 An Overview of the *Paidika* — 2
1.2 Textual Background — 3
1.3 Original Language — 6
1.4 Date — 7
1.5 Setting and Place of Composition — 12
1.6 Authorship — 13
1.7 Genre — 14
1.8 Historicity and Fiction — 18

Chapter 2
JESUS THE HOLY TERROR — 23
2.1 Literary Ineptitude? — 24
2.2 Jesus as an Intolerant Jewish Holy Man — 25
2.3 The *Paidika* as Children's Story — 28
2.4 The *Paidika* as an Anti-Christian Document — 30
2.5 Jesus as a Developing Child — 32
2.6 The Graeco-Roman Context of the *Paidika* — 33
2.7 Jesus and Infancy Narratives of the Olympians — 39
2.8 Humour in the *Paidika* — 43
2.9 Why Is Jesus Portrayed as a Killer? — 45

Chapter 3
JESUS THE CHILD — 49
3.1 Jesus the Child — 49
3.2 Jesus as *Wunderkind* — 52
3.3 Jesus as an 'Ideal Child' — 54
3.4 The Holy Terror as Divine Child — 58
3.5 A Child Reprehensible to Man and God? — 60
3.6 Childhood Development — 63
3.7 Jesus's Development — 66
3.8 Jesus the Divine Child — 70
3.9 Why Jesus the Child? — 73

Chapter 4
JESUS THE DIVINE: THE CHRISTOLOGY OF THE *PAIDIKA* — 75
- 4.1 Luke 2:41-51 — 76
- 4.2 The Gospel of John — 78
- 4.3 Jesus and Miracles — 81
- 4.4 Jesus and Nature Miracles — 83
- 4.5 Jesus and Punitive Miracles — 87
- 4.6 Jesus's Marvellous Teaching — 90
- 4.7 Jesus's Healings and Raisings from the Dead — 92
- 4.8 Gnosticism — 96
- 4.9 Docetism — 99
- 4.10 Ebionism — 100
- 4.11 The *Paidika*'s Christology — 102

Chapter 5
THE *PAIDIKA*'S JESUS IN CONTEXT — 105
- 5.1 The *Paidika*'s Audience — 105
- 5.2 The 'Great Church' — 109
- 5.3 Miracles and Agonism — 111
- 5.4 Popular Christianity — 115

Conclusion — 117
Bibliography — 121
Subject Index — 137
Index of Modern Authors — 140
Index of Ancient Authors — 142

PREFACE

Despite its established tradition in the English-speaking and scholarly world, I shall not use the title *The Infancy Gospel of Thomas* to describe the work under discussion, but refer to it instead as the *Paidika*.[1] There are solid justifications for this change in nomenclature. For one thing, the *Infancy Gospel of Thomas* is a modern title, which may have been first promulgated by Johann Albert Fabricius, who designated the work as *Evangelium Thomae* in his *Codex Apocryphus Novi Testamenti*.[2] Subsequent scholars followed his lead, and his influence is reflected in the work's designation in modern languages.[3] This designation, however, does not occur in the work itself, nor, in all likelihood, was it ever designated as such. Instead, it bore the name, *paidika* – the 'things (events, deeds) from the childhood (of the Lord)'.[4] As this traditional name is both descriptively apt and economical, it has rightly been proposed by various scholars as a more suitable title for the work.[5] This title has the added advantages of being the same in all modern scholarly languages, and of avoiding misleading connections with Thomasine literature.[6]

Two further points in its favour are that the *Paidika* is arguably not a gospel and that it has also been wrongly ascribed to Thomas. The designation of the *Paidika* as a 'gospel' is doubtful, and arose from references by patristic authors to a 'Gospel of Thomas', which were then interpreted by later readers as referring to the *Paidika*.[7] It was not until the emergence of the Coptic version of the Gospel of Thomas at Nag Hammadi that the two works were recognized as being distinct entities.

---

1. The first use of the title in English was by William Wright (1865), who entitled his translation of one of the Syriac versions of the *Paidika* 'The Gospel of Thomas the Israelite'. The first modern scholars to refer to the work as a Gospel of Thomas were Johann Albert Fabricius, *Codex Apocryphus Novi Testamenti* (1703), p. 129; Giovanni Luigi Mingarelli (1764), pp. 73–155; and Johann Karl Thilo (1832). Constantin Tischendorf's famous edition (1853; 1876) gave it scholarly currency as the *Evangelium Thomae*. See the discussions in Davis (2014), p. 235#16; Amsler (2011), pp. 433–4; Chatrand-Burke (2003), pp. 129–51.

2. Fabricius (1703), pp. 159–67.

3. In German, *Kindheitsevangelium;* in French, *Évangile de l'enfance selon Thomas*, and so on. The '*Infancy*' part of the title is a modern addition to distinguish the *Paidika* from the Coptic *Gospel of Thomas*. Cf. Hock (1995), pp. 84–5.

4. Klauck (2003), p. 73.

5. Davis (2014), p. 4; Van Oyen (2011), p. 482; Hock (1995), pp. 84–5.

6. Voicu (2011), p. 403; (1998), p. 7. As a case in point, see Landesmann (2010), pp. 2–3, who refers to the *Paidika* as the 'Thomas Evangelium'.

7. See the list of patristic references to a 'Gospel of Thomas' in Burke (2010), pp. 38–41.

By then, however, the designation had stuck, and confusion between the two works continues to take place, both in English and in other modern languages.[8]

Nor does the work ever describe itself as a gospel and, as will be shown in Chapter 1, there are substantial grounds for regarding it as being generically distinct from a gospel.[9] Given, therefore, that the title – the *Infancy Gospel of Thomas* – is essentially a misnomer in various respects, the work will be described here as the *Paidika*.[10]

One of the most determinative features of the *Paidika* is the sheer profusion of variants. Writing a book on the *Paidika*, therefore, immediately raises the question – 'Which *Paidika*?' My decision to write a monograph based chiefly on the eleventh-century, Greek manuscript Sabaiticus gr. 259 (=Gs) follows some of the reasoning advanced by Reidar Aasgaard, whose book also focuses primarily on Gs. As he observes, Gs is very close to the oldest texts attested in Latin and Syriac, and likely reflects a primitive form of the *Paidika*. Further, there is only one version of the Gs recension, which eliminates the problem of variant versions.[11]

Where possible, however, I have attempted to take account of alternative readings in the primitive Latin and Syriac versions to compare their renderings with Gs. As a result, my conclusions in this book will only pertain fully to one version of the *Paidika*, but it is hoped that some of the conclusions and inferences drawn here will cast light on other versions. I follow Aasgaard's 2010 Greek version of the *Paidika*, which is almost entirely based on Burke's 2010 edition.[12] References given with numbers only (e.g. 7.2) are to the *Paidika*; all other ancient texts are indicated. Greek and Latin translations are from the Loeb Classical Library unless otherwise indicated, and the biblical references are from the NRSV.

In this book, effort has been made to follow the designation of the *Paidika*'s pericopes suggested by Reidar Aasgaard (2010) in his Appendix 4 (pp. 245–7). For the sake of convenience, I address the author as 'he'. It is possible that the author of the *Paidika* may have been a woman, but given that the great preponderance of ancient authors were male, I presume that gender for the author of this work, too.

One cannot engage in research on *Paidika* today without being cognizant of the profound contributions made by Tony Burke.[13] His scholarship has laid solid foundations for anyone who wishes to write about the text. It will be clear to my

---

8. Voicu (2011), p. 403.

9. Only the Arabic infancy narrative calls itself a gospel: 'The Gospel of the Infancy' (*Arab. Gos. Inf.* Proem) cf. Gero (1971), p. 59.

10. See further, Davis (2014), pp. 21–6.

11. Aasgaard (2010), p. 34.

12. For the Greek text, see Aasgaard (2010), pp. 219–32; Asgaard's English translation is found on pages 233–42. For Burke's texts and translations of the various Greek versions, including Gs, see Burke (2010), pp. 300–539.

13. And before him, Sever Voicu. Tony Burke has published as Tony Burke and Tony Chartrand-Burke. When I refer to his works I use the form of the name under which he published the work in question.

readers just how much I have drawn from his works, and where I differ from him, just how much I remain indebted to his discussions. Much the same can be said for the substantial contributions of Reidar Aasgaard and Stephen Davis. Initial inspiration for my work came in part from an SBL paper proposal by David Litwa, and his later, perceptive remarks on the *Paidika* in *Iesus Deus* mesh with my own findings.[14] I would particularly like to thank Reidar Aasgaard, Jan Bremmer and Sakari Häkkinen for commenting on earlier drafts of this work, and most especially to Tony Burke for making a prepublication copy of *The Infancy Gospel of Thomas in the Syriac Tradition* available to me, and for his generous and careful reading of the entire manuscript, which saved me from a welter of errors. Thanks are also due to Kristi Upson-Saia for allowing me to piggyback on her apt title, 'Holy Terror'. Most of all I would like to thank my redoubtable editors James Hume and Dr Thomas Goud for their sterling advice and ever-insightful remarks.

Much of the research for this book was conducted in the Dalton McCaughey Library associated with the University of Melbourne. I would especially like to thank them for making their outstanding facilities available to me, and tender special thanks to Professor David Sim of the Australian Catholic University for so generously arranging for me to come to ACU as a visiting scholar, and to Professor David Runia, past master of Queen's College, University of Melbourne, for welcoming me into the college as a member of the Senior Common Room.

Finally, I would like to acknowledge my long-standing appreciation to Dominic Mattos and Sarah Blake at Bloomsbury, and to Malavika Mariswamy, who did a fine job editing an ever-changing text. The indexes were admirably crafted by Yvette Haakmeester.

14. Cousland (2015), pp. 165–89.

ABBREVIATIONS

AB	Anchor Bible
ABD	*Anchor Bible Dictionary*
AcA	Antike christliche Apokryphen in deutscher Übersetzung
ACW	Ancient Christian Writers
ANRW	*Aufstieg und Niedergang der römischen Welt*
BDAG	Bauer, W., F. W. Danker, W. F. Arndt, and F. W. Gingrich, *Greek-English Lexicon of the New Testament and Other Early Christian Literature*
BIS	Biblical Interpretation Series
BJS	Brown Judaic Studies
CBQ	*Catholic Biblical Quarterly*
CCSA	Corpus Christianorum Series Apocryphorum
CRINT	Compendia rerum iudaicarum ad Novum Testamentum
EDNT	*Exegetical Dictionary of the New Testament*
FC	Fathers of the Church
Ga	Greek Recension A (mss W V P BDML)
Gb	Greek Recension B (mss S C)
Gd	Greek Recension D (mss A T R)
Greek A	Greek Manuscript A, Athens, *Cod. Ath. gr. 355* (15th cent.)
Greek B	Greek Manuscript B, Bologna, *Univ. 2702* (15th cent.)
Gs	Greek Recension S (ms H) = Sabaiticus gr. 259
HDR	Harvard Dissertations in Religion
HTR	*Harvard Theological Review*
IGT	*Infancy Gospel of Thomas*
JECS	*Journal of Early Christian Studies*
JSHJ	*Journal for the Study of the Historical Jesus*
JSNT	*Journal for the Study of the New Testament*
JSNTSS	Journal for the Study of the New Testament Supplement Series
JRS	*Journal of Roman Studies*
JTS	*Journal of Theological Studies*
LCL	Loeb Classical Library
LIMC	*Lexicon iconographicum mythologiae classicae*
LNTS	Library of New Testament Studies
LSJ	Liddell, H. G., R. Scott, and H. S. Jones, *A Greek English Lexicon*. New Ed. Oxford, 1983
LXX	Septuagint
NHMS	Nag Hammadi and Manichean Studies
NovT	*Novum Testamentum*
NovTSup	Novum Testamentum Supplement Series

NTS	*New Testament Studies*
NTTS	New Testament Tools and Studies
OCD	*Oxford Classical Dictionary (4th Ed)*
OT	Old Testament
PG	Patrologia Graeca. Edited by J. P. Migne, 162 vols. Paris, 1857-86.
PGL	*Patristic Greek Lexicon*. Edited by G. W. H. Lampe, Oxford, 1968.
PTS	Patristische Texte und Studien
RAC	*Reallexikon für Antike und Christentum*
RHE	*Revue d'histoire ecclésiastique*
SBLTT	Society of Biblical Literature Texts and Translations
SBS	Stuttgarter Bibelstudien
SCH	Studies in Church History
SHR	Studies in the History of Religions
STAC	Studies and Texts in Antiquity and Christianity
SNTSMS	Society for New Testament Studies Monograph Series
TANZ	Texte und Arbeiten zum neutestamentlichen Zeitalter
TDNT	*Theological Dictionary of the New Testament*
TJT	*Toronto Journal of Theology*
TRE	*Theologische Realenzyclopädie*. Edited by G. Krause and G. Müller. Berlin, 1977-
TSAJ	Texte und Studium zum antiken Judentum
TU	Texte und Untersuchungen
VC	*Vigiliae Christianae*
VCSup	Vigiliae Christianae Supplement Series
WUNT	Wissenschaftliche Untersuchungen zum Neuen Testament

Chapter 1

INTRODUCTION

The *Paidika* is one of the best-known works of the early Christian Apocrypha, and certainly one of the most puzzling.[1] While it contains entrancing episodes such as when the young Jesus fashions sparrows out of clay and brings them to life with a clap of his hands (2.2-4), it also contains disturbing narratives such as when Jesus kills other children for trifling offences (Chs. 3 and 4). At one moment he is dutifully helping Mary and Joseph with their chores (Chs. 10-12), but in the next, he is gamely killing one of his teachers (Ch. 13). These contradictory characterizations of Jesus are difficult to reconcile, especially when they are compared with the Jesus of the canonical Gospels.[2]

The purpose of this book, therefore, is to address this problem and examine the figure of Jesus in the *Paidika* in more detail. Now that many of the textual difficulties associated with the work have begun to be resolved, the problems of Jesus's identity have deservedly come to the fore. The child Jesus is central to the *Paidika*'s narrative, and the significance of the work as a whole is indissolubly linked with how he should be interpreted. As will become evident in the

---

1. The standard edition of New Testament (or Early Christian) Apocrypha in English is the revised edition of Hennecke and Schneemelcher (1991). The new German edition of early Christian gospels by Markschies and Schröter appeared in 2012, and a volume of additional apocrypha in English by Burke and Landau (2016) has just been published. For recent discussion of the nature and character of apocryphal gospels see Bockmuehl (2017), pp. 31–51; S. Pellegrini (2012), pp. 886–902 and for early Christian Apocrypha as a whole, Tuckett (2015), pp. 3–11; J. K. Elliott (2013), pp. 455–78; Markschies and Schröter (2012), pp. 104–14; J. K. Elliott (2011), pp. 145–59; S. Gero (1998), pp. 3969–96.

2. It is probable that the *Paidika* was written and disseminated before the New Testament Gospels were formally canonized in the fourth century. Hence it is technically misleading to describe them as 'canonical' in discussions about the *Paidika*'s relation to them. On the other hand, it is extremely awkward to write 'the Gospels that were to become canonical' repeatedly. For what follows, therefore, I will refer to the 'canonical Gospels', recognizing full well that this designation is anachronistic. Nevertheless, it is widely recognized that before being formally canonized the four Gospels already possessed an acknowledged authority in the proto-orthodox church. Cf. Irenaeus, *Adv. Haer.* 3.11.8.

next chapter, Jesus's contradictory demeanour – both as a holy terror and as a benevolent son of God – has occasioned much scholarly discussion, but as yet has not been satisfactorily resolved.[3] This book sets out to revisit the question, and also endeavours to examine the portrayal of the child Jesus in more depth. After an introductory chapter, it will consider the *Paidika*'s figure of Jesus from three perspectives, devoting a chapter to each: Jesus the holy terror, Jesus the child and Jesus the divine. It will close with a summary chapter that explores the possible contexts of the *Paidika*.

1.1 An Overview of the Paidika

The narrative of the Gs version of the *Paidika* opens with a prologue (Ch. 1), where 'Thomas the Israelite' recounts, for the benefit of the gentile brethren, the childhood deeds performed by Jesus after he was born in the 'region of Bethlehem, in the village of Nazareth' (1.1). Jesus's first recorded deed occurs when he is five: he collects water into pools on the bank of a stream and purifies it with a word (Ch. 2). Next he fashions twelve sparrows out of mud. But because this deed is performed on a Sabbath, a Pharisee condemns Jesus to his father Joseph. Thereupon Jesus claps his hands, and the sparrows come to life and fly away (Ch. 2). At this point, the son of Annas, the High Priest, condemns Jesus for breach of the Sabbath and dries up the pools. Jesus retaliates by drying him up so that he withers and dies (Ch. 3). Jesus then curses another child who bumps into him. This child dies, too, and the child's parents decry Jesus's actions, complaining to Joseph that Jesus needs to learn how to bless and not to curse (Ch. 4). Joseph rebukes Jesus, but Jesus still blinds the child's parents, and is impervious to Joseph's recriminations – even Joseph's yanking on his ear (Ch. 5).

The next major episodes introduce the education of Jesus, where Joseph takes him to the teacher Zacchaeus to learn the alphabet. Jesus tells the two of them that he pre-existed them both. When Zacchaeus asks Jesus to recite the alphabet, Jesus affirms that he is actually more familiar with it than Zacchaeus is, and reproaches him for not knowing the true meaning of the alpha. Jesus then substantiates his claim with an elaborately esoteric disquisition on the meaning of the alpha (Ch. 6). This exposition leaves Zacchaeus totally humiliated, and wondering about Jesus's true nature – whether he was a god, an angel or something else (Ch. 7). It is at this point that Jesus becomes mindful of his heavenly calling and decides to undo his previous curses (Ch. 8).

Jesus is next described as playing with other children on the roof of a house when one of them – Zeno – falls and dies. Zeno's parents accuse Jesus of having killed him, but Jesus denies the charge and restores him to life so that Zeno can assure his parents of Jesus' own innocence. After Jesus tells Zeno to 'fall asleep',

---

3. The phrase 'holy terror' is not one that occurs in the *Paidika*, but which is used here as a convenient designation for Jesus's 'unchristian' and antisocial behaviour – particularly when he kills or harms other people. Cf. Upson-Saia (2013).

Zeno's parents glorify God and worship (προσεκύνησαν) Jesus (Ch. 9). Jesus then embarks on a series of errands for his parents: he brings home water for Mary in his cloak when the pitcher breaks (Ch. 10); he helps his father sow a crop of grain and distributes the miraculous harvest to the poor (Ch. 11); and he extends a board that is too short so that Joseph can use it to fashion a bed for a wealthy customer. Jesus's assistance prompts Joseph to kiss and embrace him, blessing God for giving him such a child (Ch. 12).

The narrative then returns to Jesus's education, with Jesus seeing another teacher who, again, wants him to recite the alphabet, beginning with alpha. Jesus responds, 'You tell me first what beta is, and I will tell you what alpha is' (Ch. 13). When the second teacher strikes Jesus for his impudence, Jesus retaliates by cursing and killing him (Ch. 13). Afterward, Jesus is sent to a third teacher who listens to him gladly and praises his abundant grace and wisdom. Jesus rewards him by restoring the second teacher to life (Ch. 14). Jesus continues this programme of salvific actions by saving his brother James from death by snakebite (Ch. 15), and bringing a woodcutter back to life after he had bled to death from an axe wound (Ch. 16). The final episode in the *Paidika* is a retelling of Luke's narrative of Jesus's visit to the temple when he was twelve. The work concludes with the doxology: 'To him be the glory!' (Ch. 17).

1.2 Textual Background

Tony Burke's survey of *Paidika* research admirably recounts the 'rediscovery' of the work in the Renaissance and the various approaches taken by its early investigators.[4] Since the *Paidika* was often confused with what has now become known as the Gospel of Thomas, it was generally deemed to be a gnostic or heretical work. This supposition has continued up to the present day, and it was only with the discovery of the Gospel of Thomas and the Nag Hammadi Library that serious doubts about its heretical character began to surface. Much of this scholarly re-evaluation has been a direct consequence of the valuable work on the textual traditions of the *Paidika* that has been undertaken over the last few decades by Burke and others.

The textual background of the *Paidika* is a topic not to be approached lightly. Ehrman and Pleše remark that 'The so-called Infancy Gospel of Thomas presents some of the most intractable textual and historical problems of the entire corpus of early Christian literature.'[5] Helmut Koester adds, 'The variety of the available evidence in Greek manuscripts and in numerous translations [of the *Paidika*] is hopelessly confusing.'[6] If the abundance of versions was not sufficiently daunting,

---

4. Burke (2010), pp. 45–126; see further the additional surveys in Davis (2014), pp. 8–14; Aasgaard (2010), pp. 1–13.

5. Ehrman and Pleše (2011), p. 3.

6. Koester (1992), p. 311. Cf. Kaiser (2012), pp. 931–34; Burke (2010), pp. 127–71; Voicu (1998), p. 10#3. Ehrman and Pleše (2011), p. 3.

the problem is further compounded by the significant number of manuscripts in various languages that continue to await proper editing and translation.[7]

Also problematic are those versions of the *Paidika* that have been widely circulated, but that are based on late and inferior manuscripts.[8] This is especially true of Tischendorf's 1853 publication of Greek and Latin editions of the text, which have proved to be enduring and influential.[9] These editions have served as the basis for most of the modern translations and editions that have appeared in the last century and a half.[10] Reliance on Tischendorf's editions has continued up until the present day, and for some moderns, Tischendorf's longer recension (Ga) of nineteen chapters effectively *is* the *Paidika*.[11]

In their recent edition of apocryphal gospels, for instance, Ehrman and Pleše contend that Tischendorf's 'fuller' version of the infancy narrative is of greater interest to contemporary readers than the earlier, succinct editions: not only is it more detailed, but also includes episodes not found in earlier versions, and displays strengthened characterization.[12] If, however, one is interested in establishing the earliest versions of the *Paidika*, then Tischendorf's editions are not especially useful.[13]

Fortunately, a number of scholars have recently begun to address these problems, and to contend with the various difficulties just noted. The pioneering work of Gero and Voicu and the recent monumental edition of the Greek *Paidika* by Tony Burke have done much to resolve these problems of transmission. All three scholars provide stemmata of the *Paidika*'s textual tradition, and even if they differ on some of the details, they offer a relatively consistent picture.[14] One of the

---

7. Kaiser (2012), pp. 931–33; Burke (2010), p. 45; Chartrand-Burke (2003), pp. 148–50.

8. Voicu (1998), p. 11. Greek A has a major lacuna in Chapter 6 amounting to 15 per cent of the entire *Paidika*, while the text of Greek B has been abbreviated and epitomized; cf. Voicu (2004), p. 16.

9. On his selection of manuscripts, see Tischendorf (1853), pp. xliii–iv. His Greek A (=Ga) version is based on four manuscripts: two are fragmentary (Paris *A.F. gr. 239* [=P] containing chs. 1–6) and Vienna, *Phil. gr. 162* (=O, now lost) and two are 'twin' manuscripts (Bologna, *Univ. 2702* [=B] and Dresden, *A 187* [=D]). Tischendorf's Greek B (=Gb) is based on a single abbreviated and rewritten manuscript (*Cod. Sinai gr. 453*). All of Tischendorf's manuscripts likely date from the fifteenth century or later. See further Chartrand-Burke (2003), pp. 130–1; Voicu (1991), p. 125.

10. They include Ehrman and Pleše (2011), Hock (1995), Schneider (1995), Elliott (1993), and Cullmann (1991). For lists of others, see Chartrand-Burke (2003), p. 131#10; Voicu (1998), p. 10#3.

11. Voicu (1998), p. 10 rightly remarks that they have attained a 'sort of canonization', though he also describes this canonization as a 'disastro sotto il profile filologico' (p. 9).

12. Ehrman and Pleše (2011), pp. 4–5.

13. Sheingorn (2012), pp. 273–4.

14. Burke (2010), p. 222; cf. Chartrand-Burke (2003), p. 145; Voicu (1998), p. 95; Voicu (1991), p. 132; Gero (1971), p. 56. See, further, Voicu's comments (2004), p. 16#15, on the stemma of Chartrand-Burke (2003), p. 145.

clearest features of the transmission history is that the text has evolved over time, changing and becoming more expansive and elaborate. The earliest versions reveal a basic core to the traditions, but later episodes become more fluid, shift position or disappear over time, with the general tendencies being accretion or assimilation with other infancy texts.[15] Later versions also demonstrate attempts to reduce the offensiveness of some of Jesus's actions.[16]

The earliest manuscripts date from the fifth or sixth century. These include a fragmentary Latin palimpsest from Vienna (5th C?)[17] and two Syriac manuscripts (6th C?).[18] Over the following centuries, apart from further Syriac and Latin manuscripts,[19] other versions appeared in Georgian,[20] Ethiopic,[21] Arabic,[22] Armenian,[23] Old Church Slavonic and a verse-form in Old Irish.[24] While the manuscripts of these versions tend to be late, the texts themselves date from centuries earlier, and largely agree with the form and content of the earliest Latin and Syriac manuscripts. The overall resemblance between this group of texts has, accordingly, given rise to the theory that there was originally a 'short recension' of the *Paidika* that featured briefer versions of the chapters than those found in Tischendorf's version, and which also omitted Tischendorf's Prologue (ch. 1) and his chapters 10, 17 and 18.[25]

Concrete evidence for 'expanded recensions' does not begin to emerge until the late eleventh century with the appearance of the earliest extant Greek manuscript (Sabaiticus Gr 259 = Gs), which adds a prologue and Tischendorf's chapter 10. Tischendorf's chapters 17 and 18 also begin to make their appearance, and it is these expanded versions that appear in his Greek A version and in the Old Church Slavonic.[26] A final stage of the textual tradition occurs with the incorporation of the so-called 'Egyptian Prologue' (Ch. 0: 1-9) into some Greek

---

15. Compare Aasgaard (2010), p. 30. On collections of Infancy Gospels, see Burke (2013b), pp. 52–3, Kaiser (2010), pp. 253–69; Vitz (2001), pp. 124–49.

16. Upson-Saia (2013), pp. 25–37.

17. Vienna *Vindob. 563*. See, further, Voicu (2004), pp. 13–21; Phillipart (1972), pp. 391–411. Two other versions in Latin are also extant; cf. Burke (2010), pp. 144–60.

18. Göttingen ms *Syr. 10* and Cod. *Brit. Mus. Add.* 14484. Cf. Horn and Phenix (2010), pp. 538–9; Baars and Helderman (1993), pp. 191–226; Wright (1865), pp. 6–16.

19. See Burke (forthcoming), pp. 25–112; (2016), pp. 53–6.

20. Burke (2010), pp. 168–9; Garitte (1956), pp. 513–20.

21. Abraha and Assafa (2010), pp. 629–33; cf. Grébaut (1919), pp. 554–652.

22. Horn (2010), pp. 592–7.

23. Burke (forthcoming), pp. 109–11.

24. Slavonic: Rosén (1997); Santos Otero (1967); Old Irish: McNamara (2010), pp. 723–5; McNamara et al. (2001), pp. 441–83.

25. Burke (2010), pp. 188–95, provides an overview of the 'short recension' (or 'short text') theory, and a synopsis of selected readings from the various manuscripts that appear to substantiate this 'short text' tradition.

26. Kaiser (2012), p. 934.

and Latin manuscripts.[27] The later Greek tradition also evidences an abridgement of the *Paidika* – Tischendorf's Greek B – which only contains eleven chapters and has eliminated most of Jesus's speeches.[28] One form or another of these 'expanded recensions' underlies most of the modern versions of the *Paidika* that have appeared since the fifteenth century.[29]

Burke argues that Greek S (Sabaiticus gr. 259 Jerusalem) – not Tischendorf's Greek texts A and B – best represents the original text: 'If read alongside the early versions, Greek S can be used to establish the original text of the IGT with some confidence.'[30] His assessment has been accepted by a number of recent scholars, with Aasgaard suggesting that it 'should be the requisite starting point for future study'. Though his recommendation has yet to find universal acceptance,[31] it will be adopted here.[32]

1.3 Original Language

Given the complicated textual background of the *Paidika*, its original language has been the topic of some dispute over the last century. The early provenance of the Syriac manuscripts led earlier scholars such as Peeters to suppose that the *Paidika* was composed in Syriac, and some more recent commentators continue to entertain this supposition.[33] While it is not possible to refute this hypothesis definitively,[34] Burke advances several solid arguments against it. One is that there are almost no early gospel-related texts that were not originally composed in

---

27. *Cod. Ath. gr. 355*. For the text, cf. Delatte (1927), pp. 24–5. On the Latin manuscripts, Voicu (2004), p. 17. The 'Egyptian Prologue' includes the flight into Egypt, Jesus's revivification of a salted fish, (yet another) conflict with a teacher, and his return to Nazareth. Burke (2010) contains an edition of Gd incorporating two additional manuscripts.

28. Burke (2010), pp. 140, 218–19.

29. Aasgaard (2010), pp. 248–51, provides a very useful overview of the versions, as well as the Greek variants.

30. Chartrand-Burke (2008b), p. 130.

31. Aasgaard (2010), p. 9#50; cf. Van Oyen (2011), pp. 484–5.

32. This entails excluding those parts of Tischendorf's chapters 17 and 18 not found in Codex H, as well as chapters 1 and 10, which are not found in the ancient versions. Cf. Davis (2014), p. 326#1.

33. Peeters (1914), vol. II, pp. xvii–xx. Burke (2010) notes that this theory was first posited by M. Nicolas shortly after Wright's (1865) publication of one of the earliest Syriac manuscripts. Schneider (1995), pp. 38–9 and Elliott (1993), p. 69, both leave open the possibility of Syriac as the original language.

34. Horn and Phenix (2010), p. 544, remark that the final word on the question has yet to be spoken. Burke's subsequent discussion (2013a), pp. 241–7, however, goes a long way towards doing just that.

Greek.³⁵ Second, he notes that translation from Syriac into Greek was very unusual in the early centuries of the Common Era.³⁶ Finally, he shows that the *Paidika*'s version of the pericope where Jesus teaches the elders in the temple, which has been adapted from Lk. 2.41-51, has far more affinities with manuscripts of Luke's Greek text than it does with any known Syriac versions of Luke.³⁷

These arguments make it likely that the *Paidika* was originally composed in Greek even if, somewhat paradoxically, the earliest Greek manuscript is late and dates from the eleventh century. The Greek archetype or archetypes would have been translated into Latin and Syriac, resulting in our earliest manuscripts of the work. It was then translated into a host of different languages as Christianity expanded.³⁸

1.4 Date

The dating of the *Paidika* is based on various criteria, and continues to be disputed. The work's extensive reliance on Lk. 2.41-52 means that it must post-date Luke's Gospel (90 CE?), while the dates of the earliest manuscripts indicate that it was extant by the fifth or sixth century CE. Within this 400-year span most scholars tend to prefer a second-century date, although they often differ over whether the work existed in whole or in part.³⁹

One criterion for the dating is the general character of the work. It is often thought that it would not have taken long for gaps in Jesus's story to be filled in, as happened, for instance, with the *Protevangelium of James*, which is usually dated to the second half of the second century.⁴⁰ Paul Achtemeier has noted that the Christian apocryphal writings tend to demonstrate a creative phase not long after the appearance of the canonical Gospels, that was then followed by a phase where the traditions underwent a form of hardening.⁴¹ Since the miracles

---

35. Chartrand-Burke notes that only *Gospel of the Hebrews* and *Gospel of the Nazareans* are thought to have been composed in a Semitic language (2008b), p. 132#24.

36. Burke (2010), pp. 175–8.

37. Burke (2013a), p. 247 and (2010), pp. 182–8.

38. While agreeing with the hypothesis of a Greek archetype, Voicu (1998), pp. 19–23 and (2011), p. 405, argues that the Ethiopic versions are the best witness to the original Greek versions. His theory, however, has not been widely accepted; cf. Abraha and Assefa (2010), pp. 632–3; Chartrand-Burke (2003), pp. 146–7.

39. For the second century: Aasgaard (2010), p. 30; Burke (2013b), p. 49; Van Aarde (2013), p. 615; Voicu (2011), p. 405; Koester (1992), p. 311; Mirecki (1992), p. 540 (cf. p. 542); Cullmann (1991), p. 442. By contrast, Gero (1971), p. 56#1 and Amsler (2011), p. 457, would date it to the fourth century.

40. Ehrman and Pleše (2011), p. 5. For various estimates of the *Protevangelium*'s date, see the scholars listed in Van Oyen (2013), p. 274#15.

41. Achtemeier (2008), pp. 178, 218.

in the *Paidika* evidence this 'creative phase', they tend to support a second-century date.[42]

Allusions to the *Paidika* in other writings are limited and equivocal.[43] The earliest possible parallel occurs in Justin Martyr's *Dialogue with Trypho* (88.8), which dates to about 150 CE, and states that Jesus was a carpenter (τέκτονος) who used to make ploughs and yokes (ἄροτρα καὶ ζυγά). This Greek phrase has echoes of *Paidika* 12.1, which relates that Joseph was a carpenter (τέκτονος Gs) who made ploughs and yokes (ἄροτρα καὶ ζυγούς). While such echoes are suggestive, 'ploughs and yokes' could well be a stock phrase used to describe the typical products of a carpenter.[44]

More promising are references in the *Epistula Apostolorum* and Irenaeus's *Adversus Haereses* that are similar to Jesus's references to the alpha found in *Paidika* 6.9 and 13.1-2.[45] The *Paidika*'s two versions read as follows:

> When the child ceased from his anger, he skilfully recited all the letters from alpha to omega on his own. Looking clearly at the teacher he said, 'Not knowing the alpha according to its nature, how can you teach another the beta? Hypocrite! If you know, first teach me the alpha and then I will trust you to speak of the beta'. (6.9)

And:

> Joseph gave him over to another teacher. And the teacher wrote the alphabet for him and said, 'Say alpha.' And the child said, 'You tell me first what beta is, and I will tell you what alpha is'. (13.1-2)

Irenaeus reads:

> Besides those passages, they [the Marcosians] adduce an untold multitude of apocryphal and spurious writings (ἀποκρύφων καὶ νόθων γραφῶν), which they have composed, to bewilder foolish men and such as do not understand the letters of the Truth. For this purpose they adduce also this falsification (ῥᾳδιούργημα):

---

42. Voicu (2004), p. 13, further points out that the ideology of the work does not comport well with that of the fourth century.

43. See the overview of external evidence in Aasgaard (2010), p. 252. Burke (2010), pp. 3–44, and Voicu (1998), pp. 38–42, consider a number of other possible parallels in addition to those mentioned below.

44. Davis (2014), p. 248#135, notes that the phrase is used this way in the *Acts of Thomas* 3 and 17.

45. Compare *Pseudo-Matthew* 31.2; 38.1 and the *Arabic Infancy Gospel* 49, both of which are reliant on the *Paidika*. McNeil (1976), pp. 126–8 points to similarities with the story of Ahikar, but the underlying point of the two narratives is different.

When the Lord was a child and was learning the alphabet, his teacher said to him – as is customary – 'Pronounce alpha.' He answered: 'Alpha.' Again the teacher ordered him to pronounce 'Beta.' Then the Lord answered: 'You tell me first what alpha is, and then I shall tell you what beta is.' This they explain in the sense that he alone knew the unknown, which he revealed in the form of the alpha. (*Adv. Haer.* 1.20.1)[46]

The passage in the *Epistula Apostolorum* reads:

This is what our Lord Jesus Christ did, who was delivered by Joseph and Mary his mother to where he might learn letters. And he who taught him said to him, 'Say Alpha.' Then the Lord answered: and said to him, 'First you tell me what Beta is.' And truly (it was) a real thing which was done. (*Epist. Apost.* 4)[47]

Both Irenaeus and the *Epistula Apostolorum* date from the second century. Book I of Irenaeus's *Adversus Haereses* dates from the 180s or before, and the *Epistula Apostolorum* likely from the mid-second century or even earlier.[48] While the relation between all three texts is far from self-evident, there are good grounds for assuming that the *Epistula* is the oldest of the three.[49] It does not seem to be reliant upon the *Paidika*, and probably adopted its teaching episode from a floating piece of tradition.[50] Its account of the alpha is very simple, whereas those versions described in Irenaeus and the *Paidika* are substantially more complex.[51] And although the *Epistula*'s saying of Jesus is very close to that in Gs 13.1-2, the frame of the apothegm differs from the *Paidika* by its inclusion of Mary in the narrative. Moreover, it seems – in contrast to the *Paidika* – to stress only the young

---

46. Unger and Dillon (1992), p. 76.
47. Translation from Elliott (1993).
48. On Irenaeus: Behr (2013), p. 68. On the *Epistula Apostolorum*: Müller (2012), pp. 1064–5. Hill (1999), p. 51, postulates a timeframe from 117 to 148. For a helpful synopsis of the episodes, see Amsler (2011), pp. 438–9.
49. Baars and Helderman (1994), p. 4, maintain that Irenaeus's account is likely the oldest.
50. Amsler (2011), p. 437. On this question, Helmut Koester (1992), p. 311, seems to reverse his earlier view (1971), p. 202#150. Hills (1990), p. 51, concurs with Hornschuh (1965), p. 10 (cited in Hills [1990], p. 51#49) that the *Epistula* adopted the tradition from elsewhere. Contrast Burke (2013b), p. 93. Hannah's (2008), p. 627, supposition that the Marcosians' version of the narrative has been 'domesticated' by the *Epistula*'s author is not convincing.
51. Bovon (2002), p. 110#11. Moreover, the *Epistula*'s puzzling ending – 'And truly (it was) a real thing which was done' – could indicate that the *Epistula*'s author is constrained by his limited material, and attempts, not altogether successfully, to heighten the impact of Jesus's utterance.

Jesus's precocity, but not necessarily his divine insight.[52] Is this a feature that the *Epistula*'s author would have deliberately omitted?

If these observations carry weight, then it is more likely that the *Paidika* is reliant on the *Epistula* or depends on the same independent traditions that the *Epistula* drew upon. It is noteworthy, however, that Irenaeus's source(s) appears to be different. Apart from his evident hostility to the material,[53] the subject matter of the two accounts varies. In Irenaeus, Jesus demands an account of alpha, but in the *Epistula* he wants to know about the beta.[54] Significantly, the *Paidika* includes both variations (6.3; 13.1-2).

What is the relation, then, between Irenaeus's account of the Marcosians' 'falsification' and *Paidika* 6.3? First of all, there is probably a textual relation between the two. Both narratives are likely too elaborate to go back to an isolated apothegm or piece of floating tradition.[55] What is more, as Burke points out, there are extensive similarities between the two accounts that would seem to imply that the Marcosians' account was based on the *Paidika*'s version or something like it.[56] In particular, the Marcosians' reference to the 'unknown' seems to be a gnostic extrapolation of Jesus's 'arcane description of the alpha'.[57] It is, of course, possible that the *Paidika* is a 'domestication' of the Marcosian version, but it is fair to say that it was more common for proto-orthodox writings to be re-appropriated or refashioned by 'heretical' forms of Christianity than the reverse.[58]

If this inference has merit, then it bears upon the existence of the *Paidika* as a whole. It is sometimes suggested that even if the Marcosians were relying on this episode from the *Paidika*, it need not imply that the entire work existed in Irenaeus's day, but merely the section dealing with the alpha.[59] Yet, the teaching episodes in the *Paidika* (chs. 6, 13, 17) appear to be closely linked together: Jesus's demand for an explanation of the beta (13.2) follows logically on his demand for an explanation of the alpha (6.1). Likewise, the third teacher's praise results in Jesus choosing to revive his second teacher (although the revival is not present in the earliest versions), while details of Jesus's first teacher – such as his beating of Jesus – are consciously replicated in the second teacher episode. In turn, these

---

52. Hannah (2008), p. 627.

53. Hill (1999), p. 25.

54. It is important to note that the *Epistula Apostolorum* is avowedly anti-gnostic.

55. Amsler (2011), p. 437, and Gero (1971), pp. 63–4, both make this argument, but fail to account for the elaborate similarities between the two narratives.

56. Burke (2010), p. 5.

57. Burke (2010), p. 5. It may be that the Marcosians take the alpha to stand for ἄγνωστον – that is, everything in the cosmos that is unknown and unrevealed, and known only to Jesus the heavenly revealer. Beta (or gamma?) on this reading would then signify the known world. Jesus's teacher is ignorant of the first elements (=letters) and principles that are foundational for everything else.

58. Voicu (1998), p. 49.

59. Kaiser (2012), p. 936.

teaching episodes prefigure Jesus's meeting with the elders in the Temple. As the Temple episode is sometimes thought to be the pericope around which the *Paidika* crystallized, it too was very likely early.[60] At the very least one would have the alpha narrative and the Temple narratives, which already furnish the core of the *Paidika*. After this, it would not have needed much time to append other episodes, such as the interrelated narratives of Chapters 2–5 or the domestic miracles (chs. 10–12).[61] Other episodes – Zeno (9.1-3), James's snakebite (15.1-2), the healing of an injured foot (16.1) – could readily be added on, as we know happened with later versions (cf. the raising of a dead baby, and of a labourer in Ga, chs. 17–18). If these episodes were extant, then a great part – if not all – of the *Paidika* could have come to exist some time before 180 CE.[62]

More explicit references are to be found in two fourth-century works: Epiphanius of Salamis's *Panarion* and Chrysostom's Homily 17 on St John. While not unequivocal, both works have some strong points of contact. The *Panarion* (51.20.2-3) reads: 'John [sc. the evangelist] does not say that Christ ... had worked any of his miracles [before] he started preaching – except, perhaps, the ones he is said to have performed as a child. (3) (For he ought to have childhood miracles [παιδικὰ ... σημεῖα] too...).'[63]

Chrysostom states:

> In short, it is plain to us that those miracles which some ascribe to Christ's childhood (τὰ σημεῖα ἐκεῖνα, ἃ παιδικὰ εἶναί φασι τοῦ Χριστοῦ) are false, and merely products of the imagination of those who bring them to our attention. If he had worked miracles beginning from his early youth, neither would John [sc. the Baptist] have failed to recognize him, nor would the rest of the crowd have needed a teacher to reveal him.[64] (*Hom.* 17)

That the two passages share the words παιδικὰ and σημεῖα is revealing, and Voicu has argued that it is 'unequivocal' that this is a reference to the *Paidika*.[65] He may be slightly overstating the case, since Chrysostom's homily does not expressly mention any written text and could be referring to oral accounts. Nevertheless, it is

---

60. Klauck (2003), p. 73: 'This is the obvious nucleus from which the whole work has grown'.

61. By contrast, Gero (1971), pp. 63–4, would postulate a centuries-long 'tunnel period' in which this process occurred. Yet, there is no reason why this process could not have happened far more quickly. The rapid assemblage of the Sayings Source Q furnishes a very different analogue.

62. Burke (2013b), p. 133, is confident that the *Paidika* is Irenaeus's source.

63. Translation from Williams (2013), p. 46. The *Panarion* dates from ca. 375–80 CE.

64. Translation from Goggin (1969). She dates the homilies to 390 (p. xv), Burke (2010), p. 6, to between 386 and 398.

65. Voicu (1998), p. 41 'inequivocabile'; Burke (2010), p. 6 describes it as 'the earliest *certain* [my italics] temporal and geographical evidence for the text'.

certainly suggestive that both Chrysostom and Epiphanius should use the unusual word *paidika* to refer to Jesus's childhood miracles,[66] as this term is the very same one used in the later Greek prologues to describe the work. Both of the above accounts strongly suggest, therefore, that they actually had the *Paidika* in view. So, while the argument is not quite unequivocal, the balance of probability indicates that one or both authors are referring to the *Paidika*.[67]

All told, a strong case can be made for the existence of the *Paidika* in Irenaeus's day, and an even stronger one for the fourth century, and the following chapters will assume, along with many other scholars, that the *Paidika* is a second-century product.

1.5 Setting and Place of Composition

Various places of origin have been postulated for the *Paidika*, but certainty on this matter remains elusive. Proposed locales range from Alexandria to Asia Minor. Baars and Helderman, for instance, suggest Alexandria or Egypt, surmising that it was the likeliest place for Buddhist and Egyptian traditions to have influenced the *Paidika*.[68] The difficulty with their view is that there is no direct evidence that these traditions actually did have direct influence on the *Paidika*. Aasgaard suggests Asia Minor because the *Paidika* demonstrates familiarity with both Luke and John, and both these gospels were widely attested in second-century Asia Minor.[69] His surmise is certainly possible, but by the second century the 'canonical Gospels' had begun to be widely disseminated.

Palestine,[70] Edessa,[71] Syrian Antioch,[72] Eastern Syria,[73] Syria as a whole[74] or the Greek East of the Roman Empire[75] have all been proposed as possible places of composition. Lapham has suggested Edessa because there the 'Thomasine tradition was persistently robust'.[76] But, as will become evident below, the associations of Thomas with the *Paidika* are quite late. Hence, although 'the Greek East of the Roman Empire' is the least specific of these proposed alternatives, it is probably

---

66. Epiphanius, *Panarion* 51.20.2-3 (trans. Williams [2013] p. 46). Compare Migne *PG* 925 which has παιδαρικὰ. Burke (2010), p. 7, dates this reference to 376 CE.

67. Davis (2014), p. 252#170.

68. Baars and Heldermann (1994), pp. 3–4, 30; Conrady (1903), pp. 403–4.

69. Aasgaard (2010), p. 135; Burke (2010), 212.

70. Voicu (1997), p. 192; Bagatti (1976), p. 487.

71. Lapham (2003), p. 130.

72. Chartrand-Burke (2008b), p. 134, 'may'; Voicu (1998), p. 53.

73. Elliott (1993), p. 69.

74. Mirecki (1992), p. 542.

75. Bockmuehl (2017), p. 76; Ehrman and Pleše (2011), p. 5; Hock (1995), p. 90.

76. Lapham (2003), p. 130.

Introduction 13

the safest.[77] The work could readily have been produced in a semi-rural (or urban) context anywhere in the Greek East.[78] Syria is certainly a possibility, given the existence of the early Syriac manuscripts, but the fifth-century Latin palimpsest implies that early versions of the *Paidika* circulated widely throughout the empire, both in the east and west.

1.6 Authorship

One would anticipate that the authorship of a work commonly entitled the *Infancy Gospel of Thomas* would not be difficult to establish. Indeed, the work is explicitly attributed to Thomas in the work's prologue: 'I, Thomas the Israelite, deemed it necessary to make known to all the Gentile brethren the things our Lord Jesus Christ did' (1.1 Gb). But which Thomas the prologue refers to is by no means clear. Burke notes that in the broader textual tradition this Thomas is variously styled as an Israelite, an Ishmaelite, an apostle and a philosopher.[79] The later date of the prologue and confused testimony make attribution difficult.

To further complicate matters, the version of the *Paidika* that includes the 'Egyptian Prologue' (Gd) attributes the work to 'James the brother of the Lord',[80] who makes for an attractive candidate. Not only was he the reputed author of other biblical writings – notably, the epistle of James – but he was also a (presumed) eyewitness to Jesus's childhood deeds, as well as an actual recipient of one of Jesus's childhood healing miracles in the *Paidika* (15.1-2). Who better, then, to write of Jesus's childhood? When one further factors in James's role as the head of the Jerusalem church and his reputation for piety, it would be difficult to find a more authoritative early Christian figure to ascribe the *Paidika* to.

The problem with all of these identifications is that the earliest versions of the *Paidika* do not have a prologue. As was noted previously, the above prologues did not appear until the medieval period, and even then they were confined to certain strands of the textual tradition.[81] It is easy to see why these figures might have been selected at that time as possible authors. Since the actual Gospel of Thomas was unknown, the patristic references to a 'Gospel of Thomas' led some

---

77. Kaiser (2012), p. 936.

78. The social realities the *Paidika* reflects seem to suggest a semi-rural context. Aasgaard (2009), p. 68, speaks of a 'village', but, given the presence of 'two to four-storey' dwellings (p. 68), the setting of the *Paidika* is better described as a town.

79. Burke (2010), p. 205. Ehrman (2003), p. 206, boldly (if implausibly) suggests that the *Paidika* is 'a forgery in the name of Jesus' reputed brother, Thomas'.

80. Yet another textual tradition mentions John the evangelist and apostle; Burke (2010), p. 205.

81. Davis (2014), p. 236#18.

to identify the *Paidika* with it.[82] Hence it is highly unlikely that the ascription to either James or Thomas is accurate, even though some scholars continue to postulate connections between the *Paidika* and the Gospel of Thomas and other Thomasine traditions.[83]

Apart from these later attributions, the contents of the *Paidika* provide little solid evidence for establishing the work's authorship. Apart from the problems noted above in establishing the book's provenance, it is difficult even to determine the author's affiliation. While he was evidently Christian, what sort of Christian was he: a Jewish, gentile or 'heretical' Christian?[84] The limited nature of the evidence allows for a considerable breadth of opinion, and it has been suggested at various times that the author was a Jewish-Christian Ebionite, a gnostic or 'with certainty' a gentile Christian.[85] Although certainty is far from possible, the author may have been a Jew, but is far more likely to have originally been a gentile convert. This question will be taken up more fully in Chapter 5.

1.7 Genre

The genre of the *Paidika* remains one of its most controverted aspects.[86] In a recent discussion of its genre, Sharon Betsworth has sought to establish whether the *Paidika* is best classified as a gospel, a form of ancient novel, or an ancient biography. She concludes that although it manifests aspects of all three, it most closely resembles ancient biography.[87] Here she follows the lead of other scholars like Tony Burke in arguing that the *Paidika* is best regarded as a *bios*– an ancient

---

82. There are some possible connections between the *Paidika* and other Thomasine literature: compare *Paidika* 7.3 with Gospel of Thomas 4, *Paidika* 11 and Gospel of Thomas 9, and *Paidika* 16 and Gospel of Thomas 77. It is also possible that the *Acts of Thomas* 79 references Jesus's teaching episodes in the *Paidika*. Cf. Burke (2010), pp. 29–31. Taken as a whole, these connections are rather muted.

83. Cullmann (1991), p. 442, would link Thomas's associations with India to 'Indian legends', which are paralleled in the *Paidika*.

84. Upson-Saia (2013), pp. 21–37, would argue that the *Paidika* was written by detractors of Christianity.

85. Ebionite: Van Aarde (2013), pp. 614–26; (2006), pp. 359–65, 376–8; (2005), pp. 834–8; Gnostic: Lapham (2003), p. 130; gentile Christian: Santos Otero (2003), p. 299; Cullmann (1991), p. 442; cf. Rebell (1992), p. 136.

86. On the genre of the *Paidika*, see: Betsworth (2015), pp. 148–50; Davis (2014), pp. 21–6; Kaiser (2012), pp. 937–8; Aasgaard (2010), pp. 49–52; Burke (2010), pp. 281–4; Hock (1995), pp. 92–7.

87. Betsworth (2015), p. 159. The *Paidika*'s associations with Greek novels are quite limited and will not be discussed here. As Aasgaard (2010), p. 49, rightly observes, there are few points of overlap between them and the *Paidika*.

form of biography.[88] The *bios*, as exemplified by Plutarch, Suetonius and others, typically gave an account of the lives of heroes such as Theseus and Romulus or exceptional humans, such as Moses or the Roman emperors. These *bioi* could include childhood episodes, but they were usually calculated to demonstrate how the individual's future greatness was already prefigured in their youth. A person's character was thought to be fixed from infancy and remained unchanged through adulthood.[89]

Recent studies of the gospel genre have convincingly argued that the gospel form can be regarded as an exemplar or a subgenre of the *bios*.[90] The question, however, is whether the *Paidika* is sufficiently similar to the gospel genre to assume that it should also be construed as an instance of the *bios*. There are substantial grounds, however, for questioning whether this is, in fact, the case. The issue depends on whether the *Paidika* was intended as a stand-alone document or was meant to be a pendant to Luke. Its replication and rewriting of Lk. 2.41-51 at chapter 17 suggest a deliberate association with Luke that allowed the *Paidika* to function in two ways. It could stand on its own and offer an independent account of Jesus's childhood or be read in conjunction with Luke to expand his portrayal. In the latter role it could assume some of Luke's authority and bask in reflected glory. But it could just as easily be presented in its own right. Yet, if the *Paidika* could stand on its own and was intended – at least in part – to do so, then it does not really fit with the *bios* genre. There are no extant, stand-alone *bioi* devoted exclusively to the lives of children. Childhood episodes, where they occur, are always ancillary to the narrative of the adult. So the essential forms of the *bios* and *Paidika* taken as a whole are generically different.

This finding raises the question of whether the *Paidika* and gospel genres are also distinct. Since the *Paidika* contains miracle narratives and sayings like those of the canonical Gospels and also covers some of the same period, does that make it a gospel? But, as was noted in the Preface, despite its common designation as a gospel, it is not a gospel. There is no indication that the *Paidika* ever intended to tell the full story of Jesus's ministry and passion. Since the basis of the canonical Gospels is generally assumed to be narratives of the kerygmatic good news of Jesus's life, death and resurrection, a gospel should have these features (even if they are implicit, as in the Gospel of Mark). Moreover, the superscriptions to the *Paidika* do not describe it as a gospel, but as 'the Mighty Childhood Deeds of Our Master and Saviour Jesus Christ' or as 'A story about the childhood and upbringing of the Lord Jesus Christ and the wonders which he performed in that time'.[91] Elliott notes that the superscriptions in other Infancy Gospels also tend to refrain from designating

---

88. Burke (2010), pp. 281–4.
89. Hägg (2012), pp. 6, 75, 330; Wiedemann (1989), pp. 49–50; Talbert (1980), pp. 129–41.
90. Frickenschmidt (1997), p. 501; Burridge (1992), p. 247.
91. The first is the superscript to Gs, cf. Burke (2010), p. 466, and the second the superscript to Syriac P, cf. Burke (2013a), p. 266. Other variants also exist.

them as gospels, a reluctance that may stem from a wish to distinguish them from the fuller canonical Gospels.[92]

Instead, it is preferable to follow Richard Burridge's assessment, who describes the Infancy Gospels as a 'tertiary stage' of gospel development.[93] His distinction, is helpful, and it can be made even more precise. The Infancy Gospels are tertiary not only in the sense that they are genetically later productions, but also in the sense that they derive their meaning from their parent works. The *Paidika*, just like the parabiblical and rewritten documents based on the Hebrew Bible, obtains some of its contextual meaning and authority from its reliance on one or more of the canonical Gospels. As Perkins aptly notes of the Infancy Gospels, 'their very existence depends upon readers familiar with a gospel canon'.[94] In particular, the *Paidika* presupposes the account of Jesus's infancy in Luke. Although it can certainly stand on its own merits as a narrative, it resembles, for instance, the LXX's supplements to Daniel by relying on a parent work to bring out its full significance. It has, therefore, a dual function.

In keeping with this dual function, the term employed here will be *parevangelical* to indicate, as with the term parabiblical, the text's relation to and distinction from the canonical Gospels. And, just as the term parabiblical does not reference a literary genre as such, but a specific literary corpus – namely, the Hebrew Bible – 'parevangelical' in this instance does not refer to a genre – that is, to a gospel genre – but indicates a relation to a distinct and self-contained group of texts, namely the four canonical Gospels. So even if Luke and John do not explicitly style themselves as gospels, the early church was quick to give them this designation, and with it, their concomitant authority. The *Paidika*'s author seems to discern this authority in at least one of the canonical Gospels: the very close rewriting of Lk. 2.41-51 in chapter 17 seems difficult to explain otherwise.

That being said, Stephen Davis, in his stimulating recent book on the *Paidika*, would contest the work's dual function. He doubts whether the *Paidika* was ever intended to act as a supplement to the canonical Gospels or intended to expand Jesus's biography by plugging the 'childhood-shaped hole in earlier Christian traditions'.[95] Such an approach, he suggests, fails to interpret the Infancy Gospels as literary works in their own right and turns them into mere appendices of the authoritative 'canonical' Gospels. Davis further contends that it is by no means clear how much access the early churches – especially rural churches – would have had to the canonical Gospels or how many members of these churches would actually have been able to read. For this reason, he maintains that interpreters should be wary of placing 'undue emphasis on the *Paidika*'s intertextual relationships to a

---

92. Elliott (1993), p. 68.
93. Burridge (2004), p. 242.
94. Perkins (2015), p. 199.
95. Davis (2014), p. 22. See also the reservations of Perkins (2015), p. 197: 'Neither the "childhood deeds" nor the "hidden sayings" were intended to complement the received gospels in presenting a "life and teaching of Jesus."'

corpus of New Testament Gospels that may not have been readily available to readers and hearers for close exegesis and comparison.'[96]

Yet, despite Davis's objections, there is ample reason to suppose that the *Paidika* does display a dual relation to Luke. Here, one need only point once again to the *Paidika*'s chapter 17, which, as a rewriting of Lk. 2.41-52, amounts to 'rewritten scripture'.[97] Geert Van Oyen has established that 'the verbal similarities unmistakably point to a written relationship between the canonical and apocryphal text'.[98] So, if the *Paidika*'s author were really intent on dissociating his book from the Gospel of Luke, why would he replicate such an extensive passage nearly verbatim? Instead, it seems likely that he is deliberately drawing on Luke's authority, and it is even possible that the author meant chapter 17 to serve as a bridge or hinge to link the *Paidika* with Luke's narrative. If nothing else, it demonstrates that the author of the *Paidika* had direct access to Luke and presumed it would be recognized.[99]

Moreover, although the work as a whole is not a *bios*, it contains biographical features. The *Paidika*'s narrative chronology – most notably its repeated references to Jesus's age – seems very much indebted to Luke, and is focused upon filling in the chronological gaps in Jesus's infancy. The *Paidika*'s preoccupation with Jesus's age is unusual in descriptions of children in antiquity, and here the author's inspiration was Lk. 2.42 ('And when he was twelve years old, they went up as usual for the festival') and Lk. 3.23 ('Jesus was about thirty years old when he began his work'). The author was certainly familiar with the former passage because he cites it himself at 17.1. Hence, on the model provided by Luke's verses, the author has continued to use a chronological framework that links Jesus's age with certain episodes. Jesus is five when he fashions the sparrows (2.1), seven when he carries water in his cloak (10.1), 'about eight' when he miraculously helps his father make a bed (12.1), and twelve when he goes to Jerusalem with his parents (17.1). Except for the last, and possibly the first enumeration of age, Jesus's actual age does not always seem to matter for the logic of the narrative – certainly the middle two references could be switched without affecting the overall tenor of the narrative.[100] Nevertheless, these chronological indications provide a framework that gives an overall structure to the work; the author has constructed and retrojected a developmental narrative derived from Luke's Gospel onto Jesus's childhood years.[101]

---

96. Davis (2014), p. 22.

97. Van Oyen (2011), p. 482. For the nature and character of 'rewritten scripture', see Aune (2003), pp. 410–14.

98. Van Oyen (2011), p. 491.

99. See the chart in Van Oyen (2011), pp. 499–503, which shows the *Paidika*'s probable reliance on John, as well.

100. On the possible significance of age twelve for the narrative, see de Jonge (1977–8), pp. 317–24; cf. Frickenschmidt (1997), p. 488.

101. These indications of age are characteristic of the earliest versions of the *Paidika*. All are found in the 'best source ... for the Syriac tradition' of the *Paidika* (Burke [2013a], p. 238), as well as the Greek in Gs. The reference to Jesus being 'about eight' is missing in the Old Irish version: McNamara et al. (2001), p. 482#66.

The same tendency can be observed in later redactors and compilers. The emergence of the Egyptian Prologue, for instance, can be seen as an attempt to complete this biographical impulse, by filling in a narrative of Jesus as a toddler, aged two or three.[102] The Prologue adds, 'And at the time Jesus went to Egypt, he was two years old' (*Egyptian Prologue* 1 Gd). The chronological emphasis established by Luke is still very much at work. Further, the later fusing of the *Paidika* with the *Protevangelium of James* to construct extensive infancy accounts, such as the *Gospel of Pseudo-Matthew*, suggests that one of the aims of later traditors was biographical completeness. Their aims, of course, may not have been the same as those of the *Paidika*'s author, but they are suggestive nevertheless.

The foregoing suggests that the author of the *Paidika* adopted Luke's nascent chronology of Jesus's life, and structured his narrative on a similar pattern. This narrative was intended to serve, in part, as a complement to Luke, by filling in some of the gaps in Jesus's life story. Its framework and content were intended to mesh with those of Luke especially, so that the two might have been read in tandem, much as (presumably) Luke and Acts were read together. Of course, it is not necessary that its audience was aware of its precise relation to Luke or the other gospels. But, equally, it may have been read independently for edification as something that was 'useful for the soul'.[103]

What, then, can be said about the *Paidika*'s genre? Describing the *Paidika* as a gospel is a modern misnomer with little historical basis. The superscriptions to the *Paidika* do not describe it as a gospel, but as 'the Mighty Childhood Deeds of Our Master and Saviour Jesus Christ' or as 'A story about the childhood and upbringing of the Lord Jesus Christ and the wonders which he performed in that time'.[104] Elliott notes that the superscriptions in other Infancy Gospels also tend to refrain from designating them as gospels, a reluctance that may stem from a wish to distinguish them from the fuller canonical Gospels.[105] That said, the *Paidika* reveals close associations with the canonical Gospels, and is best described as parevangelical, related to the Gospels but also independent of them.

1.8 Historicity and Fiction

The attribution of the *Paidika* to James, the brother of Jesus, raises some pressing questions about the work's historicity. If later traditors thought it is

---

102. One possible explanation for this absence in the *Paidika* are the difficulties involved in trying to reconcile the infancy narratives of Luke and Matthew (if, that is, the author was acquainted with Matthew).

103. Bovon (2012), pp. 125–37.

104. The first is the superscript to Gs, cf. Burke (2010), p. 466, and the second the superscript to Syriac P, cf. Burke (2013a), p. 266. Other variants also exist.

105. Elliott (1993), p. 68.

possible that Jesus's brother was the author of the work, is it conceivable that some of the stories do actually go back to authentic traditions of Jesus? If the *Paidika* in whole or in part dates from the second century, might it not contain reliable echoes of the historical Jesus? As attractive (or unattractive!) as this idea might be, it is not especially probable. The major discrepancies already present in Matthew and Luke's birth narratives raise serious questions about the historicity of the events that they describe.[106] How much more, then, for stories that are likely later by a century or more? Helmut Koester's supposition that the *Paidika*'s stories were fashioned in part from the gospel narratives themselves, and from broader folk traditions[107] is more convincing, though it also needs to be recognized that the quest to isolate individual folk stories and tie them to the *Paidika* is probably misguided.[108] Not only are folk traditions notoriously fluid, but the motifs contained in them can also emerge independently in different places. Miraculous stories, of the sort found in the *Paidika*, are particularly prone to this 'wandering'.[109]

Nor are the *Paidika* narratives simply attenuated versions of extant gospel stories. Burke has suggested that the stories originally told of the adult Jesus were refashioned as childhood tales.[110] But it is preferable to say that some of the themes encountered in the stories of the adult Jesus – such as his breach of the Sabbath – are refashioned in the narratives of the *Paidika*. The gospel stories provided a thematic matrix out of which new narratives could be constructed, as for instance, when the withered fig tree becomes the model for Annas's son.

In light of this 'wandering' and 'refashioning', the historicity of the episodes is highly questionable. Even those who have sought to argue for the presence of valid historical traditions in the *Paidika* – Richard Bauckham for one – are quick to acknowledge that it is a work of imagination, not historiography.[111] John Meier is more scathing about the prospect of finding *any* historical data in the *Paidika*, 'If we can use the *Infancy Gospel of Thomas*, we can use *Alice in Wonderland* just as well.'[112] And, not unexpectedly, some details of the *Paidika* do betray

---

106. Dunn (2003), 343 asks, 'Are there, then, no historical facts concerning Jesus' birth to be gleaned from the birth narratives? The prospects are not good.' Cf. further, Dunn (2015), pp. 92–3; Meier (1991), p. 213.

107. Koester (1992), p. 314 speaks of 'the wider store of various narratives of the ancient world'.

108. Koester (1992), p. 314. Baars and Heldermann (1993), pp. 198–204, for instance, attempt to link the *Paidika* with various Egyptian and gnosticizing traditions, but without much success.

109. Achtemeier (2008), pp. 38–9.

110. Burke (2010a), p. 199. Cf. Mussies (2008), p. 602, and Burke (1998), p. 42#53. Contrast Gero (1971), pp. 59–61.

111. Bauckham (1994), p. 696.

112. Meier (1999), p. 464. For his reasons, see Meier (1997), pp. 522–4.

its historical limitations. One is the glaring error in the (late) prologue of the *Paidika* that proclaims Jesus's birth 'in our region of Bethlehem in the village of Nazareth' (1.1).[113]

The historical problem is further compounded by the fact that the line between history and fiction in the Graeco-Roman world was far from distinct. Both forms constituted *historia*. Even in the modern world the boundaries between truth and falsehood, fiction and history, can be blurred with appeals to 'alternative facts', and this problem was much more acute in antiquity. As Glen Bowersock has memorably shown in his *Fiction and History*, various categories of discourse overlapped significantly, with myth shading imperceptibly into history and biography.[114] Moreover, there were no mechanisms in place that would enable readers of narrative to distinguish between truth and falsehood.[115] No less an authority than A. D. Nock remarks: 'One feature of the time was a marked credulity. Anything reported on any authority was to a man of education possible and to a man in the street probable or even certain.'[116]

Then as now, invention proved to be both beguiling and necessary. As Meier notes, filling in the gaps of Jesus's story was an attractive prospect because one was not bound by historical fact and could freely give vent to one's imagination.[117] And this was certainly what happened: in Achtemeier's words, 'Hellenistic imagination ran wild'.[118] Yet, the resulting apocryphal gospels were not imaginatively ironic confections like Lucian's *True History*; rather, they were regarded as accounts that were somehow true. In contrast to Lucian, there is no indication that the author was aware of the fictive quality of his narratives. Given the shifting contexts of oral and literary materials about Jesus, the author may simply have been including stories that he knew (or supposed) had been confidently circulated about Jesus. As for the author's own narratives, they were stories that *ought* to have been true. Even if they had not actually happened precisely as reported, they nevertheless expressed real truths about Jesus.

Acceptance of Jesus's miracles would have been facilitated by antiquity's near-universal belief in miracles. As almost everyone acknowledged, the 'world was full of gods' and it only made sense to suppose (Epicurus and Lucretius notwithstanding) that these gods were actively engaged in the world of humans. For Christians, of course, the pagan gods would be regarded as *daimones*, but the essentials would remain unchanged – God and his son could and did perform miracles.

What made the populace even more welcoming of the marvellous was their overwhelming need.[119] In a world where death, illness and injury were rife, Jesus

---

113. Gathercole (2015), p. 262.
114. Bowersock (1994), pp. 9–13.
115. Luther (2014), pp. 345–68.
116. A. D. Nock (1961 [1933]), p. 90.
117. Meier (1991), p. 253; cf. Foster (2009), pp. 84–5.
118. Achtemeier (2008), p. 218.
119. On the love of the marvellous, cf. Hansen (1998), pp. xix–xx; on the sheer need of the people, Hoornaert (1988), pp. 207–8.

offered the strongest hope of deliverance from these ills. And, as the *Paidika* demonstrates over and over, Jesus's power over life and death was absolute. The modern-day spectacle of needy and desperate people flocking to attend the miracle-rallies of discredited healers and charlatans is a reminder of how deeply ingrained the human need to believe and hope in the miraculous truly is. The same can be said for the unquenchable fascination with the extraordinary. Newspaper tabloids with sensationalistic and factually dubious stories sell in the tens of millions, and this is not even to mention the similar 'true stories' purveyed on the Web.[120] So, when the *Paidika* told stories about Jesus performing outlandish miracles, they were likely to be credited, even by church fathers. As was noted above, Irenaeus and Chrysostom only object to parts of the *Paidika* that seem to agree with Gnostic teaching or which contradict the canonical Gospels. If they knew of them, they did not express objections to Jesus's miraculous killings. It is not until Maximus the Confessor (*c.* 580–662) that the stories themselves appear to be condemned. He rejects a book on the 'Infancy of Christ' – presumably the *Paidika* – as the 'product of a crazed fabulist' (*Life of the Virgin* 62).[121] Such a variegated response to Jesus's miracles on the part of the church fathers is not to be wondered at since the response of modern scholars is no less diverse. The next chapter will explore the various ways in which scholars have sought to explain Jesus's actions on those occasions where the *Paidika* seems to represent him as a holy terror.

---

120. Bird (1992), p. 7.
121. Burke (2010), pp. 8–9. Frilingos (2016), p. 37 observes that 'Scandal at a "naughty" Jesus is not to be found among early Christian commentators'.

Chapter 2

JESUS THE HOLY TERROR

This chapter will focus on Jesus as a 'holy terror'. It will open by considering and evaluating many of the explanations that have been advanced over the last few decades to account for Jesus's behaviour. From there it will attempt to situate Jesus's actions within the context of Graeco-Roman conceptions of the gods. This contextualization will then serve as a preliminary to the establishment of the *Paidika*'s Christology over the course of the two chapters that follow.

Why the *Paidika* portrays Jesus as a 'holy terror' is one of the most perplexing questions in the Christian Apocrypha, and one that is not easily answered. For most readers, the description of Jesus as a killer is extremely unsettling. And if it is shocking to describe Jesus as a killer, how much more shocking is it to describe the *child* Jesus as a killer? There is little doubt, however, that the author has deliberately given prominence to Jesus's killings. For one thing, he has situated them prominently at the beginning of his narrative. In the Graeco-Roman world, authors would frequently highlight features by situating them at the beginning of a literary work; the beginning episodes would typically serve to establish the characteristics of the work and set the stage for what was to follow. The first appearance of a character is usually meant to be normative and to establish what the readers can expect from them over the course of the work.[1] Of course, there are some writings where these impressions need to be revised, but in ancient narratives this type of character transformation is uncommon. The first impression typically remains definitive. It is certainly noteworthy, therefore, that in the *Paidika* the initial narratives present us with an infant Jesus who is a wonderworker and a killer. In the *Paidika*, Jesus kills a total of three people, and two of these killings are situated at the very outset of the work.[2] Because the *Paidika*'s superscript and prologue are likely later additions to the text, the work really opens with Jesus at play, cleansing pools of water and fashioning birds out of clay (2.1-3). A short two verses later (3.3-4.1) he kills two children who had offended him.[3]

If the author had meant to emphasize Jesus's compassion at the outset of the work, this is certainly a strange way to do it. By the end of the *Paidika*, Jesus has

---

1. Frickenschmidt (1997), pp. 227–8.
2. Cf. Von Bendemann (2013), p. 833.
3. Klauck (2003), p. 73.

relented and restored the lives or sight of most or all those whom he had cursed (8.2, 14.4). These 'restorations' raise additional questions: Why would the author give such prominence to Jesus's killings at the outset of the *Paidika* only to have Jesus reverse them later on? And since the killings are not ultimately determinative for the final picture of Jesus that emerges from the *Paidika*, why did the author include them at all, especially when they appear to create such an uncomplimentary portrayal? The various versions of the text indicate that Jesus's negative deeds are a constant feature in the tradition, while his reparations for his negative deeds are not as widely represented.[4] Why, then, is Jesus so emphatically represented as such an enfant terrible?

2.1 Literary Ineptitude?

Various explanations for Jesus's unflattering behaviour have been proposed in recent years. One influential position, associated especially with Oscar Cullmann, has been to argue that the *Paidika*'s author is simply lacking in the necessary skills and good judgement required for a work of this kind. Cullmann affirms that the author is lacking 'in good taste, restraint and discretion'.[5] The *Paidika*'s miracles are a case in point: the 'cruder and more startling the miracle, the greater the pleasure the compiler finds in it'.[6] As a consequence, the author's excessive fixation on Jesus's marvels does not express spiritual profundity, but, as Gerhard Schneider maintains, 'unprecedented theological banality'.[7]

There is certainly much to be said for this point of view. While the *Paidika*'s narrative does have a natural vivacity, it also, like the young Jesus, lacks control and is wanting in discrimination. Whether this amounts to banality, however, is open to dispute. The remarks of Schneider and Cullmann imply that they are using the canonical Gospels as their literally touchstone; when they compare the *Paidika* to the Gospels, there is little doubt that it falls short in terms of balance, insight and sophistication. But in keeping with the description of the *Paidika* as a parevangelical writing, it is likely that the author was not trying to emulate the Gospels so much as put his own distinctive stamp on the narrative. And, if he did indeed produce a sensationalistic document of the kind that Cullmann describes, it is because he intended to do so. He dispensed with 'good taste, restraint and discretion' precisely so that he could appeal to an audience that revelled in comic-book-style marvels and narratives. His willingness to exploit these features allows Jesus to take on the trappings of a 'holy terror', only to discard them at the *Paidika*'s end. Lurid, perhaps, but not banal.

At the same time, there is no doubt that, despite its limitations, the *Paidika* is an effective piece of literature. If its author is overly fond of 'crude sensationalism',

---

4. Kaiser (2011), pp. 466–8.
5. Cullmann (1991), p. 442.
6. Cullmann (1991), p. 442; cf. Aasgaard (2009), p. 9; Elliott (1993), p. 68.
7. Schneider (1995), p. 37 (my translation); cf. Vielhauer (1975), p. 677.

he also displays a surprising amount of christological sophistication.[8] His precise theological position will be considered more fully in later chapters, but for the moment it is safe to say that despite certain lapses in taste, he cannot really be regarded as an inept author. The *Paidika* has even been described as 'a wonder of literature', but this valuation probably overestimates the work's literary qualities.[9]

2.2 Jesus as an Intolerant Jewish Holy Man

Tony Burke advances a different approach to Jesus's 'unchristian' behaviour, asserting that the *Paidika* portrays the petulancy and bad-tempered behaviour thought to be characteristic of Jewish holy men (*hasidim*). Burke argues that the *hasidim* constitute a distinct category in the Hebrew Bible and Jewish tradition, and are characterized by their tendency to curse rather than to bless. Their spiritual power originates with God and, just as God does not always act with mercy, nor do they.[10]

Elijah and Elisha are among the most famous of these holy men, and their actions show no reluctance to curse others. Burke notes that the 'Objects of their wrath include kings (*1 Kgs* 21,17-29; *2 Kgs* 1), prophets (*1 Kgs* 18,40; *2 Kgs* 5,20-27), messengers (*2 Kgs* 1,9-12), disobedient servants (*2 Kgs* 5,20-27), rival armies (*2 Kgs* 6,18) and even children (*2 Kgs* 2,23-24).'[11] Nor are Elijah and Elisha alone: Artapanus' fragmentary account of Moses's life describes how he cursed and revivified the Pharaoh,[12] and the famous Jewish *hasid* Honi the Circle-Drawer (*fl.* 100 BCE) was asked to inflict a curse on a contender for the Judaean throne.[13]

Burke traces this pattern right through the New Testament, where the adult Jesus also appears to display the traits of a petulant holy man. One need only mention Jesus's cursing of the fig tree (Mk 11.12-22; Mt. 21.18-19), his cursing of disbelieving towns (Lk. 10.13-15), his overturning the moneychangers' tables in the Temple (Mk 11.12-22; Mt. 21.18-19), and his authorization of the disciples to curse individuals and cities (Mt. 10.11-15; Lk. 9.5; 10.10-12). These traits are also characteristic of Jesus's disciples: Peter is involved in the deaths of Ananias and Sapphira (Acts 5.1-11), while Paul blinds Elymas, the false prophet (Acts 13.6-11). Further examples can be obtained from the Apocryphal Acts, and intolerant Christian holy men populate the Christian tradition at least until the fifth century.[14] In Chartrand-Burke's view, therefore, Jesus's intolerant behaviour in the *Paidika* – and in the Synoptic Gospels – makes sense when it

---

8. Elliott (1993), p. 68.
9. Chartrand-Burke (2008a), p. 116.
10. Burke (2010), pp. 276–8.
11. Burke (2010), p. 277.
12. Artapanus frag. 3.
13. Josephus, *Ant.* 14.22-24.
14. Burke (2010), pp. 278–9; cf. Eastman (2015), pp. 200–5; Burke, (2009), p. 41.

is contextualized within this centuries-long tradition of intolerant Jewish and Christian holy men.

This is a plausible argument, but various features render it less than compelling. For one thing, the pre-Christian examples of the 'intolerant holy man' are rather limited. Although Chartrand-Burke's argument assumes that the *Paidika*'s authors were very familiar with the Elijah and Elisha episodes in 1 and 2 Kings, the extent of the author's acquaintance with the Hebrew Bible and Septuagint (LXX) is uncertain.[15] The *Paidika*'s biblical allusions are very muted, and this factor makes it difficult to assess the extent of the author's familiarity with the LXX. It is even conceivable that the author's only acquaintance with Elijah and Elisha is what he has learnt from the Gospels of Luke and/or Matthew.[16] While this latter supposition is unlikely, the number and prominence of the curses ascribed to the prophets seem insufficient to have established a trope applied to the youthful Jesus.

The reference to Moses and the example of Honi the Circle-Drawer are not especially compelling either. For instance, in Artapanus's fragmentary life of Moses, the pharaoh collapses as a consequence of having Moses tell him Yahweh's name. Moses does not curse him; instead, the pharaoh is simply overwhelmed by Yahweh's power.[17] As for Honi, he (as Burke recognizes) actually *refuses* to pronounce any curses.[18] When all these examples are taken into account, there is only a very slender body of evidence left on which to construct a category of intolerant holy men, at least in biblical and parabiblical literature.[19]

Nor do appeals to the behaviour of Jesus and the disciples in the canonical Gospels and Acts appreciably substantiate this portrayal: Jesus does not curse, kill or harm anyone in the Gospels, and nor do his disciples. Apart from the Gadarene swine, Jesus's opprobrium is confined to inanimate objects. The only thing that he curses is the fig tree and his only act of anger is to overturn the moneychangers' tables (Mk 11.12-22; Mt. 21.18-19).[20] While he certainly upbraids disbelieving Galilean towns for rejecting his message, he does not curse them. In fact, Jesus expressly *rebukes* his disciples for wanting to call down fire on an unreceptive Samaritan village (Lk. 9.51-6), and he does not authorize the disciples to curse individuals and cities, much as they

---

15. Aasgaard (2010), p. 129; Hock (1995), p. 98.

16. Aasgaard (2010), pp. 127–30. See further the chart of Old Testament motifs and allusions in Van Oyen (2011), pp. 499–503.

17. On this phenomenon, see Holladay (1983), p. 240#90.

18. Burke (2010), pp. 277–8.

19. The references to intolerant Christian holy men all likely post-date the *Paidika*, and may themselves have been influenced by it.

20. Graham Twelftree (1999), p. 324 (cf. p. 165), observes that, apart from the fig tree, 'no other punitive miracles [are] associated with Jesus in the Gospels'. Frey (2015), p. 28, notes that with 'the punitive miracles, the Jesus of the *Inf. Gos. Thom.* strongly differs from the canonical image of Jesus'.

may have wanted to.[21] Further, Jesus's teaching is famously opposed to cursing, not to mention killing (Mt. 5.21-22), and it is especially emphatic about the sanctity and praiseworthiness of children (Mt. 11.25 // Luke 10.21; cf. Mt. 21.15-16; Luke 9.47-8).[22]

As for the book of Acts, it does not attribute the killing of Ananias and Sapphira to Peter's 'curse'; their demise originates with God, and is portrayed as a direct consequence of their lying to God and putting the Holy Spirit to the test (Acts 5.4,9); their death is a *Gottesurteil* – a judgement of God.[23] The only instance in Acts where a disciple actually inflicts harm on someone is when Paul, 'filled with the Holy Spirit', blinds Elymas. But the verse also makes it evident that Elymas's punishment is ultimately enacted by God – Paul tells him: 'the *hand of the Lord* is against you, and you will be blind for a while, unable to see the sun' (Acts 13.9,11 my italics). The category of the intolerant holy man, therefore, is largely absent from the New Testament.

This is not to overlook Jesus's prophetic warnings of judgement to come. Just as the prophets of the Hebrew Bible frequently alluded to the wrath of God and to future punishment, so, too, does Jesus. The canonical Gospels indicate that the Son of God will certainly appear in glory to judge humankind, and that those who have acted immorally and unjustly will be consigned to outer darkness. Jesus's earthly ministry, however, is not one of judgement or condemnation, but one of compassion and admonition. So while the Gospels certainly envision a future-glorified Christ who will enact divine punishments, their picture of the earthly Jesus is not one of a fierce or judgemental messiah. As was just argued, neither Jesus nor the disciples display any such actions.

Moreover, it is highly significant that the parents of the second child Jesus killed reproach Joseph and urge him to 'teach him to bless and not to curse' (4.2). This reproach helps to illustrate the fundamental distinction between the *Paidika* and Luke and the other Gospels. The latter are full of blessings, including the beatitudes (Luke), while the *Paidika* has none. Curses abound in the *Paidika*, but do not really figure in Luke and the other Gospels. According to Chartrand-Burke's theory, the infant Jesus of the *Paidika* is 'presented as a cursing wonderworker because the author considers the adult Jesus to have been a cursing wonderworker'.[24] Yet, as was just argued, such a picture of Jesus is largely absent in the canonical Gospels and related literature. It is only with considerable difficulty, therefore, that Jesus's killings and blinding of a child's parents in the *Paidika* can be regarded as paralleling the canonical Gospels' depictions of the adult Jesus.

That being said, a sort of 'codicil' to Burke's understanding of Jesus's curses has recently been advanced by Daniel Eastman, who makes several illuminating

---

21. Cf. the comments in Litwa (2014), p. 72#9.
22. Chartrand-Burke's claim (2008a), p. 115#39, that Jesus was not speaking of literal children but using the term 'as a metaphor for the powerless in society' questionable.
23. Nock (1972), pp. 327–8.
24. Chartrand-Burke (2008b), p. 137.

observations about the nature and context of these curses.[25] With respect to the former, he observes that the curses all demonstrate the same features: they 'are all invoked as responses to personal slights, all achieved instantaneously, and all reversed at a later point'.[26] He adds that these common features reveal the underlying purpose of the curses – they are intended to be didactic. Not only do they instruct their recipients, but also 'establish Jesus' special identity in his community as a teacher who possesses extraordinary powers'.[27]

Eastman refers to many of the biblical figures cited by Burke, and then follows up one of Burke's suggestions by examining the role of cursing and miracles among ancient Syrian ascetics. He finds that their punitive miracles display remarkably close similarities to the curses found in the *Paidika*, and he proposes that these stories about intolerant ascetics influenced the final composition of the *Paidika* in fourth-century Syria, and help to account for the presence of such features in the *Paidika*.[28]

Eastman's reference to the Syrian sources is instructive, especially given the attestation of the *Paidika* in the early Syriac manuscript tradition. Nevertheless, his conjectures raise various questions. What of the *Paidika*'s possible influence on the Syrian ascetic tradition? Even if one were to assume that the ascetic tradition influenced the *Paidika*, it fails to explain why its author would give preference to the stories of mere ascetics over the canonical Gospels in constructing its portrait of Jesus. Nor is it warranted to say that Jesus's curses were ultimately instructive, and therefore benevolent. What possible benevolent lesson underlies the blinding of parents who weep for the child Jesus had angrily killed – Is it: 'If you grieve for your dead child, you will be blinded'? What conceivable lesson could underlie the death of this child, who bumps into Jesus? – 'Don't bump someone or they will kill you'? The chief 'lesson' that emerges from all of Jesus's curses is essentially this: Do not offend a powerful and angry god.

2.3 The Paidika *as Children's Story*

Reidar Aasgaard's very different approach to 'Jesus the Holy Terror' proposes that the *Paidika* is actually a literary work designed for children. In fact, he suggests that it is Christianity's first children's story – 'a story for children about Jesus, true God and true child. It is a story about a Jesus with whom they could identify, a story with both seriousness and humor, and a story well fit both to entertain and to edify'.[29]

25. Eastman (2015), pp. 186–208.
26. Eastman (2015), pp. 191-2, 206.
27. Ibid. Compare the related argument by Paulissen (2004), p. 21.
28. Eastman (2015), pp. 206; 200–5. Peter Brown remarks in his celebrated article, 'The Holy Man in Late Antiquity', that the 'Syrians were notable cursers': Brown (1971), p. 87; cf. p. 88.
29. Aasgaard (2010), p. 216; Aasgaard, (2009a), pp. 1–27. For qualified acceptance of his proposal, see Dunn (2015), p. 492; Foster (2014), p. 347; Hill (2010), p. 87.

Various considerations lead him to this conclusion. One is that the episodes of the *Paidika* appear to share literary characteristics with ancient fables and fairytales.[30] Another is that the *Paidika* is virtually unique among ancient writings in focusing exclusively on the life of a child and upon child-centred concerns: its audience of children 'could identify with Jesus' anger, sympathize with his wish for revenge, and dream of having similar powers'.[31] Further, the *Paidika*'s locations and characters reflect a child's world, and the actions it describes are well adapted for an audience of children. Likewise, the chronological framework given to Jesus's development reflects his society's perceptions of how a child develops and would, as a consequence, have been of special interest to children: it is 'adapted psychologically and pedagogically to the level of children', and this pedagogy also includes theology.[32] In fact, one might describe the *Paidika* as 'theology for children'.[33]

Aasgaard's proposal is a refreshing and needed corrective to scholarly reconstructions that overlook or minimize the role played by children in Graeco-Roman antiquity.[34] It is only just recently that the place of children in antiquity has begun to receive the attention that it warrants, and as a consequence, Aasgaard's proposal is partially hobbled by the limitations of the evidence. Unfortunately, we know very little about children's literature in antiquity and its audience.[35] Is it warranted, then, to argue that because the *Paidika* is compatible with children's concerns it must, necessarily, have been directed at children and designed for their consumption?[36] The *Homeric Hymn to Hermes* 4 would suggest otherwise. All those features that are said to be of special interest to children can be found in the *Hymn*, but it is extremely unlikely that it was either addressed to children or primarily concerned with them. So far as can be established, the *Hymn* was directed at adults and had a ritual or cultic function.[37]

Also problematic is the assumption that the *Paidika* functioned as 'theology for children'. As Burke has forcefully argued, it 'strains credibility that a text in which the young protagonist maims or slays other children, disobeys his parents, and defies his teachers would be considered edifying subject matter for children by parents of that time'.[38] The *Paidika*'s author provides no emphatic moral barometer

---

30. Aasgaard (2010), pp. 93–103; cf. Aasgaard (2010a), pp. 439–44.

31. Aasgaard (2009a), p. 22.

32. Aasgaard (2010), p. 210.

33. Aasgaard (2010), p. 212; cf. Aasgaard (2009a), p. 23.

34. See for instance, Betsworth's (2015), pp. 157–8, appreciative acceptance of Aasgaard's hypothesis.

35. Anderson (2000), pp. 1–9, describes the cumulative data as a 'meagre harvest' (p. 9).

36. Aasgaard acknowledges that adults would also have been part of its audience: (2009a), p. 212.

37. See note # 87 below.

38. Burke (2012), p. 396. Cf. further, Burz-Tropper (2013), p. 723#19, and Kaiser (2010), p. 269; Clark (1994), p. 20.

that would allow a child to distinguish between appropriate and inappropriate behaviour, and for this reason, it is unlikely to have functioned as theology.

Having said that, however, it is probable that children would have found these stories every bit as entertaining and engrossing as their parents. When accompanied by their parents and in the context of the Christian community where the *Paidika* may have been read, the excesses and infelicities of the work could be readily overlooked in favour of its entertaining and devotional aspects. With adult supervision, the transformations in the maturing Jesus – not even particularly obvious to modern audiences – could be highlighted to present Jesus as a youthful role model.

Interestingly, the infancy traditions show signs of having undergone modifications in the medieval period. Pamela Scheingorn notes that the manuscript Ambrosiana SP II 64, which contains material derived from the *Paidika*, does away with many of the negative miracles, and transforms Jesus into a more explicitly suitable role model for children.[39]

2.4 *The* Paidika *as an Anti-Christian Document*

One of the key issues raised by the *Paidika* is whether its audience would have found Jesus's anger and violent actions as shocking and distasteful as a modern audience tends to.[40] The most recent assessment of the question by Kristi Upson-Saia furnishes an unequivocal answer – the ancients would have found it equally repugnant: 'Jesus' behavior would have been characterized as self-indulgent, ignoble, unmanly, and a threat to the community.'[41]

Her conclusion is based on a detailed analysis of Graeco-Roman ethical treatises from around the turn of the Common Era, including several that focus exclusively on anger. These treatises indicate that anger was universally condemned: it was considered a base emotion that characterized those of low social standing, the sick and the young.[42] Early Christian and pagan authors would have shared this aversion. Regardless of whether Jesus was conceived of as divine or human, he would have been dismissed as a slave to his own anger. His exceptional power would have counted for little if he was unable to control his own emotions.[43] A similar judgement even extended to God the Father. Patristic authors were particularly embarrassed by the references to God's wrath in the Scriptures, and pursued various strategies to represent his anger in a more positive light.[44]

---

39. Scheingorn (2012), p. 256.

40. For similar views, see Kaiser (2011), pp. 462–3. Litwa (2014), p. 70#3, draws attention to the title of another version of the *Paidika*: 'Concerning the shocking (*exaisiōn*) and hair-raising (*phriktōn*) wonders which our Lord Jesus Christ did as a child.'

41. Upson-Saia (2013), p. 3; cf. Amsler (2011), pp. 456–7.

42. Upson-Saia, (2013), p. 14.

43. Ibid., p. 16.

44. McCarthy (2009), p. 846; cf. Considine (1969), pp. 85–159.

This insight leads Upson-Saia to account for Jesus's anger in an entirely different way: the stories in the *Paidika* are unflattering because they were designed to be. They were not written by Christians at all, but by opponents of Christianity who wished to discredit Jesus by representing him as a petulant child incapable of stemming his anger or acting with self-control. Later Christians, however, came to suppose that the *Paidika* was actually a Christian production and did their best to mitigate the problems associated with Jesus's anger. By means of judicious reframing of the stories, editing and the tempering of some of the language, they did their best to reduce the offensiveness of the narratives.[45]

Upson-Saia's insights gain a certain confirmation in earlier observations by Frédéric Amsler, who finds indications of mockery associated with the *Paidika*'s episode wherein Jesus transforms the clay birds into sparrows. He suggests that the word παίζω used in this episode also means 'mock' and helps set a derisory tone. The undeniable subtext of Genesis underlying the 'separation of the waters' (to be discussed more fully in Chapter 4) also makes Jesus's actions appear trivial and ridiculous. Accordingly, this story may have originated among Jews hostile to Christian beliefs, and it is no mere coincidence that the *Toledoth Jesu* – a late antique/medieval Jewish 'gospel' that satirizes Jesus and Christianity – has similar episodes, including the vivification of the sparrows. Amsler goes on to suggest that the water imagery can be interpreted as reflecting a later dispute between Jews and Christians over the merits of ritual immersion versus baptism.[46]

These theories are bold and ingenious, and attempt to address the problem head on. Nevertheless, they raise a number of questions. Why would Christian detractors bother to represent Jesus as a child in order to denigrate him? Celsus, an early pagan critic of Christianity, attacks the adult Jesus directly (Origen, *Cels.* 2.76). Wouldn't others have done likewise? Why would they need to invent oblique and dubious stories about Jesus's infancy to condemn him? Children were popularly regarded as imperfect and irrational beings by nature, so it would have been no great victory to denigrate a child.

Moreover, what is to be made of those aspects of the infancy stories where Jesus does act with rectitude and compassion? Were they also written by those wishing to subvert Christianity? Apart from the curses, the *Paidika*'s miracles portray Jesus positively – his healings and raising people from the dead are treated straightforwardly and sympathetically. In the case of Jesus's raising of Zeno, for instance, it is not likely that detractors would describe Jesus as 'Lord' (κύριε), or implicitly advocate the worship (προσεκύνησαν) of Jesus as Zeno's parents do (9.3; cf. Mt. 14.33).

While the sparrow episode does appear in the parodic *Toledoth Jesu*, the text does not dispute Jesus's ability to perform the miracle, but merely tries to

---

45. Upson-Saia (2013), pp. 21–37; cf. Burke (2010), pp. 216–17, for an account of such changes, and McNamara (2010), pp. 724–5, for an example of some of these changes in the Irish version.
46. Amsler (2011), pp. 452–8. He cites the Vienna manuscript of the *Toledoth Jesu*. Cf. Peter Schäfer (2012), pp. 214–35, who finds a parody of Jesus's birth in *y. Ber.* 2:4/12-14.

impute it to magic (*Toledoth* 15,34-5; cf. *b. Sanh.* 107b).[47] As the same episode also appears in the Koran (3.49; 5.110) in a neutral light, it may be that it was the mere attractiveness of the narrative that led to its widespread replication in later traditions. Davis further asks whether Upson-Saia's data about anger are skewed because they are derived from a 'philosophical and patristic elite'.[48]

2.5 Jesus as a Developing Child

Other possibilities have also been considered. Some scholars have resorted to allegorical interpretation to eliminate the offensiveness of Jesus's actions. Van Aarde, for instance, argues that Jesus's intolerant actions are not meant literally, but as a warning to those who would reject the Christian message and oppose Christian communities.[49] Others appeal to gnostic interpretations that make Jesus into a heavenly revealer who has come to earth to liberate humans. Jesus's objectionable traits are actually an indication that Jesus, being a heavenly entity, reacts in an alienated manner to the earthly world.[50]

In the end, the most satisfactory solution to the problem of Jesus the Holy Terror is to suppose that the *Paidika* represents Jesus as a developing child. From this point of view Jesus's anger and curses are merely a feature of the lack of perspective, rationality and self-control that typify young children. Children in antiquity were thought to be deficient in all these attributes until the onset of adulthood.[51] Both Ursula Ulrike Kaiser and Reidar Aasgaard argue convincingly that the *Paidika* deliberately represents Jesus as possessing the characteristics and immaturity of a young boy.[52] Jesus is described as engaging in just the sorts of activities that would be typical for a youth of his age. His anger, curses and lack of proportion are merely an expression of the deficient sense of self-control that characterizes young children. Jesus, of course, is also possessed of divine powers, and it is the uneasy juxtaposition of the divine with the human child that creates some of the problematic issues in the narrative.[53] As Miller trenchantly asks, 'How would God act if he had the interests and emotions of a five-year old?'[54]

---

47. Schlichting (1982), p. 111; cf. the alternate version cited in Burke (2010), pp. 37–8.
48. Davis (2014), p. 225.
49. Van Aarde (2005), p. 842.
50. Klauck (2003), p. 77.
51. Kaiser (2011), pp. 474–9.
52. Ibid., pp. 474–5; cf. Kaiser (2010), pp. 267–9; Aasgaard (2010), pp. 99–102; (2009), pp. 9–10. Kaiser's (2010), p. 269 proposal that the *Paidika* might have served as a consolation to stressed parents with overly active children is an imaginative hypothesis.

53. Aasgaard (2009), p. 9 perceptively notes that, 'The child-like picture of Jesus in IGT throws into relief the tension between the human and divine sides even more than is the case with the description of him as adult and divine in the New Testament.'

54. Miller (2003), p. 275.

Yet, is it simply a question of divine powers residing in a five-year-old? There is no doubt that children's actions can be callous, narcissistic and uncontrolled, but the severity of Jesus's actions far outdistances all these attitudes. The depth of his indifference and the extreme savagery of his anger are perplexing and difficult to account for. The explanation for Jesus's behaviour that will be advanced here is that the young Jesus is indeed presented as a child who is both human and divine, and who matures with the passage of years. Yet, it will argue additionally that the *Paidika*'s depiction of Jesus's petulant divine nature reflects popular Graeco-Roman understandings of the gods. The way that they are depicted in myths and elsewhere further helps to explain Jesus's excessive punishments and his insensitivity to human cares. The balance of this chapter, therefore, will focus on these popular understandings, while Chapter 3 will return to address how the *Paidika* portrays the development of Jesus the child.

2.6 *The Graeco-Roman Context of the* Paidika

It was argued in Chapter 1 that the *Paidika* is parevangelical and bears a close generic relationship to the canonical Gospel of Luke. Where the *Paidika* notably departs from its reliance on Luke is in its portrayal of Jesus's character, which appears to be far removed from Luke's account. It will be argued here that the religious context of the Graeco-Roman world was a significant influence on the depiction of Jesus, particularly in its manner of representing divine beings. While the influence of Graeco-Roman models has been broached in passing before,[55] until recently it has been largely overlooked and downplayed in favour of non-Graeco-Roman traditions, including Buddhist, Hindu and Egyptian materials.[56] Although there are notable overlaps between the *Paidika* and some of these other traditions, it remains uncertain whether these stories would and could have come to influence the episodes within the *Paidika*.

The tendency to overlook a Graeco-Roman milieu underlying the *Paidika* is surprising since the work fits readily with a Greek world. As has already been noted, its earliest versions were, in all likelihood, written in Greek.[57] In the 'school narratives', Jesus's initial instruction is usually in Greek, with Hebrew or Aramaic coming second (6.15; 14.2). The *Paidika* also features at least one character – Zeno – with a non-biblical Greek name.

This oversight has been remedied recently with the publication of David Litwa's instructive consideration of the question. While our discussions diverge, we come

---

55. Klauck (2003), p. 77. Graeco-Roman parallels are briefly mentioned in Vielhauer (1978), p. 676, who describes Jesus as a 'pagan divine child', and see Burke (2010), pp. 250, 252; (2009), p. 38.

56. Burke (2009), pp. 205–12; Thundy (1993), p. 121; Thundy (1989), pp. 26, 51; Bauer (1909), pp. 97–100.

57. As noted above in Chapter 1, Burke (2010), pp. 174–88, argues convincingly that the *Paidika* was originally composed in Greek.

to similar conclusions.[58] My argument is that Jesus's actions are best interpreted in light of Graeco-Roman mythic traditions. Jesus's killings and immoderate punishments portray him with the attitudes of a Graeco-Roman deity.[59] The strong ambivalence associated with Jesus's actions corresponds to the ambivalence attributed to Graeco-Roman deities – whether it be their moral ambivalence or the ambivalence of their attitude towards humans.

From the time of the pre-Socratic philosopher Xenophanes (*fl.* sixth century BCE), the Greeks, followed by the Romans, unsuccessfully sought to reconcile the ambivalent actions of their gods with human morality and the notion of divine justice.[60] Fundamental contradictions remained a feature of the ancient mindset, and can even be found within the very same work of a given author. The gods were often viewed as the originators of human calamities, whether the humans deserved them or not.[61]

The same, of course, can be said for benefactions experienced by humans. The gods were also responsible for miraculous healings and the fulfilment of prayers. Particularly within the sphere of civic religion the gods were regularly, and even officially, viewed as benefactors who would bestow their blessings on their favourite cities and on a grateful human race.[62] This was also true for personal religion: there were numerous believers who felt a close kinship with the gods and were grateful for their care.[63] Since, however, the focus of the present discussion is on how the portrayals of the Graeco-Roman gods can be used to illuminate Jesus's intolerant actions, the balance of this chapter will focus on the gods' negative actions towards humans. While much of this discussion is reliant on evidence derived from early Greek myths, these myths continued to have currency well into late antiquity. And despite being largely disregarded or reinterpreted by the scholarly classes, myths retained their authority and resonance among the common people.[64]

The illiterate and uneducated would have heard (or seen images of) these myths from their infancy, especially those myths found in Homer, and the gods continued to dominate their understanding of the world. Particularly revealing in this respect is what Plutarch says about the superstitious (who likely overlap considerably with both the illiterate and the uneducated):

> You see what kind of thoughts the superstitious have about the gods; they assume that the gods are rash, faithless, fickle, vengeful, cruel, and easily offended; and,

---

58. Litwa (2014), pp. 69–85.

59. The justification for treating Jesus as a god rather than as a hero or 'divine man' (*theios anēr*) will be developed fully in Chapter 4.

60. Graf (2004), pp. 541–5. For various modern attempts to address the issue, see: Lloyd-Jones (1971); Dodds (1951); cf. Versnel (2011), pp. 151–237.

61. Kleinknecht (1967), pp. 385–9.

62. Parker (1996), pp. 143–60.

63. Instone (2009).

64. Lane Fox (1987), pp. 110–11. Cf. Aasgaard (2009a), pp. 12–15.

as a result, the superstitious man is bound to hate and fear the gods. And yet, though he dreads them, he worships them, and sacrifices to them and besieges their shrines; and this is nothing surprising; for it is equally true that men give welcome to despots, and pay court to them, and erect golden statues in their honour, but in their hearts they hate them. (Plutarch *Superst.* 170 D-E)

The myths of the gods in the works of Homer – particularly in the *Iliad* – and in the epic poet Hesiod regularly represent the gods as immoral and partisan, even when the poets touted them as the upholders of justice and morality. The poets' failure to reconcile divinity with morality was recognized very early on: Xenophanes lamented that 'Homer and Hesiod have attributed to the gods all things that are blameworthy and disgraceful for men: stealing, committing adultery, deceiving each other.'[65] Over the centuries attempts were made to resolve this paradox, but the rift was never fully paved over – a full millennium after the time of Homer, the emperor Julian makes a similar lament: 'The Hellenes invented their myths about the gods, incredible and monstrous (ἀπίστους καὶ τερατώδες) stories' (Julian *Galil.* 44A).

The extent of the gods' indifference to human death and suffering can be clearly seen in the *Cypria*, a part of the Greek epic cycle about the Trojan War. Zeus's pity, such as it is, is rarely directed towards humans:

There was a time when the countless races [of men] roaming [constantly] over the land were weighing down the [deep]-breasted earth's expanse. Zeus took pity when he saw it, and in his complex mind he resolved to relieve the all-nurturing earth of mankind's weight by fanning the great conflict of the Trojan War, to void the burden by death. So the warriors at Troy kept being killed, and Zeus' plan was being fulfilled.[66]

The same idea is expressed by the Greek playwrights in Euripides's *Helen* (38-41) and *Orestes* (1639-42), and in Aeschylus's *Prometheus Bound*, where Prometheus recounts how he alone had saved humans from the complete destruction that Zeus had unjustly intended to visit upon them (Aeschylus *Prom.* 233-8).

In fact, Christian apologists, such as Clement of Alexandria, would regularly demonize the pagan deities:

Come then, let us add this, that your gods are inhuman and man-hating daemons, who not only exult over the insanity of men, but go so far as to enjoy human slaughter. They provide for themselves sources of pleasure, at one time in the armed contests of the stadium, at another in the innumerable rivalries of war, in order to secure every possible opportunity of glutting themselves to the

65. Frag. 17; cf. Graham (2010), vol. I, p. 109.
66. *Cypria*, Fragment 1 in West (2003); cf. Hesiod fr. 204. 95–104: Zeus 'was already eager to annihilate most of the race of speech-endowed human beings, a pretext to destroy the lives of the semi-gods' Most (2007): *Cat.* 98–100.

full with human blood. Before now, too, they have fallen like plagues on whole cities and nations. (*Protrept.* 3.1)

Where humans did matter to the gods was when they could be used as tools or objects to fulfil a god's agenda or desires. The *Iliad* demonstrates that the gods' involvement in the Trojan War was almost exclusively an opportunity to settle their own scores, using humans as the all-too-dispensable pieces of their cosmic chess-game. The same held true outside of the context of war: if, for instance, Aphrodite's revenge on Artemis's protégé, Hippolytus, necessitated the death of his innocent stepmother, Phaedra, it was of no consequence (Euripides, *Hipp.* 48-50), just as Artemis would have no qualms about killing Aphrodite's own innocent favourite to get her revenge (Euripides, *Hipp.* 1420-22).

In addition to being pawns in the gods' elaborate games, humans were frequently the hapless victims of the gods' lusts. The stories of the gods' rapes of humans, both females and males, are among the most familiar in the Graeco-Roman tradition. Zeus, as the 'father of all', certainly does his best to merit that designation by raping humans indiscriminately. His victims, moreover, were often subjected to additional sufferings once the god had discarded them. Io, for example, was transformed into a cow and tormented by gadflies, Antiope was persecuted, Danaë was set adrift in a sealed box, Callisto was turned into a bear, just to mention a few of the better-known instances.[67] Humans were objects whom the gods could callously exploit to gratify their lusts and thirst for recognition.

Humans were also regarded as the objects of divine envy, where 'a touchy and malevolent jealousy was a conspicuous characteristic of the gods' attitude toward humanity'.[68] If, for instance, a human appeared especially happy, fortunate or prosperous, he or she was seen as encroaching on the state of blessedness that the gods considered to be their own exclusive preserve. This state of affairs would inevitably provoke divine *phthonos*: the envy or jealousy of the gods.[69] Humans, therefore, would habitually refrain from mentioning or drawing attention to their own prosperity in order to avoid divine jealousy.

Herodotus provides a number of examples of this divine jealousy, including the famous story of Croesus and Solon.[70] Croesus, the king of Lydia, paraded his wealth and good fortune before the wise Athenian, Solon, hoping to be called the most fortunate man alive. Solon replied with his celebrated observation – 'no living man is blessed', an insight that the proud Croesus pointedly ignored.[71] Not long after,

---

67. Io (Apollodorus, *Bibl.* 2.1.3; Hyginus, *Fab.* 145; Ovid, *Metam.* 1.588-746), Antiope (Apollodorus, *Bibl.* 3.5.5; Hyginus, *Fab.* 7), Danaë (Apollodorus, *Bibl.* 2.4.1-2; Hyginus, *Fab.* 145; Ovid, *Metam.* 1.588-746), Callisto (Apollodorus, *Bibl.* 2.8.2; Hyginus, *Fab.* 177; Ovid, *Metam.* 2.477-507).

68. Dover (1974), p. 77. Eidinow (2016) speaks of the 'terrible unreliability of divine behaviour' (p. 231).

69. Parker (1996), p. 151#30; Nock (1972), p. 549; Opstelten (1952), pp. 232–9.

70. Herodotus, *Hist.* 1.32; 4.40; 7.10, 46. For the extended story of Croesus, cf. 1.26-91.

71. Godley (1981) Herodotus, *Hist.*1.86 (LCL); Dodds (1951), pp. 30–1.

Croesus is deceived by Apollo's oracle and ends up defeated and despoiled, sitting on a funeral pyre, about to be burned alive. His timely recollection of Solon's advice saves him from death, but he loses the other perquisites of his once 'blessed' life.[72]

But it is divine retribution rather than divine envy that is, perhaps, most characteristic of the gods' interactions with humans in mythology. If mortals obtruded on the sphere of the gods, dishonoured or flouted them, or appropriated divine prerogatives in any way, their act was deemed *hubris* – 'arrogance in word or deed or even thought', which was almost invariably followed by divine *nemesis* – 'punishment by [a] jealous deity'.[73] Here again, thanks to Ovid and later compilers of myths, the list of humans killed, punished or blinded for their hubris can be multiplied with ease: one need only mention Niobe, Phaethon, Lycaon, Tantalus, Tityus, Salmoneus, Sisyphus, Marsyas, Arachne, Pentheus, Lycurgus and Erysichthon.[74] This list extends to historical figures, as when Herodotus theologizes the defeat of the Persian king Xerxes by the Greeks, as an example of hubris and nemesis.

In cases of hubris, the punishment is often portrayed as something far in excess of the crime. Marsyas, for having the temerity to challenge Apollo to a musical contest, is flayed alive by the god. Niobe, for daring to claim that she is superior to the goddess Leto, is forced to witness the death of all her children, and turns to stone in her grief. In Euripides's *Bacchae*, Dionysus orchestrates the savage death of his own cousin, Pentheus, by maddening a throng of Theban women – including Pentheus's own mother and his aunts – and impelling them to tear Pentheus apart. Pentheus's crime is refusing to recognize that Dionysus is a god, and when Dionysus is reproached for behaving so savagely towards humans, he shrugs off the complaint (Euripides *Bacch.* 1346-9).

Of course, all of these examples, with the exception of Herodotus, are derived from Greek mythology and do not reflect the convictions of the educated elite. The educated pagan would argue that such actions were impossible for the pagan deities, who were not – unlike Yahweh – jealous gods.[75] The same cannot be said, however, for the popular understanding of the world, where mythological concepts continued to inform the people. As Kleinknecht observes, 'In extraordinary natural events like pestilence, storm and hail, deformity and sickness, popular belief sees the operation of the ὀργή [wrath] of gods and demons'.[76] Myth popularly confirmed the truth underlying the power and anger of the gods.[77]

It is this last of the above-mentioned 'negative' qualities of the gods – divine retribution – that has the most bearing on the interpretation of Jesus's divinity

---

72. On Herodotus's use of the cycle of fortune as one of his 'master narratives', see Fowler (2010), pp. 322–3.

73. Dodds (1951), p. 31. On Nemesis as a deified abstraction, see Larson (2007), pp. 179–80.

74. See Ovid, *Metamorphoses*, and Apollodorus, *Bibliotheca*, *passim*.

75. MacMullen (1984), p. 130#9.

76. Kleinknecht (1967), p. 388; cf. Lane Fox (1986), p. 128.

77. Lane Fox (1986), p. 95.

within the *Paidika*, and helps to explain the intolerant behaviour that is attributed to him.[78] His killing and blinding of people can be readily paralleled by Graeco-Roman myths. Moreover, the excessive punishments meted out by Jesus are entirely consonant with the extreme forms of nemesis practised by the gods. When, for instance, the son of Annas deliberately destroys Jesus's arrangement of the pools, the *Paidika* assumes he has committed an act of hubris – insolent behaviour directed at a god. Annas's son has refused to acknowledge Jesus's miracle of the clay birds, and has arrogantly set out to challenge a god. The same pattern as in Graeco-Roman myths operates here: hubris is invariably followed by the destruction or punishment of the perpetrator: 'immediately that child withered away' (3.3).

In fact, when it is considered in detail, the extent of Annas's son's hubris is more far-reaching than the simple dispersion of Jesus's pools; there are at least three different features bound up in the son of Annas's actions. First, the fact that the *Paidika* identifies him as Annas's son is significant; an Annas appears as one of the 'high priests' who interrogate Jesus in Jn 18.13-24, and during this interrogation Jesus is struck in the face (Jn 18.22-3).[79] The author of the *Paidika* may, therefore, be consciously paralleling the acts of hubris committed by father and son. Alternatively, Annas in his capacity as a high priest may be seen as representing Jewish law, including the laws of ritual purity, with his son assuming a similar function. When Annas's son reproaches Jesus for committing ritual impurity, he is effectively impugning a god for disregarding human laws.[80] Either way, the accusation by Annas' son accusation is a misguided way to respond to a divinity.

In addition, like Euripides's Pentheus, the son of Annas fails to recognize the presence of a god. The text does not make it clear whether Annas's son was aware that Jesus was rendering the waters ritually clean, but if he was aware, then he was ignoring Jesus's authority once again: Who but a god could cleanse waters by a word?

Lastly, when the son of Annas disperses Jesus's pools, he symbolically negates Jesus's active emulation of God. Symbolically, then, the son of Annas is actively engaged in undoing the work of God and, by implication, choosing chaos over creation. By setting himself directly against the Son of God, he is assuming a role normally occupied by Satan.[81] His perversity in challenging Jesus's divine authority consequently results in the usual nemesis visited on acts of hubris.

The same holds true for the little boy who bumps into Jesus – he, too, has affronted a god.[82] In this instance it does not matter whether his action was

---

78. Litwa (2014), p. 85.

79. Annas's actual term of office as high priest was from 6 to 15 CE. John's use of the title 'high priest' to describe Annas (Jn 18.19, 22) was probably honorific; cf. VanderKam (2004), pp. 420–4.

80. Technically, Jesus's actions could have constituted a breach of Sabbath; cf. *m. Shab.* 7.2 and Felsch (2013), p. 828.

81. Von Bendemann (2013), p. 837, rightly expresses reservations about Aasgaard's view (2010), p. 128, who parallels the son of Annas with the serpent in Eden.

82. Riemer (2006), p. 45, using different terminology, describes it as a 'sacrilegious act'.

intentional or not. The Graeco-Roman gods were not concerned with such niceties, nor is Jesus, who responds with immediate retribution. When the boy's parents complain, they too are rashly calling into question the actions and deeds of a god. It does not matter whether the parents' complaint is just – their recriminations of Jesus also constitute hubris, and they are evidently punished with blindness precisely because they fail to recognize Jesus's divinity. Accordingly, they 'obtain their punishment' (5.1). Instead, the appropriate reaction to the boy's death is signalled by the bystanders, who ask where the child was born, since his word becomes deed (4.1). Their question shows that the point at issue is not whether the boy's death was warranted, but whether there was a divinity in their midst. The villagers, at least, are not slow to associate this violent act with the presence of a god. Finally, there is the episode of Jesus killing his second teacher. This teacher affronts Jesus by refusing to acknowledge his divine wisdom, and by striking him.

All of these examples of hubris and nemesis suggest that Jesus has been portrayed as though he were a Graeco-Roman deity. Jesus's harsh responses to any slights against his person show that he is reacting in a manner that would have been familiar – and even expected – among a popular pagan audience. This, in their view, was how a real god acted. David Litwa makes this point elegantly when he remarks that for the *Paidika* the Graeco-Roman gods had not died – their 'love of honor and violent attempt to defend it had been reborn in the child of Bethlehem'.[83]

2.7 Jesus and Infancy Narratives of the Olympians

In addition to the hubris motif, the author of the *Paidika* may be using other parallels from Graeco-Roman myths to inform his account of Jesus's infancy. Stories about the childhood of the Olympian gods were well known throughout the Graeco-Roman world, and formed part of its common store of traditions. The author could use them serve them to serve as as analogues for his own story of Jesus, not least because these stories also focus on the gods' divine power.[84]

Two of these pagan infancy narratives appear in the Homeric Hymns.[85] Although these hymns were not in fact a product of 'Homer' and likely post-dated the Homeric period, they came to be attributed to him and gained Homeric authority as a result.[86] Though the individual poems of the Hymns vary in length

---

83. Litwa (2010), p. 85.
84. See Litwa (2014), pp. 74–82 for his discussions of Heracles, Hermes and Dionysus.
85. There are two *Homeric Hymns to Hermes*: *Hymn* 4, which is lengthy narrative, and the brief *Hymn* 18. There are also two for Dionysus: the narrative *Hymn* 7 and the fragmentary *Hymn* 1. In the former, Dionysus is represented as a young teenager – 'the likeness of a youth in first manhood' (7.3 LCL).
86. Faulkner (2011), pp. 7–16.

from a mere three to hundreds of lines, they appear to have functioned in part as a ritual preludes to the public recitation of Homeric epic. A correlative function, especially in the longer hymns to Apollo and Demeter, was to provide stories of the origins of the gods' religious cults.[87]

Their supposed 'Homeric' origin meant that the Hymns acquired near-canonical status among the Greeks; consequently, their cumulative influence was prominent throughout antiquity. The standard account of the abduction of Persephone, for example, originates from the Hymn to Demeter, while the foundation-narratives of Apollo's two major cult sites, Delphi and Delos, stem from the Hymn to Apollo. These myths did much to supplement the authoritative stories of the gods found in Homer and Hesiod and, on occasion, added their own stories about the infancy and youth of the gods – a feature that is integral to the Homeric Hymns to Hermes and Dionysus.[88]

While the author of the *Paidika* is not literarily dependent on these Homeric Hymns, it is probable that he was aware of oral versions of these stories. They were perennially popular and featured prominently in the ongoing literary and iconographical culture of the Graeco-Roman world.[89] The author, like a great many of the inhabitants of the Roman Empire, would likely have been thoroughly familiar with these infancy narratives from the time of his or her own infancy.

The narrative *Homeric Hymn to Hermes* opens with the nymph Maia giving birth in a cave to Hermes, her child by Zeus: 'And she gave birth to a son resourceful and cunning, a robber, a rustler of cattle, a bringer of dreams, a night watcher, a gate-lurker, who was soon to display deeds of renown among the immortal gods: born in the morning, by midday he was playing the lyre, and in the evening he stole the cattle of far-shooting Apollo' (*HHymn* 4.13-18). As the poem indicates, Hermes's actions are anything but those of a newborn child. Immediately after his birth, he leaves his cave and encounters a tortoise. Recognizing the resonant qualities of its shell, Hermes kills it and uses it to construct a new invention – the lyre. Not content with that, he steals his half-brother Apollo's cattle, and devises various strategies to avoid pursuit. Returning to his cave, he entirely disregards his mother's parental strictures. Meanwhile, an old man named Battus reveals to Apollo that Hermes was the thief who had rustled his cattle. In later versions of the story, Hermes kills him by turning him into stone,[90] and tries, unsuccessfully,

---

87. Faulkner (2011), pp. 17–19; Richardson (2010), pp. 2–3, 24–5. This raises the interesting possibility that the *Paidika* might have functioned in a similar way, namely as a prelude to the reading of the apostles' 'memoirs'.

88. On the enormous importance of these 'archmyths', see Parker (2011), p. 25.

89. For later versions of the story, see Apollodorus, *Bibl*. 3.10.2; Antoninus Liberalis 23; Ovid, *Met*. 2.679-707; Philostratus, *Imag*. 1.26; *Schol. Il*. 15.256; Alcaeus frag. 308 (retold by Horace's Hymn to Mercury: *Carm* 1.10.9-12). For iconography, cf. Siebert (1990), *LIMC* V.2, plates 243–51.

90. The Scholiast to Antoninus Liberalis states that Hermes's punishment of Battus by turning him into stone goes back to Hesiod; cf. Clay (1989), p. 114#65. His punishment is described in Antoninus Liberalis 23 and Ovid's *Metamorphoses* 2.685-707.

to deceive Apollo about his theft. Hermes is arraigned before Zeus and forced to make restitution. In the end, Hermes and Apollo are reconciled, and Hermes gives Apollo his lyre while securing for himself an established position in the Olympian pantheon.

A comparison between the infants Hermes and Jesus reveals some suggestive similarities. Both Hermes and Jesus manifest a strong sense of divine autonomy. Almost from the moment of his birth, Hermes sets his own course and is oblivious to his mother's recriminations. He is entirely self-willed and aware of what he wants to do, whether it is inventing and playing a lyre, absconding with Apollo's herd or killing Battus. Part of his agenda involves the deliberate rejection of established morality. He is 'resourceful and cunning' and it is of no concern to him that he ought not to be stealing his brother's cattle: they are there, he wants them, so he takes them. Nor does he demonstrate any qualms about brazenly lying to Apollo or even to Zeus himself, and it is only when Zeus constrains him to do so that he makes restitution to Apollo.[91]

Such a portrayal has some interesting affinities with the Jesus of the *Paidika*. Although the *Paidika* does not describe Jesus as a newborn, its account of the youthful Jesus also reveals a self-determined and self-willed figure who, to the detriment of others, does precisely what he wants regardless of parental or societal remonstrances. He, too, is unmoved by established morality: he kills and blinds whomever he wishes. And when, later in the *Paidika*, he becomes increasingly obedient and compassionate, this transformation, too, appears entirely self-motivated.[92]

Like Hermes, Jesus is made into a kind of divine artisan. Where Hermes encounters a tortoise and immediately recognizes the possibility of creating a new musical instrument from its shell, Jesus fashions birds out of clay and brings them to life. In contrast to human children neither Jesus nor Hermes requires any instruction; they already know how to accomplish what they want to do. In fact, the bulk of the *Paidika* is devoted to demonstrating that Jesus requires no human instruction – rather, his three teachers and the elders in the Temple need to learn from him.

Both Jesus and Hermes are represented as divine figures who are already entirely – if unaccountably – familiar with the world into which they are born. Their possession of exceptional knowledge and power from the outset belies their infantile state and, despite their childlike appearance, they often act like anything but children.[93] It has been suggested that the Greeks' religious sensibilities required that 'the gods in their infancy demonstrate that their divinity was not limited by the dependency of the childhood state,'[94] and this certainly seems to be the philosophy of the *Paidika*'s author as well. It amplifies their divine abilities.

---

91. Burke (2009), p. 38, rather paradoxically includes Hermes among figures who 'are praised for their restraint'.
92. Litwa (2014), pp. 75–6, points out that both Hermes and Jesus are described as uniting word and deed in their persons; cf. *Paid*. 4.1 and 17.2 with *HHym* 4.46.
93. Weidemann (1989), p. 51.
94. Beaumont (1995), p. 361.

In addition to affinities with the *Homeric Hymn to Hermes*, similarities can also be drawn between the *Paidika* and the narrative *Homeric Hymn to Dionysus* (*HHymn* 7), although Dionysus is represented as being in the 'prime of youth' and not a child (*HHymn* 7.3-4).[95] The poem tells the story of the kidnapping of the youth Dionysus by pirates. Supposing him to be a royal prince, they propose to hold him for ransom. Once they are on board the ship, their helmsman tells them that they have committed a grievous mistake, and abducted a god not a human. He urges them to release Dionysus before the god becomes angry. The pirates ignore his warnings until the ship starts to become awash with wine, and vines with grape clusters begin to entwine themselves around the mast and sail. Dionysus transforms himself into a lion, and other wild beasts suddenly materialize on board. The lion pounces on the captain, and the rest of the sailors, in terror for their lives, jump overboard and are transformed into dolphins. Only the helmsman remains, and is commended by Dionysus for his insight.[96] The overlap between this *Hymn* and the *Paidika* is the failure of humans to recognize the presence of a divinity in their midst. The pirates receive suitable punishment for their affront to the youthful Dionysus, and the author of the *Paidika* follows a similar pattern by having Jesus kill those who affront him.[97] In both of the narratives, therefore, there is the common motif of a seemingly weak and powerless youth visiting divine punishment on hubristic adults.

In addition to the Homeric Hymns, the *Paidika* shows affinities with other Graeco-Roman narratives. One of the most notable is the story of the child Herakles and his famed lyre instructor, Linus. During his lessons, Herakles plays a false note, and Linus strikes him. Rather than submit to this correction, Herakles retaliates and kills Linus with his lyre. The literary sources for this story are relatively late, but there are numerous indications that it enjoyed a long and popular history.[98] The two stories share some common features.[99] The children's instructors strike them both for making a perceived fault, and they retaliate in an extreme fashion by killing their teachers.

These three examples suggest that the *Paidika*'s author was probably aware of pagan myths that had a bearing on his narrative. The fact that Graeco-Roman mythology gives prominence to male gods as children who are self-determined and very much in possession of divine power may have served as a useful analogue for the author in constructing his own narrative of the youthful Jesus.

95. LSJ s.v. πρωθήβης.

96. For the traditions and reception history of this Hymn, see: Apollodorus, *Bibl.* 3.5.2; Ovid, *Metam.* 3.582-691; Hyginus, *Fab.* 134; *Astr.* 2.17, and Gaspari (1986), Vol. III.2, plate 788.

97. The *Iliad* presents a similar account in the story of Lycurgus's attack on the child Dionysus and the god's horrific retribution, including the blinding of Lycurgus by Zeus (*Il.* 6.130-40); cf. Laager (1957), pp. 120-21.

98. Diodorus Siculus 3.67.2; Apollodorus, *Bibl.* 2.4.9; Gantz (1993), p. 379. For images, cf. Boardman et al. (1988), p. 4. 2 plates pp. 1666-73.

99. Kaiser (2011), pp. 470-1.

2.8 Humour in the Paidika

A third suggestive area of overlap between the *Paidika* and Graeco-Roman portrayals of the gods pertains to the humour that can be found in both. One aspect of this humour is the essential childishness of the gods. Especially as represented in Homer and the mythographers, the gods are often shown to be infantile, petty and sulky. They often react unreasonably and immoderately and are entirely consumed by their narcissism.[100]

Here again the precedents go back to Homer. The poet's juxtaposition of the power of the gods with humorous interludes was to become characteristically Greek: after Homer, it carries through Old and Middle Comedy, and continues well beyond the time of the satirist Lucian.[101] Despite the *Iliad*'s high seriousness and tragic overtones, it offers its hearer or reader much in the behaviour of the deities that could occasion smiles or amused chuckles.[102] For instance, the spectre of Zeus, the sovereign 'Father of Gods and Men' (*Il.* 5.426), responding like a henpecked husband to the querulous complaints of Hera, his sister-wife, partakes of the ridiculous (*Il.* 1.518-23). Hera's deception of Zeus in Book 14 is equally laughable, especially because she is forced to listen to an extensive catalogue of his infidelities (*Il.* 14.315-28). The blubbering of Ares, the bullying god of war, and of Aphrodite, his paramour, when they are wounded by the hero Diomedes are anything but serious (*Il.* 5.318-430; 5.5:814-898), while in the *Odyssey*, the spectacle of Ares and Aphrodite caught *in flagrante* by Hephaistus's subtle net further shows the gods to be sublimely infantile (*Od.* 8.266-366).

This humorous dimension is equally apparent in the *Homeric Hymn to Hermes* because divine infancy narratives are especially suited to comical interpretation.[103] The juxtaposition of a young infant, usually regarded as helpless, impotent, insignificant and irrational, with a mature deity who is none of these things, opens the possibility for pronounced incongruities. The infantile appearance of the god contrasts profoundly with his divine sensibility. Hermes is able to fart in Apollo's face with impunity because, although he is a god, this is the behaviour you might expect from a newborn infant (*Hymn* 4.296-7). By contrast, when Hermes finally shows Apollo his stolen cattle, Apollo is amazed how a 'new-born infant' like Hermes was able to skin two cows, and he expresses his fears about how powerful Hermes would become

---

100. Sels (2010), pp. 409–26.

101. On Homer: Griffin (1980), pp. 98–101; Old Comedy: Scullion (2014), pp. 340–55; Dover (1972), pp. 30–3; Middle Comedy: Nesselrath (1995), pp. 1–27; Lucian: Branham (1989), pp. 125–77.

102. Griffin (1980), pp. 198–201.

103. On the humour in the narrative *Homeric Hymn to Hermes*, see Vergados (2011), pp. 86–98, and Richardson (2010), pp. 19–20. On Lucian's comic use of the Hermes figure, cf. Branham (1989), pp. 147–52.

if he kept growing (*Hymn* 4.405-6). Naturally, Hermes's claim that he himself was too young 'even to know what cattle were' is transparently false, as are his repeated assurances to Apollo and Zeus that he was a naïve, innocent child who was telling the truth. Zeus immediately spotted the deception, 'and laughed out loud when he saw the wicked boy making his fine, expert denials about the cows' (*Hymn* 4.389-90).

Once it is set next to the *Homeric Hymn to Hermes*, it is easy to see that the *Paidika* also has humorous elements that result from its pronounced incongruities. Like the *Homeric Hymn*, the *Paidika*'s episodes also intensify the profound disjunction that exists between gods and humans. Not all of these disjunctions are necessarily comical, but it is difficult to overlook the humour in some of the episodes. The shockingly abrupt manner in which Jesus despatches the people who offend him provokes humour and horror in equal measure. And when Jesus is the childish victim of adults, the results are also amusing. For instance, when Joseph 'grabbed hold of [Jesus'] ear and yanked it hard' (5.2), one smiles at the extraordinary spectacle of the powerful Son of God being treated as though he were an errant toddler. The same holds true for Jesus's admission to primary school – the pre-existent creator of the universe is tasked with learning his ABCs under the tutelage of bumptious, ignorant instructors.[104] When these bumptious teachers receive their come-uppance at the hands of this 'very small child' (7.3), the result is initially comic, and then shocking. That such a very small child should be able to shame or kill his teachers comes as an incongruous jolt that becomes only partially reassuring once the teacher is restored to life by Jesus.

The narrative of Jesus raising Zeno from the dead merely to prove his own innocence offers perhaps another example of transgressive humour – especially if Jesus lets Zeno die again once he has testified to Jesus's innocence. Further, since Jesus ends by restoring all those whom he has killed and blinded, Jesus's killings have an essentially comic (as opposed to tragic) dimension and, perhaps, even a blackly humorous quality since ultimately no harm was done to anyone.

Here the *Paidika* is closer to the spirit of Graeco-Roman traditions than to the New Testament. In his extensive examination of humour in the Greek world, Stephen Halliwell remarks that 'the evidence of the New Testament as a whole suggests ... a general suspicion of laughter in the development of early Christianity'.[105] Laughter is largely absent from the New Testament, and while the Jesus of the canonical Gospels weeps (Jn. 11.35), he is not recorded as having laughed. Why, then, would the author of the *Paidika* employ humour in his life of Jesus when it is largely alien to the sensibility of early Christian writings? Once more, it makes sense to see it as an attempt to appeal to a pagan audience: 'Greeks

---

104. Aasgaard (2010), p. 48, relates that the first teaching episode has 'a distinct slapstick quality'.

105. Halliwell (2008), p. 475.

felt able to cheek the gods precisely because they did not doubt their power.'[106] Their local connections with the gods produced a sense of familiarity as well as awe, and bringing out some of the humour associated with Jesus's infancy treats him in a manner akin to the Olympians. Jesus's youth makes him familiarly human and someone who could be treated with familiarity, notwithstanding his extraordinary power and authority.

2.9 Why Is Jesus Portrayed as a Killer?

If the above observations have merit, it still remains to explain why the *Paidika*'s author would draw on Graeco-Roman conceptions. Wouldn't Christians have condemned such a depiction? If Jesus seldom acts in a Christian way, why would the *Paidika*'s author endorse such a representation? As just suggested, the optimal solution is to suppose that he wanted to make Jesus more palatable to a pagan audience.

The best way to do this was to address the stigma of Jesus's crucifixion head on. To appreciate this perspective, the best place to start is with the apostle Paul's opening statements to the Corinthians: 'We proclaim Christ crucified, a stumbling-block to Jews and foolishness to Gentiles, but to those who are the called, both Jews and Greeks, Christ the power of God and the wisdom of God' (1 Cor 1.23-4). Paul's reference to Jesus's crucifixion as 'foolishness to Gentiles' highlights the absurdity of believing that someone who let himself be crucified could be a god. This is an objection that Celsus makes repeatedly in his condemnation of Christianity: Why didn't God save him, or why didn't Jesus save himself? Isn't it patently ridiculous that a being with immeasurable power should submit to the worst form of death that the Romans could devise? If Christ was indeed 'the power of God', as Paul claims, why didn't he reveal his power and his divine nature to humanity? Paul's response tries to emphasize Jesus's divine self-sacrifice, but at the outset of the Christian movement Jesus's salvific death on the cross was an utterly foreign – and repugnant – conception to everyone.[107] How could an ignorant, impotent, dead criminal be the only son of the one universal god? Martin Hengel acutely presents the dilemma: 'That this crucified Jew, Jesus Christ, could truly be a divine being sent on earth, God's Son, the Lord of all and the coming judge of the world, must inevitably have been thought by any educated man to be utter "madness" and presumptuousness.'[108]

---

106. Parker (2005), p. 149. He is speaking here of the Athenians of the classical period, but his statement holds more generally for the Graeco-Roman world as a whole.

107. Compare Lucian's derisory reference to the 'crucified sophist' (*Peregr.* 13). Jesus's crucifixion should be distinguished from the notion of an 'atoning death', which, as Versnel (2005), pp. 213–94, argues, may have also been influenced by pagan sources.

108. Hengel (1977), p. 83.

To many pagans, the Jesus of the canonical Gospels demonstrates few of the traits that they would have considered divine.[109] In particular, Jesus does not publicly reveal his identity, nor does he fully manifest his power. Celsus pointedly asks Christ why he had done nothing 'beautiful or marvellous ... in word or deed' (Origen, *Cels.* 1.67), and why after his resurrection he was unwilling to make himself known publicly (Origen, *Cels.* 2.63,70). Celsus is prepared to accept that Jesus may have performed some notable deeds, but he thinks that they were hardly significant enough to set him apart from the great crowd of magicians who could perform similar feats.

The *Paidika* attempts to address this problem by making Jesus more Olympian than the Olympians. The opening scenes of hubris and nemesis immediately establish for gentile readers that Jesus is a deity no less powerful, touchy or wilful than their own gods. Such divine traits were entirely familiar in the Graeco-Roman world, and by showing that Jesus also conformed to them the author could establish Jesus's own 'credentials' as a powerful deity. Over the course of the *Paidika* the author actually moves away from this emphasis and embraces a more traditional gospel message of compassion, but at the outset this is the overwhelming impression that the author wishes to establish: Jesus is at least as powerful and as acutely aware of his divine nature as any of the pagan gods.

This argument presupposes that an author would deliberately meld different, even contradictory, religious traditions to accomplish his own ends. In the ancient world, however, this kind of assimilation and syncretism was commonplace. For instance, in Nonnus's late-antique epic about Dionysus, the *Dionysiaca*, there is a similar procedure to the one described here although in this case the figure of Dionysus is assimilated to the figure of Jesus, instead of the reverse. No longer an unpredictable and potentially savage deity, Dionysus is given attributes that make him resemble Christ. He feels pity for mortals, heals them and raises them from the dead. Nonnus has deliberately christianized Dionysus to make him more appealing to a late-antique Christian audience.[110]

By contrast, the author of the *Paidika* has assimilated Jesus to Dionysus, Hermes and other pagan deities in order to make him more appealing to a pagan audience. This practice, of course, hardly originates with the *Paidika* – implicit associations of Jesus with Dionysus and other pagan deities are already to be found in the Gospel of John itself.[111] Nevertheless, the *Paidika* is likely the first concerted example of this phenomenon.

So to recapitulate, why does the *Paidika* portray Jesus as a killer? Does it stem from the ineptitude of the author? Is it an attempt to cast Jesus as a Jewish holy man or to produce an attractive and palatable narrative for children? Is it anti-

---

109. Goldstein and Stroumsa (2007), p. 425 have made the interesting suggestion that Docetism originated from acute pagan discomfort with precisely this notion of a suffering deity.

110. Hernández de la Fuente (2013), p. 482.

111. Hengel (1995), pp. 293–331.

Christian polemic, or a recasting and adaptation of the Christian g[?] recognizing that there are merits to all these solutions, the argume[?] here is that the *Paidika* drew its inspiration from the Graeco-Roman conte[?]. This context would have been familiar to all inhabitants of the Roman Empire, regardless of their ethnicity. The *Paidika*'s author, therefore, drew on constructions of power and divinity that would have been entirely familiar to his audience.

Where the *Paidika* differs from these constructions is in its attribution of a moral development to Jesus. Although it has often been assumed that the figure of Jesus is unchanging, a closer analysis establishes that his character does, in fact, change significantly. It is no coincidence that the work begins with two killings on Jesus's part, and finishes with a Jesus who not only reverses his actions, but also saves at least two lives. This transformation is intended to familiarize the *Paidika*'s readers with the picture of Jesus that appears in what later become the canonical Gospels. Instead of a pagan-tinctured Jesus, they find there a god who willingly lays aside his power and is equally willing to submit to death without defending himself. In the same way that the *Paidika* introduces pagan readers to Jesus, it also introduces its audience to some features of Christian theology. It functions, therefore, as a kind of primer to Christian belief – a *praeparatio evangelica* that sketches out the preparation required on the part of believers and potential believers. They are to put aside childish things, leave their infantile deities and become Christians who have matured into moral beings, following a god who has also matured into a moral being. As the next chapter will demonstrate, Jesus's moral development is intimately linked to his human development.

Chapter 3

JESUS THE CHILD

The *Paidika*'s depiction of Jesus as a child is one of the work's most distinctive features. With the exception of the Gospel of Luke, it is the only early Christian document to focus on Jesus as a youth. The Gospel of Matthew, for instance, only refers to Joseph taking the child (παιδίον) and his mother to Nazareth when Archelaus was ruling (Mt. 2.19-23), while the *Protevangelium of James* closes its Jesus narrative with him in swaddling clothes in an ox-stall (Prot. Jas. 22). Why, then, does the *Paidika* adopt this exclusive focus, and why has the author constructed it as he has?

This chapter will examine the *Paidika*'s portrayal of Jesus as a child, and address several contested areas of the *Paidika*'s depiction of Jesus: Is Jesus represented as a human or divine child? Is he precociously wise – an idealized 'wise child' (*puer senex*) – and, if so, how does this approach correlate with his depiction as an enfant terrible? Does the *Paidika* actually sanction Jesus's antisocial behaviour, and does it chronicle any sort of development or maturation on Jesus's part? This examination of these questions will begin with a consideration of Jesus's human qualities.

3.1 Jesus the Child

The *Paidika* leaves little doubt about Jesus's identity as a human child. Its characteristic designation for Jesus is *paidion* (παιδίον), a term that occurs with considerable frequency in all of the Greek versions of the work. As Amsler notes, the phrase 'the child Jesus' (τὸ παιδίον Ἰησοῦς) occurs in every episode of the book but one.[1]

The Greek word *paidion* typically signifies a child – boy or girl – before the age of puberty.[2] It is a fitting designation for the *Paidika*'s Jesus because he is arguably represented as being in a pre-pubertal state for the entirety of the work.[3] Most recent

---

1. Amsler (2011), p. 450. Despite the awkwardness of the phrase, it occurs more frequently in Gs (26 times) than the name Jesus on its own (23 times).

2. BDAG s.v. The cognate term παιδάριον ('child' or 'little boy') is only found in Ga 6.34.

3. Data about the onset of puberty are socially constructed and vary depending on the source and whether it is males or females who are under consideration. According to the Mishnah,

scholars agree that the *Paidika* offers useful insights about childhood, especially with respect to infancy among the non-elite.[4] The portrayal of the youthful Jesus and his family 'fits within the context of ancient Judaism'; notwithstanding the family's uniqueness: they 'are special precisely because we can see the way in which they transcend the common norms'.[5] In fact, one of the happy consequences of the ongoing renaissance in *Paidika* studies is that it has stimulated the study of children in antiquity.[6]

The *Paidika*'s narrative covers Jesus's childhood, from ages five to twelve, in the context of the village or small town where he lives with his parents Mary and Joseph. The only time this basic setting changes is when Jesus accompanies his parents to Jerusalem at the age of twelve years (cf. Lk. 2.41-52). Otherwise, the activities attributed to Jesus are much the sort that might typically engage a young boy in a small town. He plays with other children, goes to school or helps his parents with their daily tasks.[7] Of course, there is a miraculous dimension to all of these actions, but Jesus's day-to-day activities are very much what one would expect from someone of his age.

School is the most characteristic setting for the *Paidika*'s Jesus, and it is significant that in Gs Joseph sends Jesus to 'school' no less than three times, emphasizing the degree to which Jesus is treated as a normal, if precocious, child.[8] Foster's recent assessment of the *Paidika*'s teaching narratives shows that they comport with 'the *realia* of the phenomenon of elementary education in the ancient world'.[9]

The youthful Jesus is also regularly portrayed as playing (ἔπαιζεν 2.1; 9.1) among other children (παιδία 2.2; παιδίων 9.1).[10] His 'playing' with other children on an

---

the age of transition for males is thirteen years and for females it is twelve years: see *m. Niddah* 5.6, and the related discussion in Horn and Martens (2009), pp. 12-13. For the Romans, male puberty began at age fourteen; cf. Betsworth (2015), pp. 34-6. It is sometimes argued that when Jesus visits the Temple at age twelve, he is regarded as an adult, but this assumption is questionable, due to conflicting estimates about the onset of maturity in antiquity.

4. Burke is not so sanguine. He contends that the *Paidika* 'reveals little about the real experiences of children in the second century' Burke (2009), p. 35.

5. Horn and Martens (2009), p. 75, speaking of the Gospels and the *Paidika*.

6. For studies of children in Graeco-Roman antiquity, see the extensive listing of sources in Davis (2014), pp. 225-7, and the helpful survey of Aasgaard (2009a), pp. 1-27, as well as Aasgaard (2006), pp. 23-46.

7. On children helping their parents with chores or trades: Balla (2003), pp. 55-6.

8. Aasgaard (2009a), p. 9. There is very extensive bibliography on education in the Graeco-Roman world. See, among many other sources, Bell, Grubbs and Parkin (2013), Cribiore (2001) and Strange (1996), pp. 12-15, 24-31.

9. Foster (2014), p. 345.

10. The word παίζω takes on a different signification at 6.7, where the word seems to suggest that Jesus has been 'toying' with his onlookers. Cf. Aasgaard (2010), p. 142. On children's play in the Graeco-Roman world, see Quintilian *Inst.* 1.3.10-11, and Aasgaard (2009a), pp. 9-12 and Strange (1996), p. 24.

upstairs roof (9.1) seems to be entirely characteristic of the kind of roughhousing that young boys engage in, and Zeno's accidental fall from the roof is an unfortunate consequence of that type of risky play.[11] Even his disputes with the son of Annas and his anger at the careless boy who bumped into him resemble the kinds of petty disputes that would happen among children (4.1). In all these interactions, Jesus's relations with his peers are highly typical of a young boy.[12] Even if his playmates abandon him at one point (9.1), he is not portrayed as a solitary figure, some kind of austere child-mage or someone who has in any way dispensed with childhood. He is one of the gang.

Also typical of the representation of Jesus as a child are his interactions with his parents.[13] The first half of the *Paidika* tends to focus on Jesus's conflicts with his parents, especially Joseph. He mocks his father and refuses to obey him. Though Jesus's disdain and intractability are certainly exceptional, conflicts among parents and children were a regular occurrence in the ancient Mediterranean. Equally familiar are the descriptions in the second half of the *Padika* of Jesus undertaking various tasks and chores on his parents' behalf.[14] These narratives constitute a mixture of the everyday and the marvellous, but their broader context is that of a child situated in the family home. Mary's request that he fetch some water is a domestic commonplace (10.1-2), as are the episodes where Jesus helps his father with his daily tasks. When Joseph goes to sow, Jesus joins him, and he also helps Joseph with his carpentry (12.1-2). Jesus's allegiance to his family is also very much in evidence when he heals his brother James, who was bitten by a snake. Jesus rushes to his aid and saves him from imminent death by blowing on the bite and raising James to his feet (15.1-2). Jesus, therefore, enacts the role of dutiful son, by assisting his parents. Mary and Joseph, in their turn, reward him for his obedience by embracing (12.2) and kissing him (10.2; 12.2). Joseph even gives thanks to God for Jesus: 'Blessed am I because God gave this son to me' (12.2). The *Paidika*'s final episode echoes Luke in affirming Jesus's continued obedience to his parents (17.5). Jesus's domestic situation, therefore, reflects a typical family context, both good and bad.

Even the conflicts between Jesus and his parents do not seem especially unusual. The ancient record contains a number of cases both trifling and grave that describe family disputes. One of the former is a letter from another child also named Jesus who petulantly threatens his father: 'If you won't take me with you to Alexandria I won't write you a letter or speak to you or say goodbye to you; and if you go to Alexandria I won't take your hand nor ever greet you again.'[15] Jesus's pique at Joseph and his teachers, therefore, does not seem especially out of the ordinary.

11. Compare the death of the child who falls to his death in John Moschus, *Prat. spir.* 233.
12. Horn and Martens (2009), p. 196.
13. Frilingos (2016), pp. 36, 55; Betsworth (2015), pp. 154–5.
14. Horn and Martens (2009), p. 180. For a dissenting view, cf. Stewart (2015), pp. 6-7, who argues that Jesus, not Joseph, is represented as the true paterfamilias and breadwinner.
15. Eyben (1991), p. 132 citing P.Oxy 1.119 (ca. 200 CE).

It is evident that, notwithstanding Jesus's divine attributes, the author has endeavoured to portray him as acting as a young boy would. The author's consistent efforts to depict Jesus in this light – extending from the beginning of the *Paidika* right through to the Temple narrative in Chapter 17 – argue that he is intent upon stressing Jesus's humanity throughout the work.[16]

Just as the miracles of the adult Jesus are largely determined by his day-to-day contexts as an adult, so it is with the youthful Jesus. The contexts in which Jesus performs his miraculous actions are those typical for a young boy. Almost all of them take place at school, at play and at home.

3.2 *Jesus as* Wunderkind

If the Jesus of the *Paidika* is a child, even a superficial reading of the *Paidika*'s episodes reveals that miracles are an essential constituent of all of the narratives. Jesus's miracles are intimately connected with the account of his infancy, and they cannot be readily separated from it. Of necessity, therefore, when one considers the child Jesus, one also needs to reflect on Jesus's superhuman words and deeds.

The *Paidika* implies that Jesus has possessed these supernatural capabilities from birth. They are not capabilities that he gradually obtains or learns – they are seemingly innate and consistently characterize Jesus from the outset of the narrative onward.[17] Larry Hurtado rightly observes that the *Paidika* advances 'a sincere (but very unsophisticated) religious inference that, as the Son of God from his birth onward, Jesus should (or can) be portrayed as already manifesting his divine powers, which include his knowledge of all that Christian faith came to claim about his transcendent status and origins'.[18]

The very first episode in the *Paidika* describes the five-year-old at play on the edge of a stream, when he gathers the unclean water into pools and makes it miraculously clean, 'not by deed but by word alone' (2.1). Already at the age of five, Jesus is able to perform miracles entirely by divine fiat. He is no mere thaumaturge or magician, nor does he call upon any other power to accomplish his will – he enacts it by virtue of his own authority and his own word.

Moreover, as was mentioned last chapter, Jesus's gathering of the water into pools and separation of the earth from the water can be paralleled with God's actions in the first chapters of Genesis. In the same way that God separates the waters from the earth, Jesus does too. And in the same way that God creates living creatures out of earth, so too does Jesus when he fashions the sparrows out of clay and brings them to life. That Jesus performs both the cleansing of the water and the vivification of the sparrows on the Sabbath implies, in addition, that he

---

16. Mussies (2008), p. 604.
17. Burkett (2011), p. 52; Lapham (2003), p. 130.
18. Hurtado (2003), p. 451.

is Lord of the Sabbath and not limited by its strictures. Such actions place him in a position similar to that of God. Whether the author of the *Paidika* was familiar with Jn 5.17 or not, Jesus's words there provide a fitting answer to the young Jesus's detractors: 'My Father is still working, and I also am working.' So from the outset of the *Paidika* Jesus is portrayed as possessing superhuman abilities – abilities that resemble the powers that characterize God. Jesus is more than a mere wonderworker: he partakes of the divine.

The same holds true for Jesus's revivification of his dead playmate, Zeno. The restored Zeno addresses Jesus as 'Lord' (κύριε), and when Zeno's parents witness his revivification they 'glorify God and worship (προσεκύνησαν) the child Jesus' (9.3 cf. Mt. 14.33). Both the designation 'Lord' and the word 'worship' have significant points of contact with the phraseology of the canonical Gospels, and represent Jesus in terms that associate him with God. The other miracles that are attributed to Jesus further establish his exceptional power. He exerts control over nature when he brings about a miraculous harvest (11.1-2). He can kill or blind people and restore them just as easily. He is able to cure a snakebite simply by blowing on the wound, can lengthen boards at will and make cloth impermeable to water. The entire natural world is seemingly subject to his will.

If Jesus's divine power seems virtually unlimited, the same holds true for his divine insight. It, too, is in evidence from the beginning of the narrative. For instance, the sophistication of the curse that Jesus inflicts on Annas's son in Chapter 3 – 'Your fruit is without root and your shoot is withered like a branch parched in a harsh wind' – is hardly typical of the playground taunts and invective of a five-year-old (3.2). Jesus's divine knowledge is also a hallmark of each of his three appearances in school. His first teacher is utterly shamed by Jesus's profound and abstruse utterances (7.1-4), his second teacher merely gets angry (13.2), while his third teacher delights in his 'marvellous words' and asks for more (14.2). In discussions with his father, Jesus points out Joseph's deep-seated ignorance and want of perception (5.3). The 'Jews', for their part, proclaim that they had never heard any utterances like those of Jesus, not even from a teacher of the law or a Pharisee (6.5), something emphasized at the end of the *Paidika*, where the teachers of the law and the Pharisees themselves acclaim Jesus's unprecedented wisdom (17.4) in the Temple.[19] In short, the *Paidika* invariably portrays Jesus's wisdom and insight as eclipsing those of anyone else in the work. As with his power, Jesus's knowledge appears to be virtually boundless.[20]

The above sketch indicates that Jesus's supernatural power and wisdom are constant features of the *Paidika*. They appear in conjunction with each other over the entirety of the work, and each of the individual episodes combines indications of Jesus's human youthfulness with examples of his extraordinary

---

19. Vielhauer (1975), p. 674.
20. So, too, Foster (2014) p. 332.

.[21] The work's litany of miracles, together with its recurrent references to Jesus's age ensure that over the course of the narrative the reader is constantly aware that Jesus is – as the German word *Wunderkind* aptly expresses it – a fusion of miracles and youth.[22]

3.3 Jesus as an 'Ideal Child'

This preliminary overview of the young Jesus as both human and miraculously endowed presents the *Paidika*'s reader with a pressing need to reconcile these two representations. In light of the above traits, how is Jesus the child to be interpreted? The remainder of this chapter will concentrate on these two issues and consider why Jesus is portrayed in the manner he is.

The first issue is whether the *Paidika*'s picture of Jesus is intended to portray him as an actual first-century child, or as an 'idealized' one – an entity socially constructed by Graeco-Roman adults to exemplify the traits that children 'ought' to possess. Burke has proposed that 'references to children in Graeco-Roman literature are of two kinds: real, reflecting the actual lives and experiences of their subjects, and ideal, reflecting the way adults would prefer children to behave'.[23] In the case of the latter, the qualities one would normally expect to see associated with children – playfulness, innocence, impulsiveness, disobedience – are absent, and replaced by qualities valued in adults – wisdom, maturity, conformity, composure.[24]

This distinction is central to Burke's investigation of the child Jesus, and he (and others following him) maintain that it is fundamental to the *Paidika*'s portrait of Jesus, which represents an *idealized* child.[25]

> [The *Paidika*'s] Jesus is consistent with the idealized portrayals of children found in the comparative literature, inscriptions, and images. He does not play, speak or act like children do. His every action is charged with meaning, his every

---

21. Hägg (2012), p. 176. Cf. Dzon (2011), p. 184: 'The types of miracles he works and the context in which they occur often illustrate his two natures at the same time.'

22. The assumptions made in this section about Jesus's divine nature will be substantiated more fully in Chapter 4.

23. Burke (2010), p. 247.

24. Ibid. Cf. Burke (2009), pp. 35–40. For a construction of the early Christian 'ideal child', see Leyerle (2013), p. 568.

25. Burke's view has proven to be very influential, although two of the most recent studies of the *Paidika* make their response to Burke less than clear. Davis (2014), p. 14 is unduly ambiguous when he says that 'this Jesus conforms to stereotypes of Graeco-Roman childhood'. To which stereotypes is Davis referring? Betsworth (2015), p. 155 is also ambiguous in her seeming acceptance of both the contrary positions of Aasgaard (2010) and Burke (2009).

word offers a lesson to be learned. His advanced intellectual abilities confound and amaze his teachers and neighbours. And his deeds foreshadow his future greatness. IGT depicts the young Jesus as mature and wise not because he is not really human but because, in the eyes of the text's author and audience, these things make him human.[26]

Burke's argument that the youthful Jesus conforms to a popular Graeco-Roman ideal of children is grounded in his presupposition that the *Paidika* is a *bios*. As noted in Chapter 1, he and others maintain that the *bios* genre exerts a dominant influence on the *Paidika* and that its accounts of Jesus as a child overlap significantly with other ancient *bioi* that contain narratives of the childhood of notable Graeco-Roman figures. The lives of these figures are idealized, and Burke maintains that the life of Jesus is no exception.

Burke also appeals to the ancient convention of the 'wise child' (*puer senex*, παῖς τέλειος), where a child is portrayed as being 'superhuman in his maturity', possessing adult attributes while being yet a child.[27] This convention was often applied to children, and is widely attested in funerary imagery, eulogies and epitaphs.[28] For Burke, Jesus's precocity puts him squarely in the company of many other ancient 'wise children', and suggests that Jesus's wisdom is not necessarily a sign of his divinity.[29] While Burke does acknowledge that Jesus possesses divine qualities, he tends to downplay them by arguing that an excessive focus on these attributes 'results in a neglect of parallels with human figures', and also leads one to misconstrue the *Paidika*'s Jesus as a 'young gnostic redeemer'.[30] He contends, instead, that Jesus should be interpreted as an exceptional youth who is endowed with divine traits. He is not an everyday child. He has been fashioned and reshaped according to adult values, whereby he has been transmuted into a virtual adult, at least with respect to his demeanour, understanding and sensibility. So even though he appears to be a child, he is actually depicted as a mini-adult, who, but for his age, is the exact counterpart of the mature Jesus of the Gospels. In Burke's view, to portray Jesus simply as a normal child instead of an idealized one would 'break with convention'.[31] Jesus's exceptional character demands an idealized *bios*.

Attractive as Burke's approach is, it is not free of problems. The first is methodological. While it is imperative that the *Paidika* be contextualized within the framework of the ancient world, it is also essential that the work itself should be allowed to comment on Jesus as a child *first*, before having recourse to larger

---

26. Burke (2010), p. 289.
27. Burke (2010), p. 223; (2009), pp. 34, 37; Chartrand-Burke (2008b), pp. 135-7.
28. Burke (2010), pp. 223-4.
29. Ibid., p. 224.
30. Ibid., p. 269.
31. Burke (2009), p. 42. See also Stewart (2015), pp. 1-2.

al and generic matrices.[32] Because Burke appears to assume that the work *is* a *bios*, he tends to utilize that lens.[33] But the *Paidika* does not identify itself as a *bios*, and questions remain about its genre. As noted earlier, in its exclusive focus on Jesus's childhood, the *Paidika* is unlike almost any *bios* known to us. And although the gospel genre is often considered a subgenre of the *bios*,[34] the *Paidika* is itself generically different from the canonical Gospels since it focuses on only one part of the Jesus story.[35]

Yet the assumption that the *Paidika* is a *bios* has a number of far-reaching consequences for interpreting the text, including the suggestion that these 'lives' do not have a developmental component. According to an often-cited article by Christopher Pelling, it was conventional to suppose that the character of an individual was already formed in one's youth and did not undergo much appreciable change.[36] As a consequence, *bioi* would provide characteristic instances of an individual character's *ethos*, but not demonstrate any appreciable development. Childhood episodes were not typically included in these *bioi*, but when they were, they formed part of the overall pattern by demonstrating the underlying consistency of the individual's character. The 'child was father of the man', and there was no appreciable difference between the two.[37] Accordingly, Burke contends that the *Paidika* shows no character development; the various *Paidika* episodes reflect the canonical Gospels and demonstrate the overall consistency of Jesus's character: 'Readers should not expect to see the young Jesus grow and mature as the text progresses – indeed, Jesus is here presented as a cursing wonderworker because the author considers the adult Jesus to have been a cursing wonderworker'.[38] But, if, as was argued in Chapter 1, the *Paidika* is not a *bios* but a tertiary, parevangelical subgenre of gospel, then Burke's argument does not apply.

Second, there are good reasons for doubting the applicability of the *puer senex* convention to the *Paidika*. It has been uncritically accepted by some *Paidika* scholars, but goes largely unmentioned in studies of ancient childhood. And while it has a very general biblical and literary application,[39] Burke's specific formulation of it is atypical.[40] More problematic yet is that Burke's appeal to the convention

---

32. It is noteworthy, for instance, that Burke (2010) devotes 45 pages to children in antiquity (pp. 223–68) before he begins his discussion of Jesus in the *Paidika*.

33. The basis for Burke's assumption is unclear.

34. Burridge (2004), pp. 246–7.

35. Ibid., pp. 242–3.

36. Pelling (1990), p. 240.

37. Hägg (2012), pp. 125–6, 253.

38. Chartrand-Burke (2008a), p. 108; Chartrand-Burke (2008b), p. 137.

39. Gnilka (1983), pp. 1077–8; Carp (1980), pp. 736–9.

40. Curtius (2013 [1953]), pp. 98–101; Keith Bradley's caveat is especially a propos in this instance: 'The literary representation of children cannot be explained by topoi alone': Bradley (2013), p. 647#8.

seems contradictory. He draws on the convention to demonstrate that the figure of the idealized Jesus in the *Paidika* is really no different from other idealized youths in the Graeco-Roman world. They are all exceptional human beings. But at the same time Burke acknowledges that the *Paidika* shows Jesus to be divine. Since, as indicated above, the very profusion of miracles ascribed to Jesus seems calculated to show him to be divine,[41] why, then, would the author invoke the *puer senex* motif, and imply that Jesus's miraculous deeds were no different from other notable humans? In the final analysis, the *puer senex* convention does not apply to the *Paidika*'s Jesus.[42] Burke emphasizes it because it stresses Jesus's humanity in contrast to a gnostic divine Jesus and because it fits with the *bios* genre.[43] But the trope is misleading. It obscures Jesus's divinity, and it also implies that Jesus is mature when it is more appropriate to acknowledge that despite his exceptional understanding, Jesus is very far from being mature – as will be seen below.

In addition to these problematic presuppositions, the assertions that Burke makes about the idealized Jesus are not borne out by the *Paidika*. One of the most questionable is Burke's claim that Jesus 'does not play ... like children do',[44] when in fact, the youthful Jesus is twice portrayed as playing (ἔπαιζεν 2.1; 9.1) in the company of other children (παιδία 2.2; παιδίων 9.1). References to children playing are uncommon in ancient literature, and the *Paidika* is distinctive precisely because it includes these references.[45]

Similarly, Burke's claim that Jesus does not display any of the impulsiveness typical of children is difficult to substantiate. Jesus's killings are all characterized by impulsiveness, a feature particularly evident in the opening of the *Paidika*, where the five-year-old Jesus peremptorily kills two youths in the space of two verses (3.3-4.1). If this were not impulsive enough, the narrative repeatedly emphasizes that his various curses took place 'immediately' (3.3; 4.1; 5.1). The same is true for Jesus's killing of his second teacher: Jesus retaliates immediately after he is struck. Moreover, the disproportionate severity of Jesus's retaliation also speaks to his impulsiveness. The very fact that he can respond to trifling offences with a draconian death sentence shows that his judgements are not considered or deliberate, but the gratification of an instinctive desire for revenge. Such examples indicate that we do not have the measured 'wisdom' and 'maturity' that Burke suggests characterize the Jesus of the *Paidika*. The very fact that Jesus goes on to reverse his judgements is decisive.

---

41. Johnson (2009), p. 185.

42. Passages like 6.5 leave open the possibility that the 'Jews' viewed him in this light, but it is clearly not the author's perspective.

43. Chartrand-Burke (2008b), p. 136.

44. Burke (2010), pp. 247, 289. As Litwa (2014, p. 73) perceptively notes, Burke tends to overstress Jesus's humanity because he is wary of claims that the *Paidika* is a gnostic document.

45. Horn and Martens (2009), p. 196.

These observations are equally pertinent to suggestions, such as one by Stephen Davis, that Jesus would 'have been understood to embody divine Reason (*Logos*) in such a way that it allows him to discipline [i.e. curse] a wayward young soul'.[46] But if the *Paidika*'s author was aware of John's divine *logos*, Jesus's actions as *logos* are hardly 'full of grace' (πλήρης χάριτος, Jn 1.14). Jesus's immediate killing of a boy who merely bumps into him is hardly a gracious or reasonable form of discipline. This observation also casts doubt on Jesus's alleged 'composure'. Where the canonical Gospels do occasionally refer to the adult Jesus's emotions,[47] the *Paidika* mentions the infant Jesus's anger or irritation on three occasions (6.8 ἠγανάκτησεν; 6.9 ὀργῆς; 8.2 παροργίσαι).[48] The last of these incidents is the most revealing, occurring just after Jesus has revoked all of his curses: 'and no one dared to anger (παροργίσαι) him from that time onward' (8.2). The passage implies, first of all, that some – if not all – of Jesus's curses had been a consequence of Jesus's anger, so we can hardly speak of Jesus cursing in a 'composed' fashion.[49] Second, it implies that people expected Jesus to continue responding to them angrily and that it was up to them to prevent this from happening. Evidently, they were not counting on Jesus's measured and temperate actions, but their own circumspection to rescue themselves from his curses.

Of a piece with this is the notion that the child Jesus is an obedient son. After Jesus kills the careless boy, the boy's parents blame Joseph. Joseph remonstrates with Jesus, who completely ignores him, prompting Joseph to grab hold of Jesus's ear and yank it (5.1-2). Later, Jesus's antisocial deeds lead Joseph and Mary to sequester him in the fear that he might harm others (13.13; 14.1-3) or bring the townspeople to put them under a ban (10.2). Jesus, therefore, is hardly an unqualified example of the ideal, obedient son.

While it is possible to mention other discrepancies in Burke's supposition of an idealized young Jesus, these examples are probably sufficient. They disclose a figure who, in certain respects, is the precise opposite of the one proposed by Burke. This obstreperous Jesus is the alter ego of the composed and mature Jesus who does fit Burke's profile.

3.4 *The Holy Terror as Divine Child*

Joseph's caution to Zacchaeus, Jesus's first teacher – 'Don't consider him a little human (μικροῦ ἀνθρώπου 6.3)!' – serves as a helpful starting place for assessing

---

46. Davis (2014), p. 86.
47. Whether any of these 'emotions' refers to Jesus's anger is uncertain.
48. Only two of these words are used of Jesus in the Gospels: ὀργή at the Pharisees (Mk 3.5) and ἀγανακτέω at the disciples (Mk 10.14). On Jesus's anger, especially in John's Gospel, cf. Voorwinde (2005), pp. 168–77.
49. The Gs version of the *Paidika* does not show a direct link between Jesus's anger and his curses, but compare Ga and Gd at 3.2, 4.1, 14.2.

the *Paidika*'s portrayal of Jesus.[50] What Joseph seems to mean is: 'Don't treat Jesus merely as a young boy: he is something considerably more.' How much more becomes clearer as the *Paidika* progresses. For instance, in the very same sentence Jesus paradoxically asserts both that Joseph was his father (πάτερ 6.4) and that he pre-existed Joseph (6.4). He later affirms that he was God's son (17.3) and that he had been sent by God from heaven to save 'those below' (8.1). Jesus clearly regards himself as having a divine identity, and as being much more than simply a 'young boy'. Further justification for this Christology will be presented below in Chapter 4; it is sufficient for the moment to recognize that Jesus is presented as being, in some measure, divine.

This recognition returns us to one of the chief interpretive dilemmas of the *Paidika*. What is to be made of Jesus's 'unchristian' actions? If Jesus is indeed divine in some sense, and his actions are divinely empowered, can his behaviour ever be faulted? Shouldn't one just say (along with Alexander Pope), 'Whatever is, is right'?[51] or that (*a priori*) 'Jesus can do no wrong'? Is the *Paidika*'s Jesus meant to serve as an ideal model for young children or not?[52]

There is little doubt that in the *Paidika* Jesus's understanding of divine realities is incontestably right. His explanation of the alpha and the other interpretations he provides attest to his heavenly insight, and he is regularly acclaimed for it. But do Jesus's deeds have a similar divine warrant? Since Jesus possesses the power to kill and to restore to life, to enact his will simply by uttering a command, and to exert his authority over nature, does not this very ability to perform such actions demonstrate his and their moral legitimacy? His healing of the afflicted, his raising people from the dead and his growth of a superabundant harvest to benefit the poor all testify to his compassion. Such actions are morally praiseworthy and fit easily with the ethos of a loving god. But what about his more questionable actions?

A number of commentators affirm categorically that Jesus's behaviour is exemplary. Kurt Erlemann proclaims in his study of *Paidika* 9 that 'Jesus was without blame, even in his early childhood'. Jeffrey Siker contends that, '[Jesus] is capable of terrible deeds, but by definition none of them is sinful.' Reidar Aasgaard, too, affirms that Jesus does not act unjustly: 'His cursing is just. For IGT, the problem is not on the part of Jesus, but on the part of those being cursed: they should already at the outset have realized who he is and thus not have challenged him. … Theological concerns take the lead over moral interest: ethics is made subordinate to Christology.'[53] Can it be, then, that the *Paidika* is really advocating an amoral Christ?

---

50. On the possible connection between Zacchaeus and Johann ben-Zakkai, see Neusner (1964), pp. 57–9. Tony Burke reminds me, however, that the original reading was likely 'little cross'.

51. Alexander Pope, *An Essay on Man* l. 292. Siker (2015), p. 85, makes this same point: 'Whatever the child Jesus does is right, because he is divine.'

52. As Aasgaard (2010), pp. 212–13, would argue.

53. Erlemann (2013), p. 845: my translation. 'Jesus war ohne Schuld, und das schon in seiner frühen Kindheit.' Cf. Siker (2015), p. 85; Aasgaard (2010), p. 161.

3.5 A Child Reprehensible to Man and God?

Despite the above chorus of opinion, there are strong reasons for asserting that the *Paidika* is not advocating an amoral Jesus. In fact, the work itself indicates that some of Jesus's deeds are reprehensible to both humans and God.[54] The very fact that Jesus twice *reconsiders* and *reverses* his actions is a prime indication that something was not right.[55] If the problem was exclusively with Jesus's beholders, why would he need to relent? But in addition to this narrative element, the *Paidika* provides further indications that some of Jesus's actions are deficient.

One clear indication is provided by Zacchaeus's plans for Jesus's education – notably his template for Jesus's *paideia*.[56] *Paideia* was a global programme of instruction in the Graeco-Roman world that involved the education and socialization of the whole child. Jesus was to be 'instructed in the alphabet and know every kind of learning and learn to show concern for his peers and honour old age and reverence his elders' (6.2; cf. 6.8). It soon emerges from the narrative that Jesus has no difficulty with the alphabet and every kind of learning – he is master of them all. But the second part of Zacchaeus's programme – Jesus's 'social *paideia*' is frequently overlooked, when it should not be.[57] Leyerle rightly remarks that the 'inculcation of correct social behaviour was as much a part of classical education as the acquisition of literacy'.[58] The following discussion, therefore, will focus on aspects of Jesus's social behaviour that the author suggests is deficient.

Although Jesus is intellectually precocious, he is a failure in the first half of the *Paidika* when it comes to the treatment of his peers, his parents and his elders. Insofar as he is divine, his miraculous knowledge and understanding are fully in evidence: Cullmann observes, 'he already possesses all divine wisdom in its fullest range'.[59] Yet, despite his understanding, Jesus is seemingly incapable of demonstrating basic human respect for others. His divine powers adversely affect all those around him, whether they are his peers or his elders. Irenaeus lauds the child Jesus of the canonical Gospels as a paragon for other children of 'piety, righteousness and submission' (Irenaeus *Adv. Haer.* 2.21.4), but the perspective of the *Paidika* is precisely the opposite. In fact, in a recent work on killing in the early church, Ronald Sider concludes that its violent portrayal of Jesus is virtually unprecedented in the Patristic period: 'An extensive

---

54. My term 'reprehensible' echoes Bauer's (1909), p. 91, observation that Jesus committed 'morally reprehensible acts'.

55. Tony Burke germanely points out, however, that Yahweh sometimes 'repents' of his actions, and occasionally reverses or undoes deeds that he has already performed (personal communication).

56. On *paideia*, see Stroumsa (2016), pp. 4–5; Clark (1994), pp. 18–23. Whitenton (2015), p. 232, has also emphasized the importance of Zacchaeus's course of instruction.

57. Davis (2014), p. 102 mentions it briefly.

58. Leyerle (2013), p. 570.

59. Cullmann (1991), p. 442.

search in the vast apocryphal Christian literature dating before the time of Constaı has located no other ... narratives of this kind.'[60]

Jesus's violent behaviour towards his peers is especially revealing. Having another child whisk away water from your pools is certainly bothersome, and to a young child lacking any concern for or insight into others, it might well seem like a capital offence. But to an adult, schooled in *paideia* and self-control, it should (rightly) appear as a mere trifle. Yet Jesus's murderous actions are unwarranted and entirely lacking in any ethical proportion.[61] Not only does Jesus fail to demonstrate Christian ethical values, but he completely disregards the *lex talionis* as well. His infantile impulses are his only moral compass. This is also apparent in the episode with the young boy who blunders into him. Jesus's vindictiveness far outstrips the offence, all the more when he fails to acknowledge the grief of the child's parents, and blinds them as well.

A similar deficiency is evident in Jesus's reaction to Zeno. It is true that this time he has nothing to do with Zeno's death; in fact, he is represented as playing with other children, which suggests a measure of social integration. Nevertheless, his reaction to the dead Zeno illustrates that a sympathetic concern for others is still not a significant part of his childish makeup. When he is blamed for Zeno's death, his overriding concern is to vindicate himself. Jesus seemingly does not bring Zeno back to life out of any concern for the dead boy, but merely so that the child can testify on his behalf. Moreover, the ambiguity surrounding Jesus's command to Zeno to 'go back to sleep' leaves open the possibility that Jesus lets Zeno die again.[62] Childish narcissism continues to dominate his attitude towards others.

The related deficiency of the youthful Jesus, as illustrated by Zacchaeus's pedagogical agenda, is Jesus's failure to venerate old age and honour his elders. If the youthful Jesus demonstrates a lack of concern for his peers, he is also wanting in respect for almost every adult he encounters. As just noted in the case of the parents of the boy who blunders into Jesus, their complaint to Joseph is entirely justified: Jesus should bless instead of curse. Yet Jesus's response is to punish them with blindness: 'These ones will receive their punishment' (5.1). He then ignores Joseph's criticisms, and when Joseph yanks on his ear (5.1-3), Jesus goes on to mock his father, claiming that Joseph needs to be taught a lesson by him (6.4).

Jesus is equally contemptuous of Zacchaeus; Jesus ridicules his reputation as a specialist in the study of the law – a *nomikos* – and asserts that he actually knows nothing about the law (τὸν νόμον 6.4). Jesus's subsequent disquisition of the alpha results in the utter shaming and humiliation of Zacchaeus: 'I dwell on my shame because although I am an old man I have been bested by a child. I have lost heart and will die or flee from this village because of this child' (7.3). Jesus's disdain also extends to the Jewish people as a whole when they marvel at his precocious utterances. Even though their astonishment is laudatory, it elicits a dismissive

---

60. Sider (2012), pp. 129–30. For later traditions, cf. Couch (2006), pp. 312–43.
61. Bagley (1985), pp. 14–15.
62. Erlemann (2013), p. 843; see also Whitenton (2015), p. 229.

response from him – he leaps about and says, 'I was toying (ἔπαιζον) with you because I know you marvel at trifles and are small-minded.'[63] His indifference creates the impression that he is dismissing a bunch of ignorant yokels, despite their apparent receptivity to what he has to say.

Jesus's second teacher experiences an even greater ordeal than the first. In his attempt to school Jesus, the teacher also strikes Jesus for his disobedience, and Jesus retaliates by killing him. Corporal punishment of students on the part of educators was a regular, if unfortunate, feature of ancient education, but Jesus's retaliation was not.[64] Jesus's reaction is totally incommensurate with the pain that he had experienced, and killing one's teacher, it goes without saying, does not conform to the respect for elders advocated by Zacchaeus's *paideia*.

In sum, the child Jesus's lack of concern for his peers and his failure to venerate his elders run totally contrary to the *paideia* expected from everyday students. While Jesus's supernatural abilities are unmatched, he is woefully deficient in ordinary humanity. What is more, his infantile petulance is amplified by his divine nature. Without his divine power, his bad-tempered outbursts would simply be regrettable acts of pique by an intractable child. With his divine power, his actions become divine disasters.

Does this failure in *paideia* imply that God the father is out of sympathy with some of Jesus's actions? Significantly, Jesus's statement of his divine mission gives precisely this impression. Jesus states that 'the one who sent me to you commanded me' to save you and 'to summon you to heaven above' (8.1). This passage is the first time in the *Paidika* where Jesus mentions his heavenly father and the task that God has enjoined upon him. At this point, apparently, Jesus is now disposed to obey this divine bidding. Once he does, there is a fundamental change in his actions to such a degree that almost all of his subsequent deeds are benevolent.[65] But the very fact that Jesus immediately relents of all of his previous actions strongly suggests that Jesus had been acting in a spirit exactly contrary to God's will.

Just how significant Jesus's failure has been up to this point can be determined from a summary of his actions: he saved nobody, but managed to kill or blind several people, mainly children. He has failed to teach others and summon them to heaven. Instead, he has mocked those who marvelled at his divine abilities, and shamed those whom he might have instructed. It would be fair to say, in fact, that at this point in the narrative he has totally alienated everyone with whom he has come into contact and has failed to enact any part of his divine commission.

That the behaviour of the young Jesus would have failed to secure God's approbation can also be inferred from Luke and John. The extent to which the

---

63. Burke (2010), p. 315, notes that the description of Jesus 'leaping about' is absent in the earlier traditions.

64. Davis (2014), pp. 96–7.

65. Johnson (2009), p. 185, also notes 'a genuine shift in emphasis beginning at 8:1'; see also, more generally, Whitenton (2015), p. 230#42. Verse 8.1 is absent from Syriac manuscript W. Cf. Burke (2016), p. 65 note e.

Paidika's author is familiar with all the canonical Gospels is unclear; nevertheless, there are sufficient grounds for assuming he had, at a minimum, an acquaintance with Luke and probably with John. Since Luke furnishes the basis for *Paidika* 17, it does not seem unwarranted to appeal to that gospel for the verdict it would cast on the young Jesus's actions. When this is done, however, the above deeds of Jesus emerge as being diametrically *opposed* to the adult Jesus's actions and teachings. Jesus's teachings in the canonical Gospels need to be taken as normative, and Jesus's words and deeds in the *Paidika* should be evaluated in light of them – not the other way around. In fact, it is highly likely that the author is actually *presupposing* some knowledge of Luke or John on the part of his readers, precisely to show where the infant Jesus falls short of the adult Jesus. The contrast between the two figures shows where the *Paidika's* Jesus emerges as deficient.

We need only consider the adult Jesus's commandment to 'Love your enemies, do good to those who hate you, bless those who curse you, pray for those who abuse you. If anyone strikes you on the cheek, offer the other also' (Lk. 6.27-29). It would be difficult to find a narrative more antithetical to the spirit of Jesus's words in Luke than the first four chapters of the *Paidika*. The child Jesus retaliates against his enemies, harms those who are against him, curses those who oppose him and brooks no provocation. In the first half of the *Paidika*, he shows no love, does nothing good, and blesses and forgives no one. Where the young Jesus kills, the adult Jesus raises from the dead (Lk. 7.11-17); where the young Jesus blinds, the adult Jesus restores sight (Lk. 18.35-43).

When all these data are taken into consideration, it emerges that the author of the *Paidika* shows some of the young Jesus's actions to be reprehensible both to man and God. Jesus falls short of the purely human standards advanced in the scheme of *paideia* outlined by Zacchaeus, as well as the divine directives that had been laid out for him by God, and the moral teachings advocated by his adult self. Despite its superficial indications otherwise, the underlying ethos of the *Paidika* does not provide Jesus with carte blanche. In the end, 'Whatever is, isn't right.'

3.6 Chilldhood Development

As already discussed in Chapter 2, the most satisfactory means of explaining Jesus's seemingly contradictory behaviour is to assume that there is a developmental schema at work in the *Paidika*. This solution, however, has been rejected by a number of commentators.[66] Burke, for instance, because of his commitment to the *bios* genre, rejects the possibility of Jesus's undergoing any development and draws attention instead to the changes that everyone else in the narrative experiences: 'The real transformation in the narrative is made in those around Jesus, not

---

66. Hock (1995), p. 96; Vielhauer (1975), p. 674.

Jesus himself.'[67] When Jesus's family and neighbours initially react to him with condemnation and disbelief, he responds by punishing them. Yet once the people around him begin to recognize his divine nature, and start to plumb his true identity, their change in attitude draws responses from Jesus that are increasingly benevolent.[68] His third teacher, for instance, exemplifies the appropriate response: one should respond with reverence and praise. These essential changes, however, occur exclusively on the part of those surrounding Jesus. Chartrand-Burke maintains that 'At no time does the text suggest that Jesus is rehabilitated; in fact, it is Jesus' teachers, neighbours, and parents who have a lesson to learn here.'[69]

This argument has some merit, and the *Paidika*'s characters do display something of a changing attitude to Jesus. Yet, just as clearly, this is not the whole story. The crowds of Jewish people, for instance, who assume a choral function in the *Paidika*, remain relatively consistent in their attitudes. From the very outset, their exclamations reveal that they sense a divine quality in Jesus: 'From where was this child born, that his word becomes deed?' (4.1). They exclaim that his divine utterances are unparalleled (6.5) and they are astonished at his words (14.2). Finally, they reflect on his healings and prophesy more to come: 'He saved many souls from death and will continue to save all the days of his life' (16.3). While this final remark does contain a positive evaluation not found in their earlier utterances, the people have nonetheless been attuned to his extraordinary qualities from the beginning. Where their attitude appreciably changes is when Jesus begins to act positively. But this is precisely the point: Jesus changes, too. The *Paidika* does not describe a one-sided transformation, rather, it sketches an ongoing dialectic between Jesus and all the other characters. None of the figures in the work is static; they react to him and he to them.

If, therefore, it can be assumed that Jesus also changes over the course of the *Paidika*, from where does this developmental tendency originate? If a non-developmental emphasis typifies the Graeco-Roman approach to biography, what induced the *Paidika*'s author to proceed along developmental lines? The answer, quite simply, is contained in a source that we are certain that the author used. While we have no certainty about his familiarity with *bioi* – we are certain he was familiar with the Gospel of Luke. What is more, these indications of Jesus's development are drawn from the passage of Luke that the *Paidika*'s author cites in Chapter 17. The *Paidika*'s reliance on Luke, chapter 2.41-51 is universally

---

67. Chartrand-Burke (2008a), p. 108. Paulissen (2004), p. 28, makes a similar point – she argues that even though the narrative gives the impression that Jesus evolved, it is actually his audience who evolve.

68. Similar arguments are also made by Davis (2014), p. 109; cf. Paulissen (2004), p. 27, who nicely states that Jesus adapts his message and miracles to his interlocuters' level of faith.

69. Chartrand-Burke (2008a), pp. 108–9. Cf. Frilingos (2016), pp. 51-2; Betsworth (2015), p. 155.

accepted by scholars, and in it Luke twice gives expression to Jesus's development: 'The child grew and became strong, filled with wisdom; and the favour of God was upon him' (Lk. 2.40, Τὸ δὲ παιδίον ηὔξανεν καὶ ἐκραταιοῦτο πληρούμενον σοφίᾳ, καὶ χάρις θεοῦ ἦν ἐπ' αὐτό), and 'Jesus increased in wisdom and in years, and in divine and human favour' (Lk. 2.52, Καὶ Ἰησοῦς προέκοπτεν [ἐν τῇ] σοφίᾳ καὶ ἡλικίᾳ καὶ χάριτι παρὰ θεῷ καὶ ἀνθρώποις).[70] The *Paidika*'s reliance on the latter verse is obvious from *Paidika* 17.5, which is nearly identical to the verse in Luke: 'And Jesus increased in wisdom and in years, and in divine and human favour' (17.5 Καὶ ὁ Ἰησοῦς προέκοπτεν σοφίᾳ καὶ ἡλικίᾳ καὶ χάριτι παρὰ θεῷ καὶ ἀνθρώποις).[71]

Hence if the author of the *Paidika* were looking for clues about how to depict Jesus as a youth, Luke's Gospel is the obvious choice. It lays out a basic template for Jesus's youthful development, both before and after Jesus's visit to the Jerusalem Temple. The word προκόπτω, which occurs in the summaries both in Luke and in the *Paidika*, typically denotes 'moral and intellectual progress' and is, therefore, describing fundamental and integral changes in Jesus's character.[72] The same holds true for Jesus's growth in human and divine favour: because of this change, both God and humans react to him with increasing approbation. Jesus matures and they become more and more favourably disposed towards him. Jesus grows in strength, wisdom and God's favour up to the age of twelve (Lk. 2.40), and the text implies that the same process continues up until his public ministry (Lk. 2.52). The *Paidika*'s author appropriates both summary statements to serve as his guidelines for his own depiction of Jesus's development.

The influence of Luke is also to be discerned in the way the author of the *Paidika* has adopted the indications of Jesus's age from Luke. Luke 2.42 and 3.23 served as the inspiration for the *Paidika*'s numerous references to Jesus's age (2.1; 10.1; 12.1; 17.1).[73] Whatever reasons may lie behind Luke's mentions of Jesus's age, the *Paidika*'s expanded references create the impression that the author has constructed a basic developmental framework for Jesus. Naturally, these temporal indicators also serve other functions, such as unifying the narrative, but it is difficult to overlook the presence of a developmental and chronological trajectory in the *Paidika*.

In short, therefore, the *Paidika*'s author has looked to Luke for a narrative template of Jesus's development. It may even be that Luke's infancy narrative actually inspired the creation of the *Paidika*. Enslin perceptively remarks of Luke's phrases that 'one can scarcely avoid the feeling that it was words such as

---

70. Luke seems to be reliant on 1 Sam. 2.26 for this depiction.

71. On the notion of spiritual maturity, cf. Horn and Martens (2009), pp. 58–61.

72. LSJ s.v. Cf. BDAG s.v. 'to move forward to an improved state, *progress, advance* in what is good or in what is bad' (italics theirs); Lampe, *PGL*: 'of moral and spiritual progress'.

73. Note, also, the temporal markers to be found in Lk. 2.21-22. I owe this observation to Thomas Goud.

these which intrigued the later writers and led them to their conjectures both as to the way he "waxed strong" and was "filled with wisdom", and as to the nature of the "grace of God" which was upon him'[74]. This solution has the advantage of simplicity. There is no need to presuppose that the author was acquainted with Plutarch or the literary conventions of Graeco-Roman biography; all he required was a familiarity with Luke Chapter 2. And this he most certainly had.

3.7 Jesus's Development

Ursula Ulrike Kaiser makes the added observation that Jesus's activities tend to correspond with his ascribed age: the five-year-old plays in pools of water with other children, the seven-year-old helps his mother, the eight-year-old Jesus helps his father in the workshop and in the fields, the twelve-year-old engages in discussions of the Scriptures with the elders.[75]

Michael Whitenton has built on Kaiser's argument even further by suggesting that Jesus's varying ages conform to various developmental stages widely recognized in antiquity. Jesus at age five reflects an immature stage where he is wanting in self-control. His characterization 'as a rowdy five-year-old boy in Gs 1-9 fits within what was expected of young boys.'[76] By the age of seven or eight, boys were thought to have reached an age where they were to embark on the road to manhood, and Jesus in the *Paidika* has begun to do precisely this by assuming responsibility, practising self-control and displaying concern for others. Lastly, by the age of twelve, adolescent boys were popularly regarded as being on the cusp of manhood and as having completed their moral character formation, and this assessment also holds true for Jesus.[77] Over the course of these stages he has moved from being a selfish five-year-old to a mature and benevolent young man.

Whitenton's societal stages of development are, perhaps, not quite so universal as he implies, but his overall arguments for Jesus's maturation and transformation over the course of the *Paidika*'s narrative comport well with the arguments that have been made here. His observations also fit with ancient understandings of Graeco-Roman childhood, which was widely regarded as an imperfect and transitional state, and in which children were viewed as deficient adults.[78] Their chief deficiency, as Gillian Clark observes, was a lack of rationality.[79] Children were commonly thought to be tyrannized by their emotions and unable to control

---

74. Enslin (1951), p. 85; cf. Hägg (2012), p. 175.

75. Kaiser (2012), p. 938#62; cf. Aasgaard (2009), p.13.

76. Whitenton (2015), p. 229. Compare Betsworth (2015), p. 154, and Aasgaard (2009), p. 12, who makes similar observations.

77. Whitenton (2015), pp. 226–35.

78. Leyerle (2013), p. 570.

79. Clark (1994), p. 20.

them through reason. Clark cites Chrysostom to this effect, and his remarks might almost have been written as a description of the *Paidika*'s five-year-old Jesus:

> For nothing is so eager for vengeance as a childish mind. For children are tyrannized by anger, since it is an irrational passion. … There is irrationality – great irrationality – and great lack of reasoning at that age, so it is not surprising that a small child is dominated by anger. Often if they bump into something or fall, they will hit their knee in rage, or kick over a stool, and in that way their pain is relieved and their anger subsides. … For all the passions are tyrannous in children, since they do not yet have any way to control them: vainglory, desire, irrationality, anger, envy.[80]

In this deficient state, Chrysostom and others consider it imperative that children receive training and correction, and affirm that it is only with the onset of maturity that reason and self-control begin to prevail.[81]

These features indicate that a developmental framework is in view. One need only compare the first of the *Paidika*'s accounts with the last: Jesus's killings and their hostile reception contrasted with the universal praise and approbation that Jesus receives in the Temple. Jesus's character at the close of the work is emphatically not the same as it was at the beginning – it has undergone a profound transformation, and this turning point happens after his teaching session with Zacchaeus (8.1).[82] Up until this juncture, Jesus has done whatever he wished, killing his peers and dishonouring his elders. His acceptance of God's directives brings about a fundamental reversal whereby he moves from killing and maiming others to saving them.

The reason for such a turning point is not certain, but the likeliest supposition is that the author, having unequivocally (and unforgettably) demonstrated Jesus's power in both deeds and word, now considers it opportune for him to embark on his divine mission and calling. So, even if it is not entirely for the right reasons, Jesus raises Zeno from the dead, and shifts from killing to saving instead. And though Jesus has a relapse with his second teacher, he again relents and restores him (in some versions) after his third teacher has praised his abilities.

It is apparent, therefore, that Jesus has resolved upon a change, and this change of heart is signalled by his subsequent actions. Here the childlike humility attributed

---

80. Chrysostom, *Homily 4.4 on Colossians*, tr. Clark (1994), p. 20. Compare Lucian, *Fug.* 19 which describes fraudulent philosophers as being infantile: 'In irascibility, pettishness, and proneness to anger they are beyond young children; indeed, they give no little amusement to onlookers when their blood boils up in them for some trivial reason, so that they look livid in colour, with a reckless, insane stare, and foam (or rather, venom) fills their mouths.'

81. Leyerle (2013), p. 570.

82. Paulissen (2004), p. 20, likewise observes that Jesus begins by cursing the inhabitants, but saves them all afterwards.

to Jesus by Irenaeus does emerge. Jesus proves dutiful and helpful to both his parents. Instead of mocking his father, he becomes instrumental in helping him perform his tasks. His acts of salvation are commemorated by the crowd, and they predict that he will continue to save others (16.3). Finally, in the last chapter of the *Paidika*, he is again commended for his obedience to his parents (17.5).

The principal objection to this developmental interpretation is that, as was just noted, Jesus kills his second teacher in retaliation for being struck after the so-called 'turning point' at 8.1-2. If Jesus was maturing and developing respect for his elders, why is this episode included so late in the process? In its essentials, his action here is no different from his earlier ones. In fact, it could even be described as worse – Jesus does not kill Zacchaeus for striking him (6.8), but he does kill his second teacher for doing so (13.2). It is true that in most versions he later reverses this killing, but this still does not justify Jesus's murder.

This is certainly a problem, but the very similarities between the first two teaching episodes may provide a solution. It is highly probable that the second-teacher episode is a doublet of the Zacchaeus episode.[83] Jesus's two rejoinders are very similar, and when the teachers strike Jesus (6.8; 13.2), the identical phrase is used: 'And becoming enraged, his teacher struck him [on the head]' (6.8, Πικρανθεὶς δὲ ὁ καθηγητὴς ἔκρουσεν αὐτὸ [εἰς τὴν κεφαλήν]). Such similarities raise the question of why the author would want to create a doublet.[84] Very possibly, he wanted to include three teaching episodes in the *Paidika* which would allow him to include the third teacher's praise, as well as both of Jesus's remarks about the alpha and the beta, which are both different. Where Jesus says to Zacchaeus, 'Not knowing the nature of the alpha, how is it that you are teaching another the beta? ... First teach me the alpha and I will believe what you say about the beta' (6.9), he says to his second teacher, 'First tell me what the beta is, and I shall tell you what the alpha is' (13.2). In the former, Jesus wants to know about the alpha, in the latter, the beta. Given the variations of this alpha-beta apothegm, it is possible that the author had two variations of the saying and may have wished to incorporate both.

But why would the author put the second episode after 8.2, if he were trying to signal a change in Jesus's attitude? On the one hand, he likely wanted to space out the three teaching episodes, which would mean inserting the second and third episodes after 8.2. On the other, the third episode requires that Jesus reward the third teacher for his insight into Jesus's divine nature: 'Since you have spoken correctly and testified correctly, the one who was struck [i.e. the second teacher] will be saved because of you' (14.4). Jesus has already reversed his hostile actions at 8.2 in response to the first teacher's inklings of his true identity (7.4),[85] and this pattern is repeated with the third teacher to stress Jesus's clemency by again

---

83. Hock (1995), p. 133; cf. Foster (2006), p. 25.

84. Compare the discussion in Voicu (1998), p. 49#131, which would argue for several different sources.

85. Cf. Burke (1998), p. 33.

reversing his punishment.[86] So in this instance the reward motif proves stronger than the developmental motif. But, whatever the reason, this one anomaly is the only significant exception to the 'developmental arc' that characterizes Jesus's process of maturing.

Along with this 'development arc', it is also possible to discern a chiastic arrangement in the episodes of the *Paidika*. This arrangement is not perfect, but there is a solid basis for viewing the second half of the work as a response and correction to the first part.

    Heading/Prologue

A   Curse on Annas's Son
B   Curse on the Careless Boy
C   Joseph Rebukes Jesus
D   First Teacher (Zacchaeus)
E   Raising of Zeno
     Carrying Water in Cloak
     Miraculously Great Harvest
C' Joseph Blesses Jesus (Repair of Bed)
D   Second Teacher
D' Third Teacher
B' Healing of James's Snakebite
A' Healing of an Injured Foot
     Jesus in the Temple

The natural dividing point for this chiastic arrangement is the end of the Zacchaeus narrative, *Paidika* 8.1 (D). After Zacchaeus has finished confessing his ignorance, Jesus makes a pronouncement: 'Now let the unfruitful bear fruit, the blind see, and the foolish in heart gain understanding.' As noted above, this command is quite clearly a revocation of his earlier curses.[87] The son of Annas, who was made unfruitful by Jesus's curse, is restored. The sight of the parents of the careless boy is returned, and the foolishness of Zacchaeus is rectified. No mention is made of the restoration of the careless boy, but the next verse makes it evident that it happened as well: 'And immediately all who had fallen under his curse were saved' (8.2).

The later part of the *Paidika* displays the significant transformation in Jesus's attitude.[88] At the time of his brother James's near-fatal snakebite, Jesus is evidently moved with deep concern for his well-being; he *runs* to James to blow on the wound (15.2). The same is true for the youth whom he raises from the dead (16.1-2). Jesus forces his way through the crowd so that he can immediately

---

86. Foster (2014), p. 347 would also argue that a developmental aspect underlies all three teaching scenes.

87. Miller (2003), pp. 275, 282–3, considers this reversal a later interpolation in the text, but the Syriac textual tradition indicates that he is mistaken.

88. Cf. Johnson (2009), p. 186.

heal the wounded foot and raise the youth from the dead. His one-time divine indifference to the deaths of his peers has matured into a deep-seated compassion for stricken humans.

Nor does it seem entirely coincidental that the final two (chronologically later) episodes of the *Paidika* (barring the Lucan Temple narrative) should be resuscitations of two young men. His brother James is on the point of death (ἀπο λλυμένου 15.2), and the woodcutter with the injured foot has already died (16.1), when Jesus restores their lives. These two episodes form a notable counterpart to the first two episodes of the *Paidika* when Jesus killed the two children. Now he gives life instead of taking it away. Later editors may have played upon this chiasmus, where Jesus has moved from being angry with his peers and doing violence to them, to caring for and saving them. He is well on his way to becoming the saviour evidenced by the canonical Gospels. The forcefulness of the crowd's final acclamation signals Jesus' changed attitude 'He saved many souls (ψυχὰς) from death and will continue to save (σῶσαι) all the days of his life' (16.3). The reference to Jesus's future saving activities is clearly an allusion to the actions of Jesus recorded in the canonical Gospels (cf. σῴζω with ψυχή Lk. 6.9//Mk 3.4; Lk. 9.56, cf. Jn 12.47). This deliberate alignment of Jesus's saving actions as a youth with those that he performs as an adult is highly evocative. In fact, it is one of the very few instances in the *Paidika* where Jesus's future ministry is actually referenced, and it is probably no coincidence that it should be situated in one of the final sections of the *Paidika*.[89] The ability and willingness to save are now normative for Jesus and will, on the evidence of the canonical Gospels, characterize his life from this point onward. Yet, precisely how does the *Paidika* relate the child Jesus to Jesus the adult?

3.8 Jesus the Divine Child

The 'heretic' Nestorius is said to have asserted: 'I deny that God is two months or three months old.'[90] If Nestorius had a problem with Jesus as a baby, one can anticipate that he would similarly have experienced difficulties with stories of Jesus as an infant. But such reservations scarcely troubled the author of the *Paidika*. Its author does not seem to doubt that the infant Jesus possessed both divine and human attributes. Yet how does he reconcile these attributes with each other, especially given that Jesus is a child? Nestorius rightly recognized that human infancy is a diminished state.

The most recent attempt to address this problem is by Sharon Betsworth. She would distinguish 'Jesus the child' from the 'Child Jesus', who, following Aasgaard's

---

89. Burke (2010), p. 334 observes that in the Greek versions Ga and Gd, the crowds' words have been re-arranged so that they will figure in the penultimate chapter.

90. Cyril of Alexandria, *Epistle* 23, cited in Strange (1996), p. 46.

definition, is both 'true God and true child'.[91] She maintains that by the end of the *Paidika*, 'Jesus the child has indeed become the Child Jesus.' Yet, despite this outcome, she does not discern any real development in the narrative.[92] Instead, Jesus's character in the *Paidika* is predicated on whether he is interacting with children or adults. When he is engaging with the former, then 'Jesus the child' is in evidence; when it is with adults, it is the 'Child Jesus' who manifests a wisdom beyond his years.[93]

Betsworth's distinction is neat, but does not work well in practice. 'Jesus the child' heals his brother James and raises the young woodcutter from the dead, not the 'Child Jesus'. 'Jesus the child' plays with Zeno, but does he then transform into the 'Child Jesus' when Zeno's parents appear and he raises Zeno from the dead? Moreover, the curse that 'Jesus the child' inflicts on Annas's son – 'Your fruit is without root and your shoot is withered like a branch parched in a harsh wind' – is hardly the playground rhetoric of a five-year-old. It may display the fury of a five-year-old, but Jesus's mindset is not childish at all.

The same difficulty of trying to separate 'Jesus the child' and the Child Jesus is also apparent in several other of the *Paidika*'s episodes. The two opening accounts of the pools and the sparrows show that the child and the Child are indissolubly bound together. On the one hand, we have Jesus engaged in the type of play that is entirely typical of young children; on the other, there is the very strong theological subtext to Jesus's actions, which parallels his actions with those of God in the first chapters of Genesis. God separates the waters from the earth, so, too, does Jesus. God creates living creatures out of earth, so too does Jesus. These examples argue that Jesus the child and the Child Jesus cannot be differentiated.

A more satisfactory approach is to recognize that the work displays a two-natures *logos* Christology of the sort found in John's Gospel. The *Paidika*, as will become clearer in Chapter 4, has been influenced by Johannine Christology, and similar emphases can be found within it. Roland Deines expresses the paradoxes attendant on this Christology well:

> The most puzzling thing about the pre-existent word was indeed this: the word made flesh was an ordinary man, in the 'likeness of an ordinary man' and to be found behaving in the way ordinary people do: he was born as a baby; he was nursed, raised, educated, he needed to drink and to eat, he could get tired and was in need of sleep; even more, he was tempted by desire, sin, and anger, as he was in need of love and fellowship. But nevertheless, besides all these commonalities, he remained different: he knew things nobody can know, he said things no sober-minded person would ever dare to say, but he said them as if they were a matter of course. And he did things that no one else could do.[94]

---

91. Betsworth (2015), pp. 153, 156, citing Aasgaard (2009), p. 157.
92. Betsworth (2015), p. 156; cf. p. 155.
93. Betsworth (2015), pp. 156–7.
94. Deines (2012), p. 112.

As is also the case in John, the author has attributed two natures to the figure of Jesus, one divine and one human. His divine nature does not change or develop, but Jesus's human character does. To be fully human, Jesus needs to undergo the same sorts of developmental changes that human children normally experience. The years of Jesus's boyhood chronicle the process whereby he attains this maturity.[95]

It needs to be said that the *Paidika*'s author is to be commended for undertaking such a problematic exercise. John the Evangelist finds it difficult enough to reconcile the divine and human in the *adult* figure of Jesus, something much more difficult to do when dealing with a child. This feature helps to account for some of the *Paidika*'s more outlandish and ridiculous features.[96] Nevertheless, it represents an imaginative and creative – if limited – approach to the dilemmas posed by the Incarnation.

The result is attractive to readers because it shows a view of the Incarnation that suggests that, notwithstanding his divinity, Jesus also experienced the normal problems that humanity faces when growing up. Jesus shared human existence with other humans. He was like us. He may not have sinned per se, but he certainly performed actions in his youthful anger that he later chose to reverse.

As we have seen, these observations suggest that the *Paidika* is not concerned with Jesus 'growing up' so much as with Jesus 'growing down', that is to say, the process whereby Jesus's Graeco-Roman divine nature is harmonized with his human nature. Jesus's obstreperous anger is quelled and set aside in favour of a compassionate and controlled bearing towards humans. Yet, over the course of this process Jesus still retains his divine insight and divine sense of identity. As Johnson nicely expresses it, the *Paidika* recounts 'a successful struggle to control the divine *dynamis* that at first appears to overwhelm him and to see Jesus' entrance into adulthood (at 12) as one in which that struggle between the good and evil uses of power has been resolved'.[97]

The author of the *Paidika*, therefore, seems to presuppose a Christology where the infant Jesus is both divine and human, and where the duality of his two-natures accounts for the ambiguity of his actions. What makes this picture more complicated is that Jesus's divine nature does not really change, whereas the sensibility of his human nature changes appreciably. To say that Jesus's divine nature does not change means that the fact of Jesus's supernatural endowments does not change. He possesses the same divine power and knowledge over the course of the *Paidika*. What does change, however, is the manner in which Jesus puts these abilities to use. With the change and maturing of his human sensibility,

---

95. In using the word 'nature', I am not referencing later christological nomenclature, but settling on a term that, in an imprecise way, alludes to the different sides of Jesus's human–divine parentage and constitution.

96. The same problem is evident in many of the paintings of the Madonna and child, where the newborn's gravitas and raised finger are meant to reveal the presence of the Pantokrator in the paradoxical figure of a helpless baby.

97. Johnson (2009), p. 185.

arising out of his human nature, he comes to use the same power for good instead of ill. Through his maturation, he learns the programme of *paideia* that Zacchaeus had outlined for him. He comes to value his peers and esteem his elders, and in this way, ironically, Zacchaeus comes to prevail.

Hence, the *Paidika* assumes from the outset that the infant Jesus is possessed of divine attributes, namely divine power and divine knowledge. They characterize his portrayal over the entirety of the *Paidika* and remain a constant. As such they represent facets of Jesus's unchanging divine nature. But, as will be discussed more fully in Chapter 4, the author has attributed a dual nature to the figure of Jesus, one divine and one human. The divine character does not change or develop, but the human character does. To be human, Jesus needs to undergo the same sorts of developmental changes that human children normally experience.

3.9 Why Jesus the Child?

What factors would have prompted this portrayal of Jesus as a child? Clearly, the popular and devotional needs of knowing more about Jesus, particularly Jesus as a child, were a factor. There is also the author's theological attempt to give expression to Jesus's dual nature. But there is a further desire to exploit the creative possibilities raised by Jesus's dual nature. Jesus's humanity allows the author to play with the limitations of childhood, particularly Jesus's weakness and insignificance. Children held a diminished role in antiquity and were generally regarded as inferior to adults. Such a diminished role allowed the author to emphasize the paradox in Jesus's circumstances by highlighting his extraordinary abilities – abilities far surpassing those of ordinary adults. Although it is perhaps anachronistic to speak of Jesus's 'superpowers', that is basically what is involved. Jesus constitutes a type of 'Superboy', and this premise allows the author to represent him as performing miracle upon miracle. And just as modern comic book readers delight in unpacking the various implications and consequences of their heroes' superpowers, the same holds true for readers and hearers of Jesus's marvels in the *Paidika*. They want to know what happens next.

To add to the piquancy of his account, however, the author employs another familiar trope from the world of myth and of comic books, namely that of the hero 'gone bad'. *Hercules furens* and 'bad Superman' are familiar enough not to require discussion, but the possibilities of the bad superhero allow the reader to explore the creative implications and ramifications of what happens when the hero uses his powers in a negative way. Jesus's immaturity allows the author to explore precisely this possibility. What would Jesus, the Son of God, do in the world of humans when possessed of immense power but also the petulance, immaturity and deficient self-control of a child? The first half of the *Paidika* provides its readers with such a spectacle.

This sort of scenario is immensely entertaining because it represents the moral Jesus of the 'canonical' Gospels involved in transgressive and immoral behaviour. There is a natural frisson and thrill of horror involved in seeing Jesus engage in deeds that are reprehensible to both God and man, just as there is with seeing Superman, sworn to use his superhuman powers to benefit humanity, threaten the very humans he has vowed to protect. And readers could happily indulge in the spectacle because, by the end of the work, Jesus has reversed his evil deeds and assumed a mature and responsible demeanour. Just how effectively he is portrayed as a divine being is the subject of the next chapter.

Chapter 4

JESUS THE DIVINE: THE CHRISTOLOGY OF THE *PAIDIKA*

Despite the amount of recent study on the *Paidika*, there remains a lack of clarity and precision about the work's Christology. This situation is perhaps not surprising given that the New Testament's Christology is itself far from uniform, and that, as we have seen, the Graeco-Roman world envisioned an exceptionally wide-ranging and multifaceted divine–human spectrum.

Chapter 3 proposed that the *Paidika* displays a two-nature Christology, where Jesus is represented as both human and divine. This chapter will consider whether such a presupposition is warranted, by examining the *Paidika*'s representation of Jesus's words and deeds. It will start by asking whether it is possible that the *Paidika* does not portray Jesus as a fully divine being but merely as a divine man (*theios anêr*) or a hero.

While such an identification is possible, there are problems with this approach. First of all, the concept of the 'divine man' has been – with justice – very largely discredited as a suitable heuristic category for the figure of Jesus in the New Testament.[1] Using it to interpret the *Paidika* is anachronistic and is certainly imprecise: the descriptor 'divine' is exceptionally vague; as Litwa observes, it 'has an appallingly broad signification in ancient discourse.'[2] As a result, the term 'divine man' has no exact denotation in antiquity: it can be applied indiscriminately to heroes, revered leaders, emperors, founders and any other number of exceptional individuals. The designation 'hero' is equally problematic.

While one could adduce other determinative factors, for our purposes the fundamental distinction between divine beings and those merely endued with godly traits is pre-existence. As Nock recognizes, the essential feature that distinguishes divine men (*theoi andres*) and heroes from deities is whether these figures had existed prior to their appearance on earth as humans.[3] The Graeco-Roman heroes, for instance, even if they had originally had divine parentage, did not exist prior to their birth on earth. Figures such as Herakles came into existence in the context

---

1. Koskenniemi (2014), pp. 169–73.
2. Litwa (2014), p. 22.
3. Nock (1972), p. 934.

of human history. After his cremation he was deified and led into Olympus by Athena, but his deification was regarded as a special act and one not normally gifted to mortals. And while it is true that other antique figures claimed that they had pre-existed their present human life, such as Pythagoras or Empedocles, they had undergone metempsychosis and so had existed before, but *as someone else*. The situation is made more complicated by the fact that the mythology of the Graeco-Roman gods indicates that they, too, had not always existed but had come into being at a certain point.[4] And although the mythological narratives are inconsistent about when the gods did come into existence, the important point is that they possessed a pre-existence (though even here there were exceptional gods like Dionysus and Asclepios who were technically demigods).

The *Paidika* makes it clear that Jesus possessed a pre-existence, a fact that he flaunts before Joseph and the Jewish people (6.4,6). The *Paidika* does not stipulate how long he had pre-existed them, but as will be shown shortly, the work displays considerable indebtedness to the Gospel of John and to its picture of the pre-existent Logos/Son of God, so this understanding likely informs the *Paidika*'s conception of pre-existence. Jesus's divine nature, therefore, is not in doubt. His behaviour may resemble that of heroes and divine men, but he is qualitatively different in appearance and behaviour from them. How, then, does the *Paidika* express this difference?

The author has drawn on the canonical Gospels to inform his depiction of Jesus, and this influence is particularly evident in his rewriting of Luke 2 and in his echoes of the Gospel of John. The Gospels' miracles are also of prime consideration and have been emulated by the *Paidika*. Luke Timothy Johnson has remarked that the *Paidika*'s 'unremitting focus on the miraculous is extraordinary', and this focus is very much bound up with the author's conception of Jesus.[5] These three strands – Luke 2, John and miracle narratives – embody the main elements of the *Paidika*'s Christology, so the following discussion will begin with an overview of the *Paidika*'s dependence on Luke and John for aspects of its Christology, and then move to a consideration of its miracle accounts. It will close with an examination of the *Paidika*'s orthodoxy.

4.1 Luke 2.41-51

As noted previously, the extent of the *Paidika*'s reliance on 'biblical' allusions is debated, and its explicit references to Scripture are very limited. There are no citations of the LXX, and the only direct New Testament citations occur in a lengthy paraphrase of Lk. 2.41-52 at *Paidika* 17 and in a brief reference to 1 Cor. 13.1 at *Paidika* 6.[6] As the latter does not have a christological focus, the *Paidika*'s

---

4. See the judicious remarks by Arnobius of Sicca, *Adv. Nat.* II.70.

5. Johnson (2009), p. 185. Cf. Wilson (1995), p. 84: 'the main interest is in the demonstration of miraculous power per se'.

6. Burke (2010), p. 203 maintains that the *Paidika* knows only Luke.

rewriting of Luke 2 takes on particular importance for assessing its Christology, not least because of its position as the work's closing chapter.[7]

Paidika 17 has both appropriated and reformulated various emphases of Luke's account. While it is literally dependent on the text of Luke, it excises some minor points within the narrative and adds other elements. Emphasis on Jesus's miraculous wisdom (σοφία) and understanding are already key constituents of Luke's account,[8] as can be determined from the verses framing the narrative: in Lk. 2.40 Jesus is 'filled with wisdom' (Lk. 2.40), while the summary following the account concludes that Jesus 'increased in wisdom' (Lk. 2.52). The narrative proper is presented as a concrete instantiation of this wisdom and understanding (σύνεσις Lk. 2.47), as exemplified by Jesus's questions and answers.[9]

While Luke forbears to outline the specifics of Jesus's wisdom, the *Paidika* has no such hesitations: in addition to listening to the teachers and elders, Jesus teaches *them*, quizzing them about the fundamentals of the law and the specifics and parables of the prophets (17.2). This dual reference to the law and to the prophets is meant to refer to the Hebrew Bible as a whole – hence, Jesus's intellectual acuity and wisdom are directly associated with his unsurpassed understanding of Scripture. Just as earlier in the *Paidika* he demonstrates a profound insight into the alphabet (Ch. 6), Jesus now reveals a similar grasp of the most important texts written with an alphabet – God's word. In fact, his exposition here is redolent of Lk. 24.27, 32, 45, and implies that he already possesses a post-resurrection understanding of the Scriptures. The *Paidika*'s introduction of a laudatory response by the scribes and Pharisees makes the point explicit by having them comment on Jesus's unparalleled wisdom: 'We have never known nor heard such wisdom' (17.5).

A second, christological feature of the narrative is its emphasis on the fatherhood of God. Here, the ambiguous phrase ἐν τοῖς τοῦ πατρός μου, which the *Paidika* (17.3) has taken over from Luke 2.49,[10] does not refer only to Jesus's presence in 'his father's house', but also to his involvement with 'God's affairs' – in this case, his knowledge of and ability to elucidate God's scriptures. Sonship, too, is one of the key strands of Luke's account. The *Paidika* develops this theme in two ways, first, by consistently discounting Joseph's role as Jesus's father and, second, by highlighting the motherhood of Mary.[11]

The result is that Jesus's divine paternity – already central to Luke's account – becomes even more emphatic. Jesus's preternatural wisdom and grasp of Scripture, hinted at in Luke, become impossible to overlook. These factors suggest that

---

7. Its importance has not gone unnoticed by commentators: see the analyses in Cousland (forthcoming), Chartrand-Burke (2008a), pp. 101–19; Robbins (2005), pp. 342–7; Schmahl (1974), pp. 249–58. For its special position in the *Paidika*, cf. Baars and Helderman (1994), p. 27: it is the 'highpoint' ('Angelpunkt').

8. Bovon (2002), p. 110.

9. Cf. Brown (1993), pp. 483–4, 490.

10. De Jonge (1977–8), pp. 331–7.

11. Cousland (forthcoming).

the Christology of the *Paidika*'s Temple narrative is largely concerned with emphasizing Jesus's divine characteristics. While Jesus's humanity is still an aspect of its presentation of Jesus, Jesus's human nature is dramatically downplayed in favour of his divine nature.

Günther Schmahl further observes that the *Paidika*'s author wishes to have his young Jesus surpass Luke's, and does so by making inclusions calculated to enhance the Christology already present in Luke's narrative.[12] Tony Burke also argues for 'improvement' in the narrative, whereby the *Paidika*'s Jesus is made more powerful, more assertive and wiser than the Jesus of Luke 2.

Taken together, these alterations to Luke's Temple narrative are chiefly christological and calculated to stress the divine characteristics of the twelve-year-old Jesus. His divine parentage is made especially emphatic here and his wisdom, too, clearly surpasses that of humans. Where these features are noticeable in Luke, they are unmistakable in the *Paidika*.

4.2 The Gospel of John

In addition to the Gospel of Luke, it is evident that the *Paidika*'s Christology has also been influenced by the Gospel of John.[13] Whether this influence was based on the written gospel or merely aural dependence is debated, but what is not in dispute is the author's indebtedness to Johannine terminology and concepts.[14] Where his reliance on Luke draws particular attention to Jesus's divine paternity and wisdom, the Johannine emphases focus chiefly on Jesus's pre-existence, heavenly origin and his being sent by God. This focus appears to be primarily conceptual, and also includes echoes of Johannine dualism.[15] Central to this understanding are the dualistic conceptions of pre-existence versus present existence, and the heavenly realms above versus the earthly regions below.

The focus on pre-existence emerges when Jesus addresses Joseph, saying, 'When you were born, I existed and came to you' (6.4). He follows this up with a remark addressed to both Joseph and his first teacher: 'I – and the one who existed before the world's creation – know exactly when you and your fathers and your fathers' fathers were born' (6.6).[16] Both statements call to mind Jn 8.56-8, where Jesus

---

12. Schmahl (1974), p. 256.

13. See Table 1 in Van Oyen (2011), pp. 499–503; Aasgaard (2010), pp. 120–1, 128; Chartrand-Burke (1998), pp. 34–6.

14. Van Oyen (2011), pp. 489, 494–5; Aasgaard (2010), pp. 120, 125; Robbins (2005), pp. 345–7. Not every Johannine echo in the *Paidika* will be discussed here – just those that are most pertinent to its Christology. Further, some of these traits may not be early.

15. Docetism, which is often regarded as a feature of John's Gospel, will be considered later in this chapter.

16. I follow Aasgaard's (2010), p. 142, emendation of the text here. Burke (2010), p. 314 has 'I know accurately, and (I know) that before the world was created'.

famously asserts: 'Before Abraham was, I am'. Each passage indicates not only that Jesus pre-existed Joseph or Abraham, but also that he was superordinate to merely human existence and that he was outside of the normal temporal continuum. This emphasis on Jesus's pre-existence is furthered by Jesus's teacher Zacchaeus, who is brought to surmise, 'Maybe this child existed before the creation of the world' (*Paid* 7.2), a suggestion that meshes with the prologue of John's Gospel and its assertion that the Word, 'was in the beginning with God' (Jn 1.2). Like John, the *Paidika* implies that Jesus pre-existed creation, and that he existed prior to being born as an infant.[17]

The dualism between the earthly and heavenly realms is also given prominence, with a notable stress on Jesus's heavenly origin. At *Paidika* 7.2 his teacher exclaims, 'The child is simply not earthborn (γηγενής)', a fact that Jesus himself confirms when he asserts, 'For I have come from above (ἄνωθεν) in order to rescue those below (κάτω) and call them to what is above (τὰ ἄνω), just as the one who sent me to you ordered me' (*Paid.* 8.1).[18]

The echoes of Johannine terminology are obvious, and evidently intended to parallel features of John's presentation of Jesus's divine origin and calling. In Jn 3.31 Jesus says to Nicodemus, 'The one who comes from above (ἄνωθεν) is above all; the one who is of the earth belongs to the earth and speaks about earthly things', while in Jn 8.23 Jesus says to the Jews, 'You are from below (κάτω), I am from above (ἐκ τῶν ἄνω εἰμὶ); you are of this world, I am not of this world.' This terminology is commonplace in John, and distinguishes the pre-existent, heavenly Jesus from the mortal human beings who dwell on earth.[19] The upper realm is characterized as the sphere of truth and knowledge, while the earthly realm below (κάτω Jn 8.23) is the place of lies and ignorance.

A related emphasis on Jesus as 'divine messenger' also underlies this segment of the *Paidika*, which depicts Jesus as a pre-existent, divine figure sent by God to summon humans to the heavenly realms. In John's Gospel, Jesus's role as the one sent by God is pivotal. As Rudolf Schnackenburg remarks, 'Perhaps the most fundamental and comprehensive assertion about Jesus Christ is that he is the one sent by the Father into the world.'[20] The Gospel frequently links the sending of Jesus with his unity with the Father, so there is an implicit glorification of Jesus's unique role in the 'sending'

---

17. It is important to note, as Tony Burke has reminded me, that the earliest versions of 7:2 read 'before Noah', which may or may not signify cosmic pre-existence. On Jesus's pre-existence in John, see Schnackenburg (1993), pp. 287–9; Hamerton-Kelly (1973), pp. 197–242.

18. *Paidika* 8.1 is only found in the later versions, including Gs. Lapham (2003), p. 130 remarks that in this passage, 'we are presented with a picture of one who is essentially not of this world'.

19. For ἄνωθεν, see Jn 3.3,7,31; 19.11; for ἐκ τοῦ οὐρανοῦ – Jn 3.13,27,31; 6.32,33, 41,42,50,51,58.

20. Schnackenburg (1993), p. 248.

phraseology.[21] God's sending legitimates Jesus as God's emissary, and in this capacity Jesus performs the will of God, especially in terms of bringing salvation – John's Jesus personifies salvation.[22] The same holds true for the *Paidika*. Jesus's 'sending' is essential for salvation since it results in the 'rescue' of those below.[23]

In addition to these, there are further notable Johannine echoes. In John, Jesus performs his first sign (ἐποίησεν ἀρχὴν τῶν σημείων, Jn 2.11) at Cana. In the Gs version of the *Paidika* the youthful Jesus is also described as performing a 'sign' (ἐποίησεν σημεῖον 10.2): Mary sends the seven-year-old Jesus to fetch water, but Jesus's pitcher gets broken in the process.[24] Instead he fills his cloak with water and brings it to his mother. Seeing the 'sign' that Jesus performed, Mary kisses him and calls forth a blessing on him (10.1-2). While this miracle is clearly distinct from the miracle at Cana, there are suggestive echoes of it in the *Paidika*. Jesus performs the task at Mary's request, and water and containers feature prominently in the story. Water and well motifs are also prominent in John's fourth chapter, and equally important is the miracle itself. Käsemann remarks that 'for John, too, miracles are indispensable. … The Johannine miracles in general are clearly and emphatically described in terms of demonstrations of the glory of Jesus'.[25] John and the *Paidika* share this emphasis.

Other emphases in John are also replicated. One of the more suggestive is Jesus's exchange with the 'Jews' in *Paidika* 6.4-8, which has points of overlap with Jesus's interactions with the Jews in John, chapters 7 and 8.[26] 'The Jews' are astonished (θαυμάζετε) at Jesus's words at *Paidika* 6.4, just as they are in Jn 7.15 (ἐθαύμαζον compare Jn 7.21's θαυμάζετε). The overall pattern of engagement between Jesus and the Jews is also similar, insofar as Jesus attributes reactions to his audience, and then responds to them using (in Käsemann's phrase) the 'literary device of absurd misunderstandings'.[27] The result is a sort of oblique dialogue that plays off the Jews' misunderstanding, enabling Jesus to provide further clarifications about his message. While the *Paidika*'s pattern is briefer and more awkward than that which characterizes the Gospel of John, it allows the author to (attempt to) introduce Johannine-style profundities that are meant to display Jesus's heavenly wisdom. The *Paidika* seems to introduce misunderstandings of its own, such as

21. Käsemann (1968), p. 11.

22. Miranda (1977), pp. 29–35, 66.

23. As Aasgaard (2010), p. 121#25 observes, the author uses ἀποστέλλω instead of πέμπω for the verb 'to send', but conceptually the sense is unchanged.

24. Robbins (2005), p. 345 identifies three. Where Ga (2.5; 9.3; 11.2) and Gd (2.5; 10.3; 11.2; 13.2) record multiple signs, Gs has only the one (Gs 10.2), which likely gave rise to the others. This suggests that the 'Johannizing' tendency of the *Paidika* was an ongoing process.

25. Käsemann (1968), p. 21.

26. Although these parallels are not noted by Van Oyen (2011), pp. 499–503 in his chart of New Testament allusions, he does show frequent parallels between John chapters 7–8 and the *Paidika* (pp. 499–501).

27. Käsemann (1968), p. 24.

when it has Jesus abuse 'the Jews' for their small-mindedness after their seemingly favourable response to him. Having reduced them to silence, he then consoles them (6.7-8). Does this mean that the author is attempting to echo the variety of responses exhibited by the Jewish crowds in John, or is he is simply showing that Jesus's responses are still infantile?[28]

These Johannine features do not characterize the entirety of the *Paidika*. In contrast to John's Gospel, where Jesus's self-disclosure is arguably the work's entire focus, Jesus's self-revelation in the *Paidika* amounts largely to one set-piece – his abstruse disquisition on the alpha, along with its preamble and conclusion. Jesus's role as saviour is also delimited. Where the goal of John's Jesus is to save the world and impart eternal life to it (Jn 3.15),[29] Jesus's salvific acts, as testified by the word 'to save' (σῴζω) in the *Paidika*, are exclusively concerned with peoples' physical lives or well-being.[30] What is more, on two of these occasions Jesus's saving actions[31] do nothing more than reverse the effects of the curses that he himself has inflicted upon those people who have displeased him (8.2; 14.4). The only other concrete instance of Jesus's saving an individual is when he raises a youth from the dead, to which the crowd responds with a summarizing acclamation, 'He saved many souls from death and will continue to save all the days of his life' (16.3).

Yet, even if these Johannine traits are limited, the author has clearly been influenced by John's Christology. Jesus's pre-existence, his role as cosmic redeemer, his ability to perform signs – these are all traits that evidence a familiarity with John and display a high Christology. Where the Synoptic Gospels do not expressly address the issue of Jesus's pre-existence and heavenly origins, the *Paidika* appropriates both these features from John. It combines them with elements of Luke's Christology, fusing them both into a fascinating hybrid. The precocious youth from Luke's Gospel is recast in the guise of an all-knowing, Johannine divine child. This fusing of two distinct Christologies is, in Bovon's view, characteristic of the second century,[32] and it marks the emergence of an increasingly divine Christ figure.

4.3 Jesus and Miracles

The most prominent christological feature of the *Paidika* is its miracles. They constitute the essential fabric of the *Paidika*, and are remarkable for both their frequency and prominence. How one enumerates them depends on the version in

---

28. On the latter possibility, Aasgaard (2010), pp. 100, 142–3.

29. For an overview of the meaning of salvation in John, Bennema (2002), pp. 2–15, 157–9.

30. This same tendency is to be seen especially in the Apocryphal Acts. In the *Acts of Andrew*, for instance, there are sixteen accounts of healings and raising from the dead that focus on the physical needs of the people. On the miracles in the Acts of John, cf. Bolyki (1995), pp. 15–35.

31. Here I am referring to the use of the passive form of σῴζω.

32. Bovon (2013), p. 31.

question, but in Gs there are five prodigies, four punitive miracles (*Strafwunder*), two raisings from the dead and one healing miracle.[33] There are, in addition, four demonstrations of Jesus's extraordinary understanding.[34] These miracles are typically focalized and amplified by the acclamation of bystanders who respond with wonder and amazement.[35] The reactions to Jesus's miracles sometimes appear as the responses of individuals (2.5; 4.2; 10.2; 12.2; 14.2), sometimes as corporate responses by the 'people' (4.1), 'Jews' (6.5), the 'crowds' (16.3), and the 'scribes and Pharisees' (17.4). These motifs and their accompanying terminology are indebted to the canonical Gospels, but given the higher percentage of miracles in the *Paidika*, these responses are proportionately more frequent than in the Gospels, and constitute a regular refrain for Jesus's words and deeds.[36]

Astonishment and wonder are typical reactions to the extraordinary, and become a characteristic feature of Christian and pagan miracle stories.[37] As a rule, expressions of amazement constitute a preliminary reaction to the numinous and do not reflect either approbation or condemnation – merely the extraordinary character of the event.[38] When the Pharisee of Chapter 2 marvels, telling all his friends about Jesus's miracle of the sparrows, it does not necessarily mean that he has come to believe in Jesus or that he considers him divine. The witnesses to Jesus's miracles merely express a knee-jerk reaction to the marvellous. They realize that something remarkable and unprecedented has taken place, but they have yet to evaluate the occurrence and to respond to it either positively or negatively. Nevertheless, as happens in the canonical Gospels, this reaction often prompts further speculation about Jesus's identity. When Jesus kills the careless boy, the people (ὁ λαός) cry out, 'Where was this child born, such that his word is deed?' (Πόθεν τὸ παιδίον τοῦτο ἐγεννήθη ὅτι τὸ ῥῆμα αὐτοῦ ἔργον ἐστίν; 4.1). Their query raises the issue of Jesus's origins, and then begins to shade into acclamation when the people begin to recognize that he must be divine.

Acclamation typically follows upon the audience's initial reaction of astonishment, since it begins to focus on the wonderworker rather than simply the wonder itself.[39] There are three other such reactions in the *Paidika*. The next is when 'Jews' (Ἰουδαῖοι) overhear Jesus's utterances to Zacchaeus and Joseph, and

---

33. Tischendorf's version includes two more raisings from the dead (17.1-2; 18) to give a total of four. The NT attributes three to Jesus – the daughter of Jairus; the son of the widow of Nain (Lk. 7.11-17) and Lazarus (Jn 11.1-46) – and one each to Peter (Tabitha: Acts 9.36-42) and Paul (Eutychus: Acts 20.9-12).

34. For an overview of the miracles in the *Paidika* based on Tischendorf's version, see Hartenstein (2013), pp. 790–1.

35. Theissen (1983), pp. 69–72. Cf. Cousland (2002), pp. 125–44; Blackburn (1991), pp. 225–8; Koch (1975), pp. 19–26; H. van der Loos (1965), pp. 128–33.

36. Theissen (1983). On acclamation in direct speech, Cousland (2002), pp. 136–40.

37. Theissen (1983), pp. 69–71. Cf. Guez (2009), pp. 244–8.

38. Cousland (2002), pp. 135–6.

39. Koch (1975), p. 25.

exclaim, 'Oh, what a new and wonderful marvel! The child is maybe five years old and – Oh! – the kind of words he utters! We know that we have never heard words being spoken such as this child speaks – not even by a teacher of the law or a Pharisee' (6.5). A third reaction by the crowds (οἱ ὄχλοι) also expresses amazement: 'He saved many souls from death, and will continue to save all the days of his life' (16.3). Lastly, the scribes and Pharisees respond to Jesus's wisdom by blessing Mary: 'Blessed are you because the Lord God has blessed the fruit of your womb. We have never seen nor heard such wisdom and glory of virtue' (17.4). In these instances the 'people', 'Jews' and 'crowds' are meant to serve as rough equivalents of each other.[40] Taken together, these collective responses emphasize the Jewish identity of Jesus's audience and the global impact of his actions.[41]

They further emphasize the unprecedented character of Jesus's words and deeds – they 'have never seen nor heard' anything like it. The people are witnesses to a divine epiphany, as testified by Jesus's ability to accomplish deeds with a word. Their responses may even suggest a progression in understanding. Their first acclamation refers to Jesus's past, asking, 'Where was this child born?' Their second refers to his age of five years, while the last finishes with a programmatic account of Jesus's future: he 'will continue to save all the days of his life'. The people's emphasis does shift from the marvellous qualities of Jesus's actions to Jesus himself and then to the significance of those actions. Their responses close with a tacit note of glorification, praising Jesus's saving acts: 'He saved (ἔσωσεν) many souls from death, and will continue to save (σῶσαι).' In this way, the public dimension of the child's deeds is conspicuously stressed. Even in circumstances where one would not expect a large crowd to be assembled, they feature prominently within the narrative. Narro plausibly argues that the crowds represent those future believers who will testify to and validate Jesus's actions.[42] And while the crowd's acclamations are not precisely an aretology, it is perhaps warranted to say that they (and the individual narratives of the *Paidika* themselves) possess an aretological dimension. They constitute a public acclamation of the deity's marvels.

4.4 Jesus and Nature Miracles

Although the designation 'nature miracles' is far from precise, it serves as a convenient heading for various wonders in the *Paidika*. The work's first miracles are Jesus's cleansing of the water in the pools and his vivification of the clay sparrows.

---

40. In Gs, the 'Jews' likely does not include the 'scribes and Pharisees', because the 'Jews' allude to the 'teachers of the law and Pharisees' as a group distinct from themselves. The analysis of Narro (2013), pp. 628–33 differs from the one above because he bases his findings on Tischendorf's version.

41. On the latent ethnic dimension often found in the word λαός, with particular reference to Matthew, see Cousland (2002), pp. 75–86.

42. Narro (2013), pp. 637–8.

These narratives have two miraculous components to them, both of which have a significant bearing on the *Paidika*'s depiction of Jesus. One is his creative capacity and the other his authority over the issues of purity and the Sabbath.[43] As has been noted before, the *Paidika*'s opening narrative of Jesus at play illustrates this theme by providing a stylized account of the entire creative process, recalling God's actions at the beginning of Genesis.[44] When the *Paidika*'s Jesus separates the sand from the water, he is echoing God's division of the water from the earth (Gen. 1.9-10).[45] Likewise, Jesus's fashioning of the sparrows from clay calls to mind not only God's creation of the birds and wild animals (Gen. 1.20-25), but also his creation of Adam from the dust of the earth (Gen. 2.7).[46] God imparts life to all creatures, and Jesus is portrayed as doing the same things that his Father had done. What is more, like his Father, he executes these deeds by divine fiat. When he vivifies the sparrows, Jesus claps his hands and commands the birds to become living creatures and fly away, which they do (2.4).[47]

The same holds true for Jesus's cleansing of the waters, which he does 'by word alone' (2.1). God himself established what is unclean for the people of Israel, and instituted mechanisms whereby they could be purified from their uncleanness (see especially Leviticus, chs. 11–16). Here Jesus's mere command is sufficient to render the water clean (καθαρὰ καὶ ἐνάρετα 2.1), just as, in the canonical Gospels, his command is sufficient to render the lepers clean (Mk 1.44; Lk. 17.14).[48] Although unlikely, it is possible that there are other underlying scriptural echoes here. Jesus's purification of the waters may reference Exod. 15.22-5, where Moses

---

43. Jesus's cleansing of the waters could also be included, but as Burke (2010), p. 302 observes, the episode – which may echo Elisha's cleansing the waters of Jericho (2 Kings 2.19-22) – is not in the earliest versions. Hock (1995), p. 105 regards the episode as a foreshadowing of the adult Jesus's control over nature. Cf. Mt. 8.2-3.

44. Both Gen. 1.9 (LXX) and *Paid.* 2.1 use the verb συνάγω of the gathering together of the waters; cf. Felsch (2013), p. 828.

45. There is widespread agreement about the presence of the Genesis allusion. See, inter alia: Davis (2014), p. 50; Felsch (2013), pp. 828–9; Davis (2012), pp. 130–1; Amsler (2011), pp. 453–4; Aasgaard (2010), p. 128; Robbins (2005), pp. 344–5; Bauckham (2000), p. 797; Baars and Helderman (1993), p. 205.

46. Gen. 2.7 (LXX) and *Paid.* 2.2 both employ the same verb-form: ἔπλασεν; cf. Felsch (2013), pp. 828–9. Aasgaard (2010), pp. 162–3 cites the *kosmopoiia* of 7.2 and 6.6, which would implicitly align Jesus's creative acts with those of God. The twelve birds are also thought to foreshadow Jesus's sending out of the twelve disciples; cf. Hock (1995), p. 107; Burke (2010), p. 305.

47. On God's creation by means of the word, cf. Westermann (1984), pp. 38–41.

48. Why the water should be regarded as unclean to Jews is not entirely clear since it seems to be running rainwater that Jesus is gathering into pools. It may be, however, that the author assumed that they were standing pools of non-running water. In any case, the rabbinic schools were divided over the cleanliness of a 'rain-stream'; cf. *m. Miqw.* 5.6. Perhaps, however, the cleansing is nothing more than the fact that Jesus removed silt from the water.

makes the bitter waters of Marah 'sweet' by throwing in a piece of wood, or 2 Kings 2.21, where Elisha purifies a spring near Jericho that has 'bad' water. Elisha tosses a bowlful of salt into it and proclaims, 'Thus says the Lord, I have made this water wholesome' (ἴαμαι τὰ ὕδατα ταῦτα 2 Kings 2.21). Although the word 'clean' is not used in either of these passages, both have obvious affinities with the *Paidika* narrative. That being said, the differences between these episodes and Jesus's deeds are also abundantly clear: Jesus does not use any physical remedies to effect the purification, nor does he perform the cleansing in the Lord's name. If Jesus is being tacitly compared to Moses or Elisha, then he eclipses them in terms of his miraculous abilities.

The controversy over Jesus's fashioning of the sparrows also reflects various Sabbath controversies recorded in the gospels.[49] The closest correspondence is with the healing of the man born blind in John 9 – both episodes refer to Jesus taking up clay (πηλὸν) and fashioning it.[50] The infant Jesus models the sparrows from clay (2.2), while the adult Jesus spits on the ground to make clay and apply it to the eyes of the blind man (Jn 9.6 *bis*, 11, 14, 15). In both narratives it is a Pharisee or Pharisees who condemn Jesus for breaking the Sabbath (2.3,5//Jn 9.16).[51] The very same charge is levelled against Jesus, namely that he 'made clay' (πηλὸν ἐποίησεν) on the Sabbath (2.3//Jn 9.14). These overlaps could indicate not only that the author was familiar with the Sabbath controversy in John 9, but also that he wished to address the issue of Jesus's authority over the Sabbath. This same breach of Sabbath is referred to again in the next episode of the *Paidika*, where the son of Annas, the high priest, condemns Jesus's failure to observe the Sabbath (3.1).

The young Jesus provides no explicit rationale for his actions; he simply responds by bringing the sparrows to life. This act in itself constitutes his justification. Who but God can impart life to inanimate matter? Jesus's ability to bestow life reveals his divine nature and eliminates the need for any explanation. Just as Jesus's miraculous healings serve as the warrant for his actions in the Sabbath controversies, so his vivification of the sparrows is a sufficient rejoinder to questions about his authority.[52]

---

49. They include the pericope that mentions harvesting on the Sabbath (Mt. 12.1-8; Mk 2.23-8; Lk. 6.1-5); the healing of the man with the withered hand (Mt. 12.9-14; Mk 3.1-6; Lk. 6.6-11); the healing of the crippled woman (Lk. 13.10-17); the healing of the man with dropsy (Lk. 14.1-6); the healing of the paralysed man (Jn 5.1-18); Jesus's reference to healing on the Sabbath (Jn 7.19-24), and the healing of the man born blind (Jn 9; cf. 9.14-16).

50. Apart from Rom. 9.21, the only references to clay (πηλός) in the New Testament are found in John 9.

51. This surmise assumes that the 'Jew' in *Paidika* 2.3 is to be identified with the Pharisee in verse 2.5.

52. In their analyses of miracle stories, Kahl (1994), pp. 76, 234–5 and Eve (2002), pp. 15–16 both distinguish between the 'bearer of natural power', the 'mediator of numinous power', and the 'petitioner of numinous power'. Eve notes that in Jewish accounts of nature

It may be, however, that there are also echoes of another Sabbath controversy in John. After healing the paralysed man, Jesus justifies his actions by saying, 'Just as the Father raises the dead and gives them life, so also the Son gives life to whomever he wishes' (Jn 5.21). Given the above-mentioned parallels with the creation account in Genesis, John's Jesus is drawing a strong parallel between God and himself (Jn 5.18), and between God's ability to impart life and his own capacity to do so. Their authority is the source of life. The only problem with this argument is that God rested on the seventh day (Gen. 2.2-3; cf. Exod. 20.11, 31.17), so how is Jesus's own act of creation on the Sabbath to be justified? In Jn 5.17, Jesus provides the answer, 'My Father is still working, and I also am working' (Jn 5.17). His answer may be alluding to interpretations, also attested in Philo and later rabbinic *haggadah*, which claimed that God never ceased from his creative and sustaining activity.[53] If the *Paidika*'s author has this understanding in mind, then Jesus's act of creation on the Sabbath is nothing more than his doing 'what he sees the Father doing' (Jn 5.19). In this case, the best analogue to Jesus's activity is not figures like Moses or Elijah, but God himself. The Christology of this portion of the *Paidika* hints not at a thaumaturge or magician, but a creator with absolute authority over the natural world.

At the same time, the author does not let us forget Jesus's juvenile state by cleverly reducing the majesty of the creation account in Genesis to a more modest scale. The infant Jesus is not fashioning an entire cosmos, but merely a series of pools on the riverside. Nor is he creating every living thing that exists, but twelve model birds made from clay. The incongruity between the two creation accounts is amusing and humorous,[54] but also has a serious subtext to it. The author is trying to be true not only to both of Jesus's natures, but also to the fact that he is only five years of age. He has ensured, therefore, that Jesus's games, such as playing in the 'sandbox' at the river's edge, or modelling toy birds out of clay for himself, are consistent with the behaviour and activities of other little five-year-old boys.

The remaining three nature miracles performed by Jesus are largely limited to the domestic sphere and have distinct folk-tale overtones.[55] Their common theme concerns Jesus's various actions to help his parents with their domestic tasks, a feature that would explain their being grouped together in the text. These prodigies represent the first unequivocally altruistic miracles performed by Jesus for the benefit of others. They can be described as prodigies insofar as they contravene the 'laws of nature', and while they display one or two features in common with biblical stories and themes, for the most part they are independent.

Jesus's carrying water back to Mary in a cloak (Ch. 10) may depend on Proverbs 30.4 'Who has wrapped up the waters in a garment?' The miracle also has parallels

---

miracles the bearer of natural power 'is nearly always God' except for Jesus in the canonical Gospels (384). In the *Paidika*, Jesus invariably figures as the bearer of numinous power.

53. Felsch (2011), pp. 77–80.

54. Felsch (2013), pp. 829–30.

55. Münch (2013) describes Jesus as a 'heimlicher Wohltäter'; cf. Schneider (1995), p. 4.

with a *Jeremiah Apocryphon*, where Ezra fills his robe with water when his vessel breaks.[56] Jesus's miracle of the miraculous harvest (Ch. 11) recalls both the multiplication of the loaves and the parable of the sower. It may even be that, as Münch suggests, the young Jesus has been identified with the sower in the parable, and is described as producing a 'hundredfold' harvest.[57] Some of the vocabulary also appears to be derived from Luke,[58] as does, perhaps, the focus on the poor and the needy. Apart from possible reminiscences of Jesus's later feedings of the four and five thousand, there are echoes of Elisha's command to give bread and fresh ears of grain 'to the people and let them eat' (2 Kings 4.42-4), where the amounts expand sufficiently to feed a hundred people. Here, though, the emphasis is on Jesus's control of the growth process.

Jesus's miraculous stretching of a board to help Joseph make a rich man's bed (Ch. 12) also has folk-tale features and recalls some of the minor domestic miracles of Elisha, such as making an axe-head float (2 Kings 6.1-7), or removing the poison from a pot of stewed gourds (2 Kings 4.38-41). Burke also cites the parallel story told of Hanina ben Dosa, who is called upon to lengthen roof beams that are too short, and finds that through prayer he can lengthen the beams.[59] Susanne Luther's examination of that miracle suggests that the underlying christological interpretation is hortatory, and that it calls for confidence in Jesus's divine ability to perform miracles. Jesus's counsel to Joseph, 'Don't worry, but do what you wish' (12.2), exhorts the believer to have confidence in Jesus's ability to intervene on their behalf.[60] Joseph's subsequent macarism, 'Blessed am I that God gave me this son' (12.2), seems to demonstrate that he is increasingly aware of his son's capabilities.

While these three domestic miracles are limited in terms of their christological impact, the picture they produce is not inconsistent with the pool and sparrow episodes. Jesus is a wonderworker with a difference. While his abilities include minor instances of manipulation of the physical world such as the cloak and the board, they can also govern larger natural processes, such as the harvest.

4.5 Jesus and Punitive Miracles

Four of Jesus's miracles in the *Paidika* can be designated as 'punitive miracles' (*Strafwunder*), and are associated with Jesus's curses.[61] As noted before, the only instance of a punitive miracle in the gospels is the Cursing of the Fig Tree

---

56. Burke (2010), pp. 324–5.
57. Münch (2013), p. 850.
58. Münch (2013), p. 849 notes that the reference to a 'hundredfold' harvest may reflect Lk. 8.8 and the 'kor' Lk. 16.7.
59. Burke (2010), p. 327.
60. Luther (2013), pp. 857–8.
61. Aune (2006), pp. 414–16. Weinreich (1909), pp. 57–62.

(Mt. 21.18-22//Mk 11.12-14).[62] Burke and Eastman have sought to draw connections between the *Paidika* and the increasing role of punitive miracles in the book of Acts and post-biblical tradition,[63] while Stephen Davis, for his part, relates the curses to Graeco-Roman agonism, reflecting the deeply competitive social contexts of Jesus's day.[64] Within this agonistic context, the *Paidika*'s curse narratives leave no doubts about Jesus's repeated victories in these contests.

To return to the passage discussed earlier, Jesus's curses in the *Paidika* follow immediately upon the miracles of the pools and sparrows:

> The son of Annas, the high priest, said to him: 'Why are you doing this on the Sabbath?' And he took a branch of willow and dispersed the pools and made the water which Jesus had gathered together flow away. And he dried up the pools. When Jesus saw what had happened, he said to him: 'Your fruit (καρπὸς) is without root and your shoot is withered like a branch parched in a harsh wind.' And that youth was withered up (ἐξηράνθη) at once. (3.1-3)

This particular episode appears to demonstrate the author's knowledge of the canonical Gospels. In addition to the name Annas (Lk. 3.2; Jn 18.13,24; Acts 4.6), the withering of Annas's son has several striking parallels with Matthew's version of the cursing of the fig tree.[65] Matthew relates that when Jesus finds no figs on it, he says: "'May no fruit (καρπὸς) ever come from you again!', whereupon the fig tree withered (ἐξηράνθη) at once", (Mt. 21.19 cf. Mk 11.12-14). The similarity of this episode to the cursing of the fig tree, and the shared references to 'fruit' (καρπὸς), could lead one to suppose that the boy's failure to 'produce fruit' was the basis for the boy's judgement. However, the triple reference to root, shoot and fruit is better taken as a curse embodying the totality of the boy's existence. He is withered entirely, and his past, present and future are eliminated. Why, then, is Jesus's judgement so extreme?

If, as noted before, the *Paidika*'s author was consciously exploiting the underlying parallels with creation, then Annas's son's activities actually set him against divine creation. His dissipation of the pools not only constitutes a real breach of the Sabbath, but it also symbolically subverts Jesus's creative actions. Because the process of creation is one whereby the individual features of a featureless chaos are separated and given a distinct existence, the dispersion of the pools symbolically destroys the boundaries and distinctions that had been put in place by God. Annas's son is punished for having effaced the distinction between water and land: desiccation for desecration. The very fact that he is Annas's son

---

62. Meier (1994), p. 895; van der Loos (1965), pp. 688-98. For a listing of the curse miracles in the Bible, see Meier (1994), p. 895. The destruction of the Gadarene swine is not usually regarded as a punitive miracle.

63. Eastman (2015), pp. 206; 200-5; Burke (2010), pp. 278-9; cf. Burke (2009), p. 41.

64. Davis (2014), pp. 64-91.

65. Aasgaard (2010), p. 124 notes that the phrase 'Your fruit be without root' has echoes of Lk. 3.9//and Gos. Thom. 40.

hints to the audience that he is his father's counterpart, and participates in his father's wickedness. A later inscription from Corinth actually invokes 'the curse of Annas and Caiaphas', who were regarded as permanent denizens of Hell.[66] If this tradition is an early one, then the selection of Annas's son as a victim is not surprising, even if his punishment is not really merited.[67]

What is also notable about this episode is that Jesus curses Annas's son on his own authority. One of the hallmarks of cursing in the Graeco-Roman world is that the curser often calls upon a deity to implement the curse.[68] This pattern is found in the Hebrew Bible, as when Elisha curses the children for calling him 'baldhead': 'He cursed them in the name of the Lord' (2 Kings 2.23-4). But Jesus withers Annas's son entirely on his own authority; he makes no mention of God. His is not the act of a human, whose wish is implemented by a deity, but a divine act in its own right. Otherwise, it is difficult to explain how the infant Jesus is able to wither Annas's son 'immediately' by word alone. There is no indication here or in any of the other curses in the *Paidika* that God has implemented Jesus's curse: Jesus has acted on his own behalf in response to hubris.[69] Annas's son's affront to the divine Jesus results in his judgement.

Hubris is also very much a feature of the pericope that follows the withering of Annas's son. The version of Gs reads:

> When he and his father, Joseph, went from there, a person ran and crashed into his shoulder. And Jesus said to him, 'Your guiding principle is under divine condemnation.'[70] And immediately he died. And straightway the people, seeing that he had died, cried out and said, 'Where was this child born, such that his word becomes deed?' But the parents of the dead child, seeing what had happened, blamed his father, Joseph, saying, 'From wherever you have this child, you are not able to live with us in this village. If you wish to remain here, teach him to bless (εὐλογεῖν) and not to curse' (καταρᾶσθαι) (4.1-2).

---

66. Winter (2001), p. 173.

67. By contrast, Whitenton (2015), p. 226 argues that 'the use of conduplicatio here suggests that the audience is meant to feel pity for the boy'.

68. Versnel (2015), pp. 453–9; Eidinow (2007), pp. 146–9; Winter (2001), pp. 164–83. Curse tablets (*defixiones*) are a slightly different category: here the gods function 'as the authoritative centre where the curse is being delivered for final implementation' – Versnel (2015), p. 458. In early Christian curses, Jesus is himself invoked as the operative deity. Cf. Acts 19.13 where the sons of Sceva adjure Jesus in an exorcism. As Irenaeus relates (Iren. *Adv. Haer.* 2.32.4-5), the church also performs its miracles in the name of Jesus Christ.

69. Eastman (2015), pp. 191, 206 appeals to the 'educational value' of Jesus's curses, but it is difficult to discern a didactic application in this particular instance.

70. The reading of Gs here is difficult; cf. Von Bendemann (2013), p. 839. Davis (2014), pp. 79–87 makes a good case for viewing 'guiding principle' as one's 'ruling faculty'. In this instance, the careless boy's faculty has proved to be deficient.

The astonished question of the people is instructive for the light it casts on the Christology of the passage. It is possible that they are asking about Jesus's actual place of birth in a fashion reminiscent of Nathaniel's question about Jesus in John: 'Can anything good come out of Nazareth?' (Jn 1.46). But it is more likely that the query is meant to refer to Jesus's non-earthly origin, and it is specifically his divine fiat that prompts this recognition (cf. Ps. 33.9).[71]

Jesus's blinding of the careless boy's parents continues his harsh acts of retribution.[72] Although the parallels are limited, there may be an underlying echo of Elisha when he takes sight away from the attacking Arameans and then restores it (2 Kings 6.15-23). Elisha accomplishes these deeds by appeals to the Lord (2 Kings 6.18, 20; cf. 6.17). There may also be reference to Paul's blinding of Elymas, the false prophet in Acts 13.6-11.[73] Here, too, the blinding is a temporary punishment. Like all of Jesus's curses, this curse is enacted on his own authority, and shows Jesus in possession of pure, unmediated power.

4.6 Jesus's Marvellous Teaching

As has been noted before, the young Jesus is shown as possessing extraordinary intelligence from the very outset of the *Paidika*.[74] The four distinct teaching episodes, both in their number and the space devoted to them in the narrative give special prominence to Jesus's divine knowledge and wisdom.[75] They are all intended to demonstrate Jesus's divine comprehension, and consistently represent Jesus as being possessed of supernatural insight and understanding.[76] The Temple episode emphasizes Jesus's extraordinary understanding of Scripture, while the three earlier teaching narratives display Jesus's command of the alphabet. Yet it is not simply his knowledge of the alphabet *per se* that is in view, but rather his command of the metaphysical realities that underlie the alpha and the beta.

---

71. Von Bendemann (2013), pp. 833, 839 observes that this is one of the leading questions of the entire narrative, and that it is closely allied with elements of John's Gospel; cf. Jn 7.27, 34-6; 8.14; 9.29.

72. For similar acts, cf. Gen. 19.11; Val. Max. 1.1.17; Juv. *Sat.* 13.93. Weinreich (1909), pp. 189-94.

73. Nock (1972), pp. 328-30 describes Paul's action as a curse followed by a judgement of God (*Gottesurteil*).

74. Davis (2014), pp. 111-12 speaks about Jesus's academic 'progress', and his 'outstripping his peers', but the text gives no indication of this developmental aspect – Jesus possesses his knowledge from the outset. In his rejoinder to Zacchaeus, Jesus asserts that he knows the letters far better than Zacchaeus does.

75. On the teaching episodes see: Holzbach (2013), pp. 862-9; Foster (2006), pp. 22-5; Paulissen (2003), pp. 153-75; on pedagogy in antiquity, Davis (2014), pp. 92-125.

76. Foster (2014), pp. 338, 347.

Jesus's lecture to Zacchaeus on the alpha is the classic instance (even if it is just as celebrated for its obscurity, as well as its textual difficulties.).[77]

One of the terms that the *Paidika* uses as a synonym for the alpha is the word στοιχεῖον. It means a 'constituent element of something', such as a letter of the alphabet, but it also has broader connotations and can refer, among other things, to heavenly bodies, metaphysical principles or even elemental transcendental powers.[78] Speculation on the letters of the alphabet (*stoicheia* = 'elements') is attested in the classical tradition by various authors such as Euripides and Athenaeus (Eurip., *Frag.* 382; Athen. *Deipn.* 10.454b-f), and it was a widespread phenomenon in the ancient world and practised among groups of various stripes.[79] The Marcosians' strong predilection for the practice helps to explain their associations with the story of the infant Jesus and the alpha.[80] It is doubtful, however, whether this association points to the story's actual origin with the Marcosians.

Jesus's interactions with his teachers shift the ground of their discussion from simple acquisition of the alphabet to a discussion about the underlying mysteries of the cosmos. Jesus does not refer to the alpha or beta as a letter of the alphabet – a γράμμα – but treats them instead as 'first principles' – στοιχεῖα. Hence, when he faults Zacchaeus and his second teacher for being unable to impart the meaning of the alpha or beta, he is condemning their ignorance of first principles. What principles Jesus is referring to is not self-evident, but various options present themselves. Jesus's exposition of the alpha reads:

> Hear, master, and understand the order of the first element (στοιχεῖον). Pay close attention here how it has sharp lines and a middle stroke, which you see pointing, standing with legs apart, meeting, spreading, drawn aside, elevated, dancing in chorus ... in triple rhythm, two-cornered, of the same form, of the same thickness, of the same family, holding the measuring cord, in charge of the balance, of equal measure, of equal proportions – these are the lines of the alpha.[81]

Lucie Paulissen argues that Jesus is not referring to elemental beings, but to the Trinity itself. She concludes that 'the [Greek word] *taxis* represents the rank in the

---

77. Obscurity and textual difficulties: Davis (2014), pp. 112, 285#142; Aasgaard (2010), p. 237; Burke (2010), p. 319; Hock (1995), pp. 118–19.
78. BDAG s.v.
79. Dornseiff (1925), pp. 14–17; cf. Davis (2014), pp. 113–14; Aasgaard (2010), p. 143#21.
80. Dornseiff (1925), pp. 126–33.
81. Burke's translation of Gs (2010), p. 318. Compare his rendering from the Syriac: 'Then Jesus began to enquire concerning the form of each character, and he began with the letters. Concerning the first, for what reason it has many angles and characters, pointed, thick and prostrate and projected and extended; and their summits [are] gathered together and sharp and ornamented and erect and squared and inverted; and transformed and folded over and bent at their sides and fixed in a triangle and crowned and clothed in life'; Burke (2013a) p. 280.

hierarchy of each of the persons in the heart of the Trinity. And the Greek word *phusis* pertains to divinity. These persons form an entity; they are separated but reunited; they are elevated in glory as far as the heavens, where they dance in a triple rhythm; threefold, they are of the same family, in a perfect equilibrium, each one having the same measure.'[82]

Paulissen's reading would help to explain the threefold emphasis that runs through the exposition. Moreover, it makes sense that God would be described as the first element. Zacchaeus knows nothing about God, 'neither the beginning nor the end' (7.3) – and he is unable to identify Jesus, whom he describes as 'a god or angel or I don't know what' (7.2).[83] Since Jesus clearly knows the elements, it is no surprise that his third teacher and the elders of the Temple hear him gladly and laud his knowledge.

Jesus's account of the elements, therefore, appears to reveal his profound understanding of reality, whether it be truths about the nature of the Trinity, the cosmos and its origins, the heavenly beings that dwell in it or some other primal truths. His interactions with his teachers are only superficially concerned with learning the alphabet, and Jesus counters their feeble understanding of the letters of the alphabet with a comprehensive understanding of divine and human reality.

The author has sought to develop a broad sense of humour and irony here: Jesus is made to go through the drudgery of the most basic and rudimentary pedagogical techniques when he himself harbours the most profound truths that humans could hope to hear.[84] When Jesus cites from 1 Cor. 13.1 and parallels Zacchaeus's instruction on the alphabet to a noisy gong or a clashing cymbal, he may well be anticipating 13.11, where Paul speaks of having put away childish things. Jesus is not thinking as a child and Zacchaeus needs to cease doing so.

The christological dimension of the teaching narratives, therefore, suggests that the young Jesus has a categorical and divine understanding of the cosmos and of Scripture. Jesus is endowed with what might be described as a Johannine understanding, whereby he is not limited by normal human comprehension, but displays a heavenly awareness that he has evidently possessed from early childhood.

4.7 Jesus's Healings and Raisings from the Dead

The primary healing account in the *Paidika* is when Jesus heals his dying brother James, from a snakebite.[85] It relates that Jesus 'ran to James and breathed upon (κατεφύσησεν) the bite and the bite was healed immediately. The creature

---

82. Paulissen (2003), pp. 162–3. My translation.

83. If God is the first element, is the text suggesting that the second element (beta) is the cosmos that God has created?

84. For an account of this basic pedagogy, see Cribiore (2001), pp. 167–72.

85. For a magical papyrus against scorpion stings, see *PGM* VII 193-6, *PGM* XXVIIIa–c;, *PGM* CXII, *PGM* CXIII; for dog-bites *PDM* xiv. 563-74. For the vast pharmacopoeia of

perished and James was saved' (15.2). The sandviper (ἔχιδνα) was a poisonous snake whose bites were often lethal.[86] It is the same snake that bit Paul on Malta, and prompted amazement among the locals when he merely brushed it off and did not fall down dead (Acts 28.3–6).

Blowing on James's snakebite might be regarded as a form of magical manipulation; Celsus offers a parallel when he references Egyptian magicians who 'blow away diseases' (νόσους ἀποφυσώντων Origen, *Cels.* 1.68). If manipulation is involved, the narrative does not explain how blowing on the bite should result in the snake's death (unless, perhaps, by means of sympathetic magic Jesus's breath causes the snake to explode) or 'heal' (ἰάομαι) the snakebite. It is also possible, indeed it is more likely, that Jn 20.22 is being referenced, where Jesus breathes on the disciples to endow them with the Holy Spirit. The Spirit gives life (Jn 6.33), and Jesus's breath saves James's life.

Given the parallels already present in the *Paidika* with the early chapters of Genesis, Jesus' breath could be a reference to the creation of man. Gen. 2.7 relates that God 'breathed into his nostrils the breath of life'. While the Greek words used are not identical, they are cognate.[87] God's breath is also associated with life elsewhere in the Septuagint (cf. Job 34.14-15; Ps. 104.29-30), and by imparting it to his creatures, he causes them to live. Of course, in this instance, Jesus is not breathing into James's mouth, but onto the bite itself. Nevertheless, just as God's breath is a source of life, so also is Jesus's breath: James is saved (ἐσώθη). If this parallel is warranted, then the young Jesus is again aligned with the creative activity of his divine Father.[88]

The episode has further parallels with the story of Hanina ben Dosa, who was a first-century counterpart to Jesus.[89] The narrative of Hanina famously recounts how he was bitten by a snake (or lizard) but survived unharmed, whereas the snake died, prompting the maxim, 'Woe to the man bitten by a snake, but woe to the snake which has bitten Rabbi Hanina ben Dosa.'[90] Here the sanctity or power of Jesus and Hanina renders the snakebites harmless and results in the demise of the snakes, although no healing actually occurs in the Hanina episode.

---

remedies for snakebite, see Pliny, *N.H.* book 20, though blowing on a snakebite does not figure here. For an encyclopedic discussion of the viper, see Keener (2015), pp. 3670–6.

86. Gitter and De Vries, (1968), pp. 363–4.

87. Καταφυσάω (15.2) and ἀναφυσάω (Gen. 2.7).

88. The comparison with Genesis also opens up other possible echoes, such as the viper with Genesis's serpent – in which case the cosmic demise of Satan is intimated in the viper's death here. Likewise, Jesus might be regarded as the divine antithesis to Cain, who saves his brother instead of killing him – thus undoing the cycle of violence initiated by Cain's fratricide. However attractive these echoes may be, they probably read too much into the text.

89. Burke (2010), p. 332.

90. Cited in Burke (2010), p. 332. Cf. *b. Ber.* 20.3; *y. Ber.* 5.1. It is unclear whether the '*arod*' that bit him was a snake or a lizard.

All told, the healing of James seems most likely to have a biblical substrate, where Jesus's breath is intended to call to mind God's activity or that of the adult Jesus. Magic may be in view, but in light of its pronounced absence elsewhere in the *Paidika*, a biblical parallel is more convincing.

In addition to this healing miracle, the Gs version of the *Paidika* contains references to the raising of five people from the dead. Proportionally speaking, these raisings from the dead occur with far more frequency in the *Paidika* than they do in the New Testament. As Meier notes, the 'Markan, Lucan, and Johannine traditions each knew of only one story',[91] whereas the *Paidika* has two distinct accounts (9.1-3; 16.1-3) and references three other instances where he has raised from the dead (8.1-2; 14.4). In effect, the dominance of Jesus's healings in the canonical Gospels is replaced by raisings from the dead in the *Paidika*. The reason for this alteration is easy enough to discern: healings are exceptional, but the ability to raise people from the dead is extraordinary and marks the child Jesus out as someone whose deeds are almost without comparison.[92]

As just noted, three raisings are implicit within the *Paidika* – the restoration of the son of Annas, that of the careless boy (8.1-2) and that of his second teacher (14.4) – and two occur as actual narratives. The first of these is when he restores his playmate Zeno to life (9.1-3), and the second when he brings back a woodcutter from the dead (16.1-3). The placement of the episodes is probably significant, and helps to signal the reversal whereby Jesus moves from an association with death to one with life. The actual purpose of these narratives is debated. Bovon maintains that they are intended not so much to elicit conversions as to promote a focus on God's spiritual world.[93] Yet it is difficult to overlook the correlation between conversion as new life and the restoration of life.

In the Zeno episode, Jesus begins to display his stature in contrast to his friends. They run away when Zeno falls to his death; Jesus alone remains behind to face the consequences. Whether this anticipates his future role as scapegoat, as Erlemann supposes, is unclear, but at the very least, it gives expression to Jesus's change in attitude. He assumes responsibility and, faced with the recriminations of Zeno's parents, goes on to bring Zeno back to life.[94] As noted before, Jesus's motivations may have been mixed, especially as it is unclear whether in Gs Zeno is merely revivified for a moment or fully restored.[95]

---

91. For Jesus's acts of raising the dead in the Gospels, see Meier (1994), pp. 773–873. Cf. *PGM* XVIIb. 1–23 on Hermes being able to raise some of the dead again (19).

92. Twelftree (1999), pp. 304–10, 424; van der Loos (1965), pp. 559–66. For other ancient accounts of raisings from the dead, see: Philostratos, *Vit. Apoll.* 4.45; Apuleius, *Flor.*19; Origen, *Cels.* 2.55; 3.26, 32–3. For discussion of pagan accounts: Anderson (2004), pp. 94–5; Remus (1983), p. 8; Grant (1952), pp. 235–7; Weinreich (1909), pp. 171–4.

93. For a detailed listing of all the resurrection accounts, see Bovon (2005), p. 257#34.

94. Erlemann (2013), p. 845.

95. Burke (2010), p. 324 remarks that Zeno's return to death is only found in Gs and the Old Irish version. While it is clear from the latter that Zeno dies again, it is much more ambivalent in Gs. Jesus tells Zeno to 'sleep' (κοιμοῦ).

What is striking in this account from a christological standpoint are the terms applied to Jesus. Jesus asks the revivified Zeno whether he had pushed him down, and Zeno replies, 'No, Lord' (Οὐχί, κύριε 9.3). Given that they are playmates, Zeno's use of the vocative 'Lord' (κύριε) in the secular sense of 'sir' is highly unlikely in this context, especially as Mary addresses God only two verses later (10.2) as 'Lord' (Κύριε). Rather, the designation has a definite religious nuance, reflecting both Jesus's divine nature and a post-resurrection sensibility.[96] This inference is further supported by the amazed response of Zeno's parents at their child's revivification: they 'glorify God and worship the child Jesus' (ἐδόξασαν τὸν Θεὸν καὶ προσεκύνησαν τὸ παιδίον Ἰησοῦν). The two parallel actions – glorifying God and worshipping Jesus – set God and Jesus on a similar footing, and it is notable that Zeno's parents *worship* Jesus himself. While it is conceivable that προσκυνέω here means 'honour' or 'do homage', the likelier signification of the verb is to 'worship as a divine being' (Cf. Mt. 14.33; 28.17; Lk. 24.52).[97]

The intimations about Jesus's divine nature raised earlier by the people (4.1) and by Zacchaeus (7.2) are now confirmed. Zeno's parents' misunderstanding of Jesus is corrected and Jesus's authority over life and death prompts their recognition of him as Lord, establishing that he is worthy of worship. That the living and the recently dead join in their veneration of Jesus expresses his all-encompassing authority. This passage is one of the most explicitly christological in the Gs version of the *Paidika*, and it anticipates Jesus's later identification of God as his Father at 17.3. It equally foreshadows Jesus's future public ministry and his status as resurrected Lord. Finally, it models for the book's audience the appropriate response to Jesus and his marvellous deeds. It is not merely astonishment that is required; but reverence and worship.

A further raising from the dead in the *Paidika* is the woodcutter episode (16.1-2 = Ga, Gd 10.1-2; Gb 9.1-3), which recounts Jesus's saving of a young man who had died from loss of blood after splitting his foot open with an axe.[98] Jesus runs to his rescue, heals his foot and then bids him to go split his wood. The crowd marvels when they see it and, as noted above, Gs appends the accolade about Jesus's salvific activities: 'He saved many souls from death, and will continue to save' (16.3 cf. Ga and Gd 18.2). While this passage is less explicitly christological than the Zeno narrative, it portends future examples of Jesus's healing and raising from the dead. This acclamation helps to close out the *Paidika*, and, as stated before, is clearly meant to allude to the healings and raisings from the dead that Jesus will perform as an adult, as recounted in the canonical Gospels.

It is highly significant, therefore, that the two actual narratives that show Jesus raising people from the dead are the ones that portray him as a saviour figure, and one who ought to be worshipped. That is to say, the events in the *Paidika* that most unequivocally demonstrate his extraordinary power are the ones that elicit the

---

96. See the discussion in Fitzmyer (1991), p. 329.

97. Cf. BDAG s.v. Lk. 24.52 (v.l.) the sole occurrence of προσκυνέω in Luke that has Jesus as the direct object occurs after the resurrection (Lk. 24.52 v. l.). Cf. Bousset (1970), p. 330.

98. This episode does not occur in the earliest traditions.

clearest apprehension of his divine identity on the part of his audience. While this pattern is also to be found in the canonical Gospels, it is more pronounced here: power (*dunamis*) and divinity are intimately linked in the text.

What, then, is to be said about miracles in the *Paidika*? The first observation concerns the dominant place occupied by miracles in the *Paidika* – they follow one another in a sheer and unceasing barrage. There are three takings of life and five restorations of life, all accomplished with a word. There is, in addition, one blinding and restoration of sight, a healing and various nature miracles and prodigies. These marvels dominate the portrayal of Jesus from beginning to end, and are the most consistent and characteristic aspect of the *Paidika*'s Christology. As Walter Bauer long ago noted, in the *Paidika*, 'the mania to portray the Lord as a wonderworker has reached such a pitch that next to it all other concerns are muted'.[99] Some of the wonders described are basic and straightforward – such as Jesus collecting water. Others, like Jesus's dividing the waters, are much more theologically complex. But if one assumes with most commentators that the assemblage of the *Paidika*'s miracles was a gradual process, then such variegation makes sense. What the miracles all share in common is the author's delight in the marvellous. Cullmann's observation that the 'cruder and more startling the miracle, the greater the pleasure the compiler finds in it' is certainly true.[100] So long as the miracle is entertaining and emphasizes Jesus's power, it seems to suit the author's purpose admirably, whether it is profound or pedestrian.

Such a superabundance of miracles seems to be the author's way of stressing both Jesus's singularity and his divinity. So many wonders are provided that the reader is hard pressed to explain Jesus's abilities except to view him as a divinity. In keeping with this perception, there is an almost complete absence of magic. Except for Jesus's healing of his brother James by blowing on the snakebite, there are no manipulations or magical techniques involved. Almost all of Jesus's wonders are accomplished by a word alone. Jesus is further represented as having the divine perquisites of granting life and taking it away, and of creating or destroying.[101] In all of this he is not represented as a conduit for divine power and authority – the power and authority originate with him. The upshot of all this is that the *Paidika* presents Jesus as being divine. He is not a magician, thaumaturge or *theios anêr*. He is the son of God (17.3).

4.8 Gnosticism

Such a 'high' Christology raises the question of the (proto-)orthodoxy of the work.[102] As was mentioned in Chapter 1, the *Paidika*'s apparent associations

---

99. Bauer (1909), p. 91. My translation.
100. Cullmann (1991), p. 442.
101. Cf. Bagatti (1976), p. 489.
102. See Burke (2010), pp. 45-126.

with the Marcosians gave rise to enduring suppositions that the work displays a heterodox view of Jesus. Several scholars continue to argue for this view, with the most popular alternatives being some form of Gnosticism, Docetism or Ebionism. Each of these possibilities will be considered in turn here.

As Burke has effectively demonstrated in his history of scholarship on the *Paidika*, the most long-standing interpretation of its Christology has been the supposition that it is a gnostic document.[103] Part of this tendency arose from the association of the *Paidika* with the Gospel of Thomas. Despite the now widespread recognition that the *Paidika* and the Gospel of Thomas are two distinct documents, some scholars continue to suppose that the *Paidika* is gnostic.[104] The most sustained cases are advanced by Santos Otero and Baars and Helderman. Santos Otero focuses on various Greek expressions that appear to reflect gnostic terminology. He argues that phrases such as the 'power of the spirit' (δύναμις τῆς ψυχῆς) or 'elements' (στοιχεῖα) recall standard gnostic terminology, as do the images of the young Jesus mocking his hearers or assuming a polymorphic form where he sometimes appears to his adherents in the form of a child.

The approach of Baars and Helderman is to examine some of the passages of the *Paidika* in light of religious-historical parallels. As was just mentioned, they place particular importance upon Jesus's exposition on the alpha because of its possible associations with the Valentinian Gnostics, the Marcosians. They do recognize that, because a similar exposition also occurs in the anti-gnostic *Epistula Apostolorum*, it may not necessarily originate from a gnostic milieu.[105] Nevertheless, they maintain that in the Syriac version of the *Paidika* Jesus's criticism of Zacchaeus and Jesus's silence before the ignorant and uninitiated 'breathe a gnostic spirit'.[106] Zacchaeus's ignorance further betrays his connections with the world of the Demiurge. Baars and Helderman posit a threefold process

---

103. Burke (2010), pp. 46–7, 58, 69–70, 80, 83, 88, 91–5, 105–7,112–13, 119, 124–6. Cf. also Davis (2014), pp. 6–7. In using the controverted terms 'gnostic' and 'Gnosticism', I largely respond to how the *Paidika*'s commentators use these designations. For problems associated with using the term 'Gnosticism' in an unqualified sense, see Williams (1999).

104. Lapham (2003), p. 130; Baars and Helderman (1993, 1994); Cullmann (1991), pp. 441–2; Vielhauer (1975), p. 676; Santos Otero (1967), pp. 172–84. Klauck (2003), p. 77 remarks that the *Paidika* could have been read in a gnostic manner. Elliott (1993), p. 69 and Rebell (1992), pp. 134–5 postulate that it may have been originally gnostic, but was later purged of its gnostic elements.

105. Baars and Helderman (1994), pp. 5, 8; Santos Otero (1967), pp. 173–84. See further Hartenstein (2010).

106. Baars and Helderman (1994), pp. 8–9. This association with the Demiurge extends to the anger displayed by Jesus's teachers (p. 11#163). For a complete listing of features they deem to be gnostic, cf. (1994), p. 31.

in which the alpha tradition developed: Buddhist and Egyptian traditions supplied the basic features that were then gnosticized by the Marcosians, and then subsequently de-gnosticized to such an extent that the author of the *Epistula* was unaware of its gnostic past.[107]

This hypothetical trajectory is conceivable but, as Wilson remarks, the type of process they propose is too complicated. It is preferable to suppose that the *Paidika* as a whole was slightly influenced by a gnostic milieu, but not significantly so.[108]

Further, features that were sometimes regarded as inherently gnostic turn out not to be gnostic after all. For instance, there is nothing specifically gnostic about speculating on the elemental character and shape of the letters of the alphabet.[109] Dornseiff chronicles numerous examples of elemental speculations that range from Pythagoreans to Neoplatonists, and from Jews to orthodox Christians.[110] This type of theorizing was much more characteristic of the age than of any particular group. Other features such as Jesus's development and maturation actually speak against gnostic influence. Typical gnostic portrayals of Jesus would suggest that he was a being exempt from the constraints and limitations of human development.[111] Yet, if the argument of Chapter 3 is accepted, then the very opposite holds true in the *Paidika*: Jesus is delimited by his incarnation as a human and by the stages of maturation through which humans pass.

Another feature that could speak to a gnostic origin is the absence in the *Paidika* of any citations of the Septuagint. In contrast, for instance, to the canonical Gospels, which are replete with citations and allusions, the parevangelical *Paidika* demonstrates no such thing. It could be, therefore, that gnostic disdain for the Demiurge is the reason for the *Paidika*'s failure to mention the Septuagint. The problem with this supposition is that, as was shown earlier, the episode of the pools seems to align Jesus with the creative activity of Yahweh. Jesus's rendering the pools 'clean', moreover, seems to echo Yahweh's approval: 'And God saw that it was good' (Gen. 1.10). Neither episode displays a rejection of matter or of creation as something aberrant – on the contrary, both are affirmed. Yet, it is most unlikely that a gnostic presentation of Jesus would want to parallel Jesus with the Demiurge or have him intimately involved with the world of matter. Finally, as will be shown next, there are no significant indications of Docetism in the *Paidika*.

---

107. Baars and Helderman (1994), pp. 10–11.

108. Wilson (1978), p. 335.

109. Gero (1971), pp. 75–6. Having said that, there is no disputing the importance of elemental speculation to the Marcosians; cf. Frankfurter (1994), p. 201; Dornseiff (1925), pp. 126–33. Hannah (2008), p. 627 would still argue for a gnostic provenance.

110. Dornseiff (1925), pp. 22–30.

111. Meyer (1904), p. 64.

4.9 Docetism

It is occasionally suggested that the *Paidika* displays a Docetism[112] not unlike that which is said to characterize the Johannine literature.[113] Is this likely? Do the *Paidika*'s similarities to John's Gospel suggest that it is also displaying a form of 'naïve Docetism'?[114] Käsemann regarded the problem as one arising from John's 'Christology of glory'. Yet, as Frey and others have shown, Käsemann's view slightly overstates the case.[115]

Docetism is characterized by a variety of forms. Georg Strecker isolates three different types of Docetism. One is attributed to Basilides, who suggests that a human other than Jesus (Simon of Cyrene) was crucified in Jesus's place. A second, associated with Cerinthus, suggests that the divine nature of Jesus – the 'Christ' – left Jesus before the passion, while the third (monophysite Docetism) holds that Jesus, being unified with the Christ's divine nature, was a mere phantasm who could not suffer because he was divine.[116]

Cerinthus's description of Jesus is, perhaps, closest to that found in the *Paidika*.[117] According to Irenaeus, Cerinthus claims that Jesus was not born of a virgin, but had been 'born the son of Joseph and Mary like all other men. ... Then [Jesus] preached the unknown and worked wonders.'[118] Like Cerinthus, the *Paidika* stresses Jesus's parentage, his wonderworking and his exposition of heavenly wisdom. At the same time, however, the *Paidika* does not explicitly reject the virgin birth. Nor, significantly, does it conform to Cerinthus's view that Christ descended on Jesus at the baptism and then left him prior to the crucifixion because, being a spirit, Christ was impassible (Irenaeus, *Adv. Haer.* 1.26.1). The *Paidika* repeatedly emphasizes that Jesus's divine nature was present throughout his childhood.[119] And while

---

112. For recent overviews of Docetism see: Von Wahlde (2015), pp. 62–5; Stroumsa (2004), pp. 267–88; Strecker (1996), pp. 69–76; Schnelle (1992), pp. 63–70. On Docetism's origins: Goldstein and Stroumsa (2004), pp. 267–88.

113. Cullmann (1991), p. 442; 'docetic tendency', cf. Voicu (1997), p. 193; Currie (1993), pp. 206–8.

114. The term is that of Käsemann (1968), pp. 26, 70.

115. Frey (2011), pp. 202–7.

116. Strecker (1996), pp. 72–3.

117. The Ethiopic version may speak for a form of monophysite Docetism. In it Jesus says, 'Je suis autre que vous; je ne possède pas comme vous une famille de chair': *Miracles of Jesus* 7; trans Grébaut (1919). Gs, by contrast, relates that Jesus has 'a noble birth (σαρκικὴν εὐγενίαν) in the flesh', a reading that certainly speaks against Docetism. Cf. Aasgaard (2010), p. 141.

118. Irenaeus, *Adv. Haer.* I.26.1; translation slightly modified from Unger and Dillon (1992), p. 90.

119. It is true that the monophysite Docetism of the *Acts of John* also feature a child Jesus, but this figure is only one of the forms that Jesus assumes as part of the work's polymorphic Christology.

Cerinthus persistently distinguishes the human and divine natures of Jesus, in the *Paidika* they are combined.

The clearest indication that the *Paidika* is not docetic, however, is that Jesus appears to experience pain and physical discomfort.[120] Jesus is angered when he is struck by Zacchaeus (6.8), and both his retaliation against the careless boy and his second teacher result from his being physically struck. He also appears to feel pain in G*a* 5.2-3 when Joseph yanks on his ear.[121] All these episodes speak to a Jesus who is physically present, not to a docetic Christ.

4.10 Ebionism

Among the most recent attempts to characterize the *Paidika*'s Christology are arguments claiming that it represents a form of Ebionism. Both Sever Voicu and Andries Van Aarde have advanced such claims.[122] Voicu contends that the *Paidika*'s frequent allusions to Joseph as Jesus's father and to James as Jesus's actual brother correspond to an ebionite Christology, which says that Jesus was born human but became divine through his obedience to the Law.[123] Van Aarde seizes on a number of features that suggest an ebionite focus to him.

Both arguments face various difficulties, not the least being the problems that arise from attempting to define Ebionism. Our understanding of the movement (or movements) is constructed from patristic authors – Justin Martyr, Irenaeus, Hippolytus, Origen, Eusebius and Epiphanius – and while there are some areas of commonality in the beliefs they describe, there are very considerable differences as well. So, one of the first questions that faces scholars trying to define Ebionism is: What form of Ebionism are they describing?[124] A synthetic construction is inevitably a distortion.

Voicu's view builds on one of the more common ebionite assumptions, found in Hippolytus, namely that Jesus had a normal not a divine birth and, therefore, belonged to a normal family. The difficulty with this view is that Voicu underestimates Jesus's divine origin. He claims that the *Paidika* 'never explicitly affirms his divine origin'.[125] While this is true, the *Paidika* never affirms his human paternity either. It does, however, imply his divine origin in the Syriac, where Jesus says to Joseph, 'But you think that you are my father,' implying thereby that Joseph

---

120. Holzbach (2013), p. 865; Klauck (2003), p. 77. Cf. Burke (2010), p. 275.

121. Burke (2010), p. 275.

122. Voicu (1998), p. 50, (1997), p. 193. Cf. Van Aarde (2013, 2006, 2005).

123. Voicu (1998), p. 50; (1997), p. 193.

124. For recent discussion of Ebionism, see Paget (2010), pp. 325–79; Luomanen (2007), pp. 81–118; Skarsaune (2007), pp. 419–62; Häkkinen (2005), pp. 247–78; Klijn and Reinink (1973), pp. 19–43.

125. Voicu (1998), p. 50.

is mistaken.[126] And when one further takes into account Jesus's reference to God as his father (17.3) and to his own pre-existence (6.4), it becomes difficult to assume that Jesus is a normal human.

Van Aarde's position is also problematic. For one thing, his understanding of Ebionism is entirely based on Stanley Jones's brief and synthetic dictionary article on the Ebionites.[127] After consulting it, Van Aarde isolates the following features by which he defines the Ebionites:

> they were opposed to Paul, among other things because of his critical perspective on the soteriological value of the Law. On the other hand, the 'Ebionites' held the Gospel of Matthew in high regard because Matthew emphasized the soteriological value of the Law (see inter al. Matt. 5,17-20). Furthermore, Jerusalem and the central position that the Temple in Judaism filled in Israelite society were important to the 'Ebionites'. The Israelite way of life was also fully upheld. They were attached to Jesus' ties with his biological relatives, and with Israel as extended family.[128]

To Van Aarde these features confirm the ebionite character of the *Paidika*. They include 'Jesus' obeisance [*sic*] to the Law, salvation being restricted to Israel, and the close and positive relation with his biological family'.[129]

Van Aarde's arguments have been discussed in detail by Frédéric Amsler, who raises some serious concerns about his hypothesis.[130] Amsler asks why, if Matthew is so valued by the Ebionites, the *Paidika* does not cite it, but refers to Luke instead, and why the only other direct citation in the work is by the despised Paul (1 Cor. 13.1 at *Paid.* 6.2)? And why, if the Jewish way of life is upheld, does the *Paidika* portray Jesus as breaking the Sabbath? Amsler adds that the 'strong family ties' that Van Aarde adduces – Mary and Joseph hugging and kissing Jesus – are not themselves sufficient to establish a uniquely ebionite connection. Finally, Van Aarde does not account for Jesus's harsh temperament toward his father.[131]

In addition to those features commented on by Amsler, Van Aarde can be faulted for not defining Ebionism with sufficient nuance. The primary sources themselves need to be consulted, especially since they are far from consistent. Likewise, Van Aarde's attempts to delimit the *Paidika* to a Jewish audience by emending the text of the work's (late) preamble are not convincing and fail to explain why his

---

126. Translation by Burke (2013a), p. 276.
127. Jones (1990), pp. 287–8.
128. Van Aarde (2013), p. 616#23; (2005), pp. 831–2.
129. Van Aarde (2013), p. 617; cf. (2006), p. 362.
130. Amsler (2011), pp. 447–9. Amsler addresses only the first two articles of Van Aarde. While Van Aarde (2013), p. 611#1 cites Amsler's article, he does not engage with the issues it raises. See, further, the remarks by Burke (2010), pp. 115–17.
131. Amsler (2011), p. 449.

emendation would refer to the 'Jews', an ethnic designation that is commonly used by non-Jews.[132]

In conclusion, it is possible that the *Paidika* or portions of it did at one time demonstrate a more heterodox Christology, but in its present form it is unquestionably orthodox. The *Paidika* may manifest tinctures of Gnosticism and Docetism, but no more than are found in the Gospel of John. And if John's Christology is considered orthodox notwithstanding these tinctures, then the same holds true for the *Paidika*'s Christology.

4.11 The Paidika's Christology

The picture of Jesus's divine nature that emerges from the various facets of the *Paidika*, therefore, is of a consistently 'high' Christology. What makes this representation unusual, as Burke has noted, is that the author has largely refrained from using 'theologically-loaded titles such as Lord, Messiah, Christ or Saviour'.[133] As just noted, the only title used of Jesus is 'Lord' (κύριε) in 9.3. Instead, the focus is very much upon a narrative Christology comprising deeds. Such an emphasis may be designed to forefront Jesus's miraculous acts and also suggest a movement away from terms with a distinctively Jewish emphasis (e.g. Christ, Messiah).

Notwithstanding the absence of the usual christological terminology, the *Paidika*'s three major christological strands all emphasize an exalted view of Jesus. In fact, one of the reasons that the work has frequently been regarded as gnostic or docetic is because of its intensive focus on the divine nature of Jesus, such as when the *Paidika*'s author rewrites Lk. 2.41-51 in such a way that he enhances Jesus's abilities and bequeaths him a Johannine omniscience. As for the echoes of John, they strongly attest to Jesus's heavenly and pre-existent origins, as well as his mission as divine emissary. Finally, the miracle stories, despite their diversity, often dwell on the parallels between Jesus and God. Jesus's divine creativity is emphasized, as is his authority to enact his will by divine fiat. Jesus's deeds repeatedly demonstrate his divine knowledge, his control over nature, and dominion over life and death itself. Although different in focus, all three of these christological strands complement each other and combine to portray Jesus as a divine figure, who, although he is human, is also much more than human. The *Paidika*'s author has consistently sought to construct a picture of Jesus that expresses his divine authority and his power.

Just how resolutely the author has adhered to this particular focus can be established from a consideration of christological features that do not appear. When it is compared to the canonical Gospels, the *Paidika*'s Christology is remarkably lacunose, a feature that has led Ulrike Kaiser to speak of a 'reduced

---

132. Van Aarde (2013), pp. 617–20.
133. Burke (2010), p. 200. Gd 10.2 has: 'our Lord Jesus Christ'.

Christology'.[134] Many features that are typical of gospel Christologies simply appear. As noted above, the titles of Jesus that are so characteristic of the canonical Gospels are largely missing. The strong connection with the Septuagint is absent. In the *Paidika*, salvation possesses a this-worldly dimension, and there is little pneumatology.[135] The message of the Kingdom so typical of the Synoptic Gospels is not found, and only occasionally do Jesus's words resemble the self-revelations that dominate John. While some of the miracles echo episodes in the canonical Gospels, there are no exorcisms (as is also the case with John), but numerous curses in their stead.

The reason for the absence of these features is straightforward: the *Paidika*'s author does not want to detract or distract from his central focus on Jesus's mighty deeds and his astonishing words. While the theology expressed by the author is proto-orthodox, much of it – such as the allusions to creation in Genesis – is left implicit and not expressed, even though the author seems to have at least some familiarity with the Jesus of the canonical Gospels. Nevertheless, he downplays all of this in favour of a non-stop barrage of miracles and wonders. Such features are unusual – why would the author or redactor have constructed the work in such a fashion? The most promising answer is that the Christology with its particular focus on miracles and marvellous deeds was produced with a certain audience in mind. Just who this audience was is the subject of the next chapter.

---

134. Kaiser (2012), p. 940.
135. However, see the other Greek traditions which do mention the cross: Ga and Gd 6.2b.

Chapter 5

THE *PAIDIKA*'S JESUS IN CONTEXT

5.1 *The* Paidika's *Audience*

It was suggested in Chapter 2 that the *Paidika* was written as an implicit comment on and rejoinder to Graeco-Roman stories of the gods. Such an assessment presupposes that the *Paidika* was written, at least in part, with a pagan audience in mind. But is such an assumption warranted? In stark contrast with the canonical Gospels, no Gentiles appear and none are mentioned in the *Paidika*. And, as was noted in the last chapter, the 'crowds' and 'people' are understood to be synonymous with 'Jews'. Moreover, the *Paidika*'s immediate setting is a Jewish village or small town, and the narrative provides readers with various details that clearly indicate a Jewish provenance. The Temple narrative is the most explicit in furnishing such details. Apart from the mention of the Temple and the Passover pilgrimage that echo Luke 2, the *Paidika* also includes various references to the Jewish authorities – scribes, Pharisees, elders and 'teachers of the Law' (cf. Lk. 2.41-51). Pharisees are mentioned several times (2.3,5; 6.5), and there are also references to Annas the High Priest (3.1). Other mentions of Jewish *realia* include the reference to the 'Book of the Law' (14.2)[1] and several allusions to the keeping of the Sabbath (2.2-4; 3.1).[2]

While these details are certainly significant, other features suggest less of a Jewish focus. The coordinated use of the terms 'Jews' (6.5) and the 'people' (λαός 6.7) in *Paidika* chapter 6 make one wonder whether this work is really intended for a Jewish audience. The two terms are used synonymously, but their connotations are quite different. The term 'Jews' (Ἰουδαῖοι) is a designation usually employed by non-Jews, whereas Jewish authors tend to refer to themselves as 'Israelites'. The use of this terminology in the *Paidika* raises the question about whether the Jewish features actually reflect a Jewish context or whether they are meant to serve as an

---

1. It is noteworthy that unlike Ga and Gd, Jesus in Gs does not 'teach the law' to those present in the classroom.

2. It is possible that the subtext of the clay sparrows on the Sabbath is a revocation of the Sabbath. Young Jesus is not simply 'saving life' on the Sabbath, but giving unfettered life to things that never had it before – namely, to Gentiles.

ethnic backdrop. If Lowe is correct in his contention that negative references to the 'Jews' in the *Paidika* increased over time, then there appears to have been an ever-increasing movement away from Judaism.³ Such positive references as there are to Judaism may be intended to demonstrate to non-Jewish readers that Jesus had been acclaimed by the more insightful of his co-religionists. The author has made efforts to establish Jesus's apparent reverence for the law, his presence in the Temple and these features might mean that his links with Judaism had not been entirely severed, and that he still retained the hope that he would convince some of them.

In this respect, the *Paidika* would resemble the canonical Gospels in entertaining the possibility of Jewish converts, but be focusing primarily on Gentile audiences to promulgate their message. In all likelihood, the *Paidika* was not aimed primarily at a Jewish audience. No mention is made of Israel's history or of God's salvific deeds on behalf of Israel.⁴ The references to Yahweh are relatively limited: God (θεός 7.4; 9.3; 12.2; 14.2; 17.5); Lord God (κύριος ὁ θεός 10.2; 17.4); and Father (πατήρ 17.3). While these designations are used of God in Jewish writings, they are not specifically Jewish.⁵ The *Paidika* makes only muted allusions to Jewish scripture (such as the echoes of the creation story) and no direct appeals to prophecy. This absence of explicit citations from the LXX is especially striking, particularly when the *Paidika* is contrasted with the *Protevangelium of James*, which has frequent references to the LXX,⁶ and to the later *Gospel of Pseudo-Matthew* (based in part on the *Paidika*) that deliberately emphasizes the fulfilment of prophecy by adding six fulfilment citations.⁷ One would anticipate that appealing to the authority of the Jewish scriptures – as Justin does in the *Dialogue with Trypho* – would be an essential technique for engaging with a Jewish audience. Even if they were illiterate, they would still have had sufficient familiarity with the Scriptures as a result of participating in weekly Sabbath readings in the synagogues, scriptural readings on the holidays and on other sacred occasions.⁸ The absence of citations and distinctive allusions from the Septuagint, therefore, is a strong indication that the *Paidika* was directed at pagans or Christians with a non-Jewish background, a large constituent of whom were likely recent gentile converts to Christianity.⁹

This is not to exclude Jewish or explicitly pagan audiences, but to suggest that the main recipients were new believers or interested pagans. Such a supposition

---

3. Lowe (1981), pp. 84–5. Casey (2007), pp. 8–9 shows that in the medieval iconography of the infancy stories anti-Jewish tendencies begin to reassert themselves conspicuously.

4. Bockmuehl (2017), p. 75; Hock (1995), pp. 97–8.

5. Contrast Gd 10.2 'our Lord Jesus Christ'.

6. See the notes in Cullmann (1991a), pp. 437–9.

7. Miller (2003), pp. 308–9.

8. Hezser (2001), pp. 452–3; Shinan (1996), pp. 132–4. On the practice of weekly readings from the law of Moses: Acts 15.21; Josephus, *C. Ap.* 2.175.

9. I am using gentile and pagan as rough synonyms. For a discussion and warrant for using this terminology, see Jones (2014), pp. 2–6.

would help to account for the text's virtual absence of references to the Septuagint. An audience of recent converts or interested pagans may have heard of Jesus's upbringing as a Jew, but been unfamiliar with the Jewish Scriptures. Paul's letter to the Thessalonians reflects a similar situation in certain respects. Although it is possible to recognize several underlying echoes of the LXX in Paul's letter, the epistle is remarkable for its absence of scriptural references, especially when it is compared to Romans or Galatians, which are replete with citations. Despite his own extensive familiarity with the LXX, Paul does not expressly cite or refer to it in Thessalonians, presumably because it would not have been particularly meaningful for his church of recent converts. In particular, the LXX's putative authority would have been rendered unnecessary by Paul's own authoritative presence. In his letter Paul has tailored his message to his audience by appealing to his own authority and example to instruct the Thessalonians instead of referring to Scripture.

The *Paidika*'s prologue also suggests an audience of pagan converts: 'I, Thomas the Israelite, deemed it necessary to make known to all the gentile brethren (πᾶσιν τοῖς ἐξ ἐθνῶν ἀδελφοῖς) those things that our Lord Jesus Christ did' (1.1). Although this prologue is considerably later than the rest of the *Paidika*, it is possible that it nevertheless offers an accurate reminiscence (or reading) of the work's intended audience.[10] If so, it indicates that the work was intended to acquaint one-time pagans who had become Christians with supplemental details about the life of Jesus and his boyhood.[11]

Nevertheless, the *Paidika*'s strong focus on Jesus's authority and miracles would suggest that its main intention was to persuade the unpersuaded of Jesus's divinity, and confirm the decision of those who had recently converted. Again, one need only compare its relative absence of devotional elements with a work like the *Protevangelium of James*. A few features of the *Paidika* suggest a context of worship, such as the crowd's acclamation at 16.3 and the scribes and Pharisees' macarism at 17.4, but the only act of worship described is by Zeno's parents (9.3).[12] Of course, the text does provide a model for believers, but it seems to be a model for people who had not previously been believers who were brought to worship Jesus by virtue of his extraordinary deeds.

The *Paidika* allows other inferences about the work's audience. Its lack of literary sophistication is revealing. Greek novels are sometimes ranged alongside the Apocryphal Acts and the *Protevangelium* as more-or-less direct literary comparanda.[13] This comparison, however, is misleading. While it is highly likely

---

10. Burke (2010), p. 215; p. 302 notes that the addition of the prologue 'is difficult to date'.

11. *Pace* Van Aarde (2013), pp. 619-20.

12. The final benediction at 17.5 is a later addition.

13. Konstan and Ramelli (2014), pp. 26-43; Cameron (1991), pp. 90-119; Pervo (1996), pp. 685-711; (1987), pp. 122-31. On the more general overlaps between Christian and pagan narrative forms, see Bowersock (1994), pp. 123-4.

that the Greek novels could also have been enjoyed by an unsophisticated and illiterate audience, they were written by an intellectual elite who envisioned a diverse spectrum of readers and auditors – intelligentsia and uneducated alike.[14] It is doubtful, however, that the Apocryphal Acts or *Protevangelium* demonstrate a similar pedigree and, in terms of sophistication, the *Paidika* is probably a further step below them.[15] Its author was able to write, and was not without some literary skill, but it is highly probable that the intended focus of his labours was an unlettered and unschooled populace. Richard Horsley has asserted that the story of Mark's Gospel 'emerged from among ordinary people ... [and was] oriented to the interests of ordinary people',[16] and much the same could be said for the *Paidika*. Its author has fashioned the story in such a way so as to emphasize its popular character.

Herein lies the distinction between what might be described as truly 'popular' writing – in the sense that it was written with an uneducated populace in mind – and most of the Christian writing of the second century. The latter, apologetic and otherwise, was almost exclusively produced for an educated readership,[17] and was largely designed to express the intellectual merits of the Christian 'philosophy' or 'school'.[18] The *Paidika*'s author had no such pretensions. Although he may have been familiar with at least some of his peers' more reasoned approaches to Christianity, they do not figure in his narrative. Lip service is frequently paid to the place of education in the *Paidika*, but, apart from the set-pieces on the alpha, there is not much evidence of it – no theological agendas, no discussions of prophetic fulfilment, no moral diatribes. Despite their prominence in the narrative, the educational passages do not focus upon Jesus's reasoning, so much as his deeds. The author, like Mark, seems to write in the knowledge that his miraculous stories about Jesus are going to be far more pleasing to his audience than any teaching he could offer.

As has been stressed in previous chapters, the *Paidika*'s emphases and enthusiasms appear to be directed at an unsophisticated populace. Jesus's 'superpowers', his 'bad-boy' antics, his divine oblivion to the concerns of mere humans, his besting of all authority figures – these are the features that seemingly appeal to and engage the *Paidika*'s audience; that grip them and leave them wanting more. That the stories are redolent with the exoticism of Jewish wisdom makes them similarly attractive (without the necessity of the audience needing to know much about Judaism except, perhaps, for relatively familiar features such as the famous

---

14. Hägg (2004), pp. 109–40. Hall (2004), pp. 1–10 argues convincingly that the generation of early Christian writings was very different from the production of pagan literature.

15. On the Apocryphal Acts, see Söder (1969 [1932]), p. 186.

16. Horsley (2015), p. 151.

17. How successful they were in reaching their intended audience of educated pagans is unclear; Tertullian remarks that 'no one turns to our literature who is not already a Christian'. Cf. Tert. *Test. Animae* 1, cited in MacMullen (1983), p. 37#6.

18. MacMullen (2009), p. xi puts Christian writers' work into context when he remarks that all the celebrated early Christian authors 'together count as no more than a hundredth of one per cent of the Christian population at any given moment'.

Jewish Temple, the existence of holy Scripture, and customs like the Sabbath).[19] And best of all, the *Paidika*'s overlap with the authoritative Gospel of Luke means that gentile converts can listen to its amusingly subversive narratives and be edified at the same time.

5.2 The 'Great Church'

The above factors, therefore, suggest that the *Paidika* was written, at least in part, with the 'Great Church' in view.[20] These were the mass of one-time pagans who had or were in the process of converting to proto-orthodox Christianity. Justin claims that an 'uncountable crowd' (ἀναρίθμητον πλῆθος) of pagans had converted (*1 Apol.* 15.7; cf. 16.4). This crowd typically belonged to the lower classes of society – slaves, freedmen, tradespeople – and were, as a rule, uneducated, credulous and often ignorant of the most basic Christian beliefs. They were the *simpliciores*, 'the simpler folk', who were well-intentioned, but often ill-informed about Christianity.[21] In fact, the common Christians' lack of education and disdain for learning were legendary among Christianity's detractors. Porphyry (*Christ.* Fr. 67 apud Jerome *Commentarii in Joel* 2.28ff) comments on their simple-mindedness and lack of knowledge. This ignorance might not necessarily have been a cause of reproach except that the Christians actively abjured education of any kind. Celsus frustratedly asks, 'Why is it bad to have been educated and to have studied the best doctrines, and both to be and to appear intelligent?' (*Cels.* 3.49). But, according to him, the Christians deliberately courted ignorance:

> Their injunctions are like this. 'Let no one educated, no one wise, no one sensible draw near. For these abilities are thought by us to be evils. But as for anyone ignorant, anyone stupid, anyone uneducated, anyone who is a child, let him come boldly.' By the fact that they themselves admit that these people are worthy of their God they show that they want and are able to convince only the foolish, dishonourable and stupid, and only slaves, women, and little children. (*Cels.* 3.44)

Instead, he says, Christians were counselled by their teachers to disdain knowledge and to accept everything on faith (*Cels.* 3.55,75). Galen makes the very same

---

19. It is telling how inadequate and misinformed accounts of the Jews were, even among the educated. See, for instance, Tacitus's celebrated account in *Histories* 5.1-5.

20. Lampe (1965), p. 383 remarks that 'Behind "orthodoxy" stands the mass of uneducated Christian folk ... orthodoxy, easily comprehended by the masses, constituted the "Great Church"'. The phrase 'Great Church' originates with Celsus (Origen, *Cels.* 5.59; cf. 5.60 'those of the multitude'). MacMullen (2009) employs the term, the 'Second Church'.

21. MacMullen (2009), p. 109. See, further, Kraus (1999), pp. 434–49 on the significance of the terminology used to describe John and Peter's lack of education at Acts 4.13.

complaint.[22] Tertullian, however, embraces this disdain as a matter of pride: 'With our faith, we desire no further belief. For this is our pre-eminent faith, that there is nothing which we ought to believe besides' (*Praescr.* 7). And to ensure that the *simpliciores* dispensed with conventional learning, their fellow Christians deliberately sought to undermine whatever they were taught. Celsus complains:

> In private houses also we see wool-workers, cobblers, laundry workers, and the most illiterate and bucolic yokels, who would not dare to say anything at all in front of their elders and more intelligent masters. But whenever they get hold of children in private and some stupid women with them, they let out some astounding statements as, for example, that they should not pay attention to their father and school-teachers. (*Cels.* 3.55)

Such a deliberate pooling of ignorance guaranteed that Christians were exploited by frauds. Lucian recounts at length how the Christians were deceived and cheated by Peregrinus (*Peregr.* 11-13, 16), noting that, 'if any charlatan and trickster … comes among them, he quickly acquires sudden wealth by imposing upon simple (ἰδιώταις) folk' (*Peregr.* 13). Celsus remarks on the same phenomenon: 'Scoundrels frequently take advantage of the lack of education of gullible people and … this happens among the Christians' (*Cels.*1.9).

Remarkably, the common Christians' deficient understanding extended to the details of their own faith. Tertullian remarks that the unwise and uneducated Christians who constituted the majority of believers were 'startled' at the doctrine of the Trinity (*Prax.* 3). Origen also comments on this circumstance, noting that since the necessities of life and human weakness discouraged rational thought, 'What better way of helping the multitude could be found other than that given to the nations by Jesus?' (*Cels.* 1.9). Jesus provided such a ready form of salvation that one did not need to engage in study. Conversion was easy – as Tertullian remarks, any manual worker could readily find God (*Apol.* 46.9). The consequence of these attitudes was a marked ignorance among Christians. In fact, some believers' acquaintance with Christianity was so sketchy that their bishops deliberated about whether they even merited the designation 'Christian'.[23]

This problem of unschooled believers was naturally compounded by the fact that the vast majority of early Christians were illiterate. Notwithstanding regional variations and differing modern evaluations of what constitutes literacy, most recent assessments would place literacy rates in the ancient world at about 10 per cent or less. Despite the centrality of sacred writings to their faith, this

---

22. The passage of Galen from an Arabic source reads: 'If I had in mind people who taught their pupils in the same way as the followers of Moses and Christ teach theirs – for they order them to accept everything on faith – I should not have given you a definition.' Cited in Chadwick (1965), p. 12#3.

23. MacMullen (2009), p. 109.

percentage also includes Christians and Jews.[24] It necessarily follows that almost all of Christian believers would have heard Christian writings delivered in an oral (and aural) context. The usual practice was to have group readings; such a context would obviously favour those who could not read, since they could hear the works for themselves. And although it is possible to envision situations where the *Paidika* might have been read outside of organized Christian settings, such as after-dinner readings designed for general entertainment, the likeliest context for public readings of the *Paidika* would have been church or Christian gatherings.[25] Justin Martyr famously describes the reading-aloud of the evangelists' 'memoirs': 'And on the day called Sunday, all who live in cities or in the country gather together in one place, and the memoirs of the apostles or the writings of the prophets are read, as long as time permits; then when the reader has ceased, the president verbally instructs, and exhorts to the imitation of these good things' (*1 Apol*. 67.3 cf. 66.3). While the *City of God* is probably considerably later than the *Paidika*, Augustine mentions the public reading-aloud in church of earlier miracle accounts that had been 'pounded into the memory by frequent reading so as not to slip from the mind' (*Civ*. 22.8). This portrait of the 'Great Church' suggests that there was a large segment of Christians who by nature or inclination were uneducated.

5.3 Miracles and Agonism

If, the 'Great Church' did, in fact, constitute a ready audience for popular Christian literature – especially the *Paidika* – then the geographer Strabo helps to explain why miracles were such prominent features within it – namely, the fact that an uneducated audience delighted in stories that focused on the miraculous:

> Now every illiterate and uneducated man is, in a sense, a child, and, like a child, he is fond of stories; and for that matter, so is the half-educated man, for his reasoning faculty has not been fully developed, and, besides, the mental habits of his childhood persist in him. Now since the portentous (τὸ τερατῶδες) is not only pleasing, but fear-inspiring as well, we can employ both kinds of myth for children, and for grown-up people, too. .... For in dealing with a crowd ... a philosopher cannot influence them by reason ... there is need of religious fear (δεισιδαιμονίας) also, and this cannot be aroused without myths and marvels (τερατείας).[26] (Strabo, *Geogr*. 1.2.8)

---

24. Harris (1989), p. 328. For Jews, see Hezser (2001), p. 496, and for Christians, Gamble (1995), p. 10.

25. Paul refers to non-believers attending church gatherings in 1 Corinthians and this may have been taken by later readers as prescriptive for future communities – to bring along prospective converts. Adams (2013), pp. 116–19 argues that early Christian teaching took place, indoors and out, in a wide variety of locales, not simply in houses.

26. Lucian's *Philopseudes* (5) suggests that the dissemination of numerous marvels (πολλὰ τεράστια) to wide-eyed auditors was a sufficiently frequent occurrence to warrant

It is revealing how Strabo makes the same conjunction of children and the illiterate that is mentioned above, and how he sees the key to the popular palate as being a combination of sweet and savoury: the sweetness of the pleasing story mixed with the piquancy of the astonishing and awe-inspiring.[27]

Of the two, the latter quality dominates the *Paidika*. Homer had affirmed, 'All things were possible for the gods' (*Od.* 10.306), and this idea continued to inform the religious landscape of the early Common Era.[28] In this respect, popular Christian expectations were comparable to those of the pagans: miracles and marvels were a commonly accepted sign of the divine for both groups.[29] Robin Lane Fox notes that 'the simpler, pious majority were not detached from the myths and expectations which surrounded their gods'.[30] They fully expected marvels and acts of power, since the power to perform miracles was the essence of divinity. The acclamation of Paul and Barnabas as Hermes and Zeus in the book of Acts after their performance of a healing demonstrates just how close to the surface of popular consciousness such ideas actually were (Acts 14.8-18). Hence, if one were interested in validating Jesus's divine claims among the common people, there would hardly be a more effective means of advancing claims about Jesus than to show him possessed of miraculous power. As MacMullen puts it, 'Miracles further served as a proof, not only of divine authority behind Christian teachings, but as a proof of God's unique claim to his title, whereas other supernatural beings deserved only to be called daimones.'[31] This type of 'competitive thaumaturgy' was commonplace and, not surprisingly, Origen indicates that miracles were influential in the conversion of uneducated believers.[32]

Just how influential Christian miracles were in promoting conversions is disputed. Lane Fox is sceptical about whether pagans were won to Christianity by witnessing a miracle. He suggests instead that Christianity won pagan converts 'by conviction and persuasion, long and detailed sequels to the initial proof that faith could work'.[33] This assessment, however, is too reductive. Religious

being satirized. Certainly, the paradoxography of people like Phlegon of Tralles is ample testimony of the popularity of marvels; cf. Hansen (1998), pp. 249-58.

27. This focus on children aligns well with Aasgaard's supposition of an audience of children for the *Paidika*.

28. Lane Fox (1986), p. 115.

29. Cf. Origen, *Cels.* 1.9,18; 5.15,19,29; Minucius Felix, *Oct.* 19.15, and Leppin (2007), p. 97; MacMullen (1983), p. 187: 'proofs of power'. Educated Christians tended to be warier of relying upon miracles as divine proofs – cf. Hanson (1980), p. 930.

30. Lane Fox (1986), p. 98. See, more fully, Nock (1972), pp. 34-45; Grant (1952), pp. 127-34.

31. MacMullen (1984), p. 108; Cf. Frend (2005), pp. 11-21; Den Boeft (2004), pp. 51-62.

32. On competitive thaumaturgy, cf. Nock (1972), pp. 327-8; Snyder (1999), 199-201; Origen, *Cels.* 1.46; 2.38, 49. Against miracles as a factor in conversion, see Lane Fox (1986), p. 317, 329.

33. Lane Fox (1986), p. 330.

conversion was a diverse and variegated process in antiquity, and carried a range of different implications. A case in point can be seen in a recent article by Ramsay MacMullen. He observes that Nock seems to subscribe to two contradictory views of conversion, which appears to be an oversight by Nock.[34] On the one hand, Nock, like Lane Fox, considers conversion to Christianity to be an elaborate and involved process: 'conversion entailed "renunciation and a new start", and adherence "body and soul"' to church authority. Yet on the other, Nock describes it as taking up 'an attitude of submissive reliance in the new δύναμις [power] and its representatives'.[35] Instead of being an oversight, however, Nock is likely referring to conversion as it applies to different strata of society. For the more educated populace, conversion is a considered and deliberative process, whereby one chooses a 'higher' philosophical mode of life. For the unschooled population, however, it would be a spontaneous and emotive reaction to the numinous, involving a rapid change of heart. Given, however, that this second type of conversion is much more of a superficial and spontaneous reaction than the first type, it may not endure. And since it is not an intellectual decision, it is no wonder that some converts were faulted for their ignorance of Christian doctrine. It is likely for this latter group that the *Paidika* was written, and the text was presumably hoping both to elicit such conversions and to sustain those who had been converted, by means of its miraculous narratives.

Educated Christians tended to be much warier of relying upon miracles as divine proofs because both pagan and Jewish critics could – and did – disparage Jesus as a magician (γόης) and a deceiver.[36] At the more popular level, however, the tendency was to pit Jesus or the disciples against their spiritual adversaries in the form of contests. This type of contestation or agonism was an established feature of the Graeco-Roman world, and extended from the poorest slaves to the emperors, and to the gods beyond.[37] Zeus famously challenged all the other Olympian gods to a tug-of-war with a golden chain, asserting that he had power enough to defeat them all (Homer, *Il.* 8.18-28), and this agonism characterized the mindset that defined religious attitudes in the ancient world and embodied the primitive religious hierarchy that was often thought to underlie the universe.[38] Divine power was the essential commodity here, so whoever possessed the greatest amounts of power would inevitably prove victorious over those with less.

In the *Paidika*, Jesus's power to perform miracles is a fundamental constituent of his divine identity. While his miracles are not explicitly agonistic, insofar as they do not show Jesus competing with other miracle workers, they still range Jesus against opposing forces, be they social, physical or metaphysical. The assembled corpus of the miracles described in the *Paidika* constitutes a kind of aretalogy of

34. MacMullen (1985/1986), pp. 74–5.
35. For conversion as a 'new start', see Nock (1961 [1933]), p. 14; for 'submissive reliance', cf. Nock (1972), pp. 327–8.
36. MacMullen (1984), p. 23.
37. Davis (2014), pp. 67–91.
38. MacMullen (1984), pp. 12–13.

the young Jesus that can be contrasted with those of other gods. Jesus is invariably triumphant in his endeavours and emerges victorious in every contest in which he is involved. He triumphs over all his teachers, Zeno's parents, those who have affronted him, over nature, and over death itself. The continued acclamation of the people or crowd in all of these situations testifies to the agonistic dimension of these miracles. Each one of them is a contest in which Jesus has emerged as the victor, whether it is against his peers, teachers and adult figures of authority. The importance placed on these encounters can be adjudged from Zacchaeus's protracted lament after he is bested by Jesus. He dwells at length on his public shaming and loss of honour,[39] and the radical expedients he proposes to deal with his disgrace – such as leaving the community – illustrate how precious a commodity such honour was thought to be. Jesus's superiority is such that a pagan audience would not be in doubt long about the efficacy of his words or his works. A case in point would be his reported raisings of people from the dead. These narratives – as with those told about Apollonius of Tyana – could hardly fail to have a profound impact on a pagan audience.

It is true that the infant Jesus does not engage in the kind of miraculous agonism seen, for instance, in the book of Acts, and in the Apocryphal Acts, but this is a necessary consequence of the Jewish setting of the *Paidika*.[40] Once the setting changes to the pagan world, the competition between Christian 'miracles' and pagan 'magic' becomes more explicit. Conflict is a defining feature of the second century especially, and it is no less a distinctive element of the Christian challenge.[41] This conflict is already very much in evidence in the book of Acts, where Peter's outgunning of Simon Magus and Paul's rebuke of Jesus Elymas assume paradigmatic status.[42] Within the Apocryphal Acts, miraculous deeds and contents regularly dominate the narratives.[43]

The *Paidika* likely constitutes a literary precursor to the Apocryphal Acts, even if it belongs to the gospel genre instead of that of acts. Its implicit appeal to miracles and agonism foreshadows the dominant role that they come to play within the Apocryphal Acts. The triumphal victory of Jesus's apostles is of the same order as that of the youthful Jesus; so, too, is the continued acclamatory score-keeping of the crowds. That this acclamation a constant in both in the *Paidika* and in the Apocryphal Acts suggests that they all were written for a similar audience – the uneducated population at large – who would ideally assume an acclamatory role themselves.

39. On shame and honour, see Neyrey (1998), pp. 14–34.
40. For Acts, see Penner (2012), pp. 169–73; for the Apocryphal Acts, Söder ([1932] Rp. 1969), pp. 51–102. Nock (1972), p. 44 remarks that the 'popular hagiographical stories of the conflict [sc. between Christianity and paganism] are couched in terms of the victory of a superior δύναμις'.
41. Riemer (2006), p. 47; Rhee (2005), pp. 72–9.
42. Nock (1972), pp. 327–9.
43. Bovon (2005), pp. 253–70; Davies (1980), pp. 17–28; Söder ([1932] Rp. 1969), pp. 51–102.

What makes the *Paidika* distinctive is that it was very likely one of the first non-canonical narratives to have been specifically written for the Great Church and unsophisticated pagan audiences. The (proto-orthodox) author has deliberately fashioned an account of the young Jesus that would appeal to their thirst for the marvellous, their delight in the shocking and humorous, and – not least – their raw credulity, all calculated to make them believers or sustain them in their Christian faith. That he does this so effectively is no small achievement.

5.4 Popular Christianity

The popularity of this message among the Christian masses may help to explain the *Paidika*'s chequered reception within and among the church fathers. The problem with the agonism in the *Paidika*'s narrative is that it is ultimately overpowering. Jesus's miraculous victories become so domineering that, even with his change in attitude, they end up presenting a message that is fundamentally subversive to the established authorities. Jesus's message as it features in the canonical Gospels is already subversive.[44] His support for the disenfranchised and his corresponding rejection of the social, political and religious elites seriously threatened the status quo.[45] His radical Christian message called for a relativizing of family loyalties (Mt. 10:35-7; 12:46-50; cf. Lk. 12:52-3), of civic values and authorities (Lk. 13:32), of conventional teachers and elders (Mt. Ch. 23), and even of life itself (Matt 10:38-9).

The *Paidika*, however, takes a message that is already subversive and further amplifies it. For one thing, it amplifies the effect by calling into question humanity as a whole. Rudolf Otto famously described the holy as 'entirely other', and there is a sense in which the infant Jesus's divine otherness challenges and undermines human institutions. His very presence in the town is viewed as an ongoing threat to the townspeople and to civic order (4.2; 13.3) – that is, to those values that humans subscribe to in order to co-exist. These include refraining from unwarranted violence, and respecting the sanctity of human families and relationships. Jesus's alterity unsettles all these values.

The same holds true for Jesus's relationship with his parents, especially Joseph. His rejection of Joseph's parental authority over him is determinative. He disregards Joseph's remonstrances (5.1-3) and even in the Temple narrative he asserts that his obligation to his heavenly father outstrips his obligations to his parents (17.3). More evocative yet is his partial disavowal of Joseph's paternity. By stressing his own pre-existence (6.6), Jesus relativizes the essential human bond between a

---

44. Konstan and Walsh (2016), pp. 39–42.
45. Francis (1995), p. 138 points out that to some pagans, such as Celsus, Jesus was subversive for different reasons, namely as an immoral charlatan and a magician. Cf. Origen, *Cels*. 1.71.

rent and child, and again indicates that the divine relationship with the father eclipses any purely human relationship he has with Joseph.

...ious institutions are also relativized and undercut. The wisdom of the elde... in the Temple emerges as something of little account, and the same can be said for the three teachers Jesus encounters. Human pretensions to learning and understanding become negligible in the face of divine realities and even the best that humans can produce fails to plumb God's truths. Human learning is a superficial cipher compared to the divine truths that are to be discovered in the alphabet.

All of the foregoing radically subverts everything that is human and relativizes it all in the face of Jesus's advent and earthly existence as a child. Humanity is reduced to a mere foil to demonstrate the surpassingly marvellous nature of Jesus.

One can imagine that as Christianity spread through the pagan world the message of the *Paidika* would be welcomed. The attractiveness of breaking with conventional pagan social hierarchies and strictures would have given the message a strong popular appeal, especially when adherents knew that they were on the winning side. Once, however, these various families, villages, teachers and institutions began to be Christianized, this subversiveness could well have proved too corrosive. The Christian religious hierarchy not pagan leaders or teachers would now be the butt of popular derision. The importance of Christian families and Christian hierarchies would now be in question. One can see how Christian leaders might no longer welcome its radical qualities. Moreover, its anti-authoritarian qualities and rejection of received wisdom might make it especially welcome in gnostic and other 'heretical' circles.

It is possible, therefore, that the *Paidika*, began as an approved text of the proto-orthodox Christian communities, lost its cachet among Christian teachers and was displaced by more amenable writings.[46] Even though it may have retained its popular appeal, it would have moved to the peripheries of the Christian mission where the displacement of pagan institutions remained a concern.

Obviously such a reading is highly conjectural, but this model might help to explain in part why the *Paidika* was largely rejected by the church fathers, but nevertheless enjoyed widespread currency, as attested by the abundance of ancient versions and manuscripts. In other words, it enjoyed an ambivalent reception. Over the course of two millennia little has changed: Jesus the holy terror still promotes profound ambivalence among the *Paidika*'s readers.

---

46. Konstan and Walsh (2016) helpfully discuss how later hagiographical writings fuse the subversive elements of the Gospels with straightforward civic virtues.

CONCLUSION

The purpose of this book was to examine the figure of Jesus in the *Paidika*. In particular, it set out to explain why it portrays Jesus as a 'holy terror' who frequently seems to act in an 'unchristian' manner. While the topic has been discussed frequently in recent years, there is no general consensus about why Jesus is portrayed in such a fashion. Nor, for that matter is there any substantial examination of the figure of Jesus extant, so this study also set out to examine the *Paidika*'s portrayal of Jesus from three perspectives, devoting a chapter to each: Jesus the holy terror, Jesus the child and Jesus the divine.

As one would anticipate, there are likely a variety of reasons for Jesus's 'unchristian' actions, many of which were considered in Chapter 2. Chapter 3 argues that the 'unchristian' deeds of Jesus the holy terror can best be explained as the result of several factors. One such factor is the child Jesus's immaturity. The infant Jesus possesses divine attributes – heavenly power and knowledge – from the outset, but insofar as he is a human child, he lacks maturity, self-control and concern for others. The volatile mixture of almost unlimited divine power combined with an infantile human sensibility means that the young Jesus begins by behaving with an insouciant disregard for anyone other than himself. His untrammelled egotism dominates almost all of his actions until he eventually decides to implement the will of his divine Father. From this point, with one notable exception – the killing of his second teacher – Jesus amends his actions and shifts to a uniformly benevolent pattern of behaviour. This change of attitude corresponds with his maturation as a human child. Although his divine nature remains unchanged, his growth, which is a consequence of his human nature, results in a fundamental reversal of his previous antisocial deeds, as witnessed by his decisions to bring those whom he had killed back to life and by his treatment of his peers and elders with respect and compassion. This maturation process up to the age of twelve anticipates the compassionate ministry of Jesus seen in the canonical Gospels.

Chapter 4 demonstrates that the author's decision to portray the young Jesus in a developmental light is obviously indebted to Luke's Temple narrative (Lk. 2.41-51), but also shows strong influence from the Gospel of John. Where Luke seems to retroject Jesus's divine knowledge and self-awareness back as far as the age of twelve, the *Paidika*'s author takes it all the way back to Jesus's infancy and beyond that to Jesus's pre-existence. That is to say, he has fused the Christologies of Luke and John to fashion his own distinctive Christology. It is his particular ative gift to have surmised how uneasily the divine and human aspects s might fit together. Using human maturation as a lens through which to view the gradual cohering of Jesus's humanity and divinity, he emerges with a picture of the young Jesus that is conflicted, dramatic and not always flattering. He succeeds in showing Jesus's fallible humanity, but also his extraordinary divine power for both good and evil.

Chapter 2 argued that it was not just Jesus's humanity that produced the conflicted picture of Jesus, but also the author's representation of the divine temperament. It is probable that the initial depiction of the harsh and tyrannical Jesus owes a great deal to popular Graeco-Roman mythical conceptions of the gods. Jesus's intolerance, self-absorption and ruthless retaliation against personal affronts are precisely what one would expect from a Greek deity. The fact the Graeco-Roman tradition included stories of male gods in their infancy and youth provides a further point of comparison between the young Jesus and the gods. The upshot of these similarities is that Jesus appears at least as powerful and knowledgeable as the Graeco-Roman deities.

In fact, the *Paidika* implies that Jesus surpasses the gods of the pantheon. While Jesus's references to his pre-existence are vague, they may suggest that he had always existed – something none of the Graeco-Roman gods could claim. More explicitly, the infant Jesus matures. By contrast, the young Hermes and Dionysus and other divine infants may grow up, but they never mature. They retain their infantile intolerance, narcissism and immorality. The author's implication is that the Greek gods remain eternal children who will never attain morality or compassion for humans. Christianity, however, advocates the putting away of childish things. As God's son, Jesus surpasses the mere divine affectations of power and arrogance, and substitutes them with responsibility and humility. Christianity, in other words, is a religion for adults.

If this reading is warranted, it suggests that the author has used the *Paidika* as an apology. Although the agonism between Christianity and paganism does not come to the fore in individual episodes or contests as happens in the Apocryphal Acts, the developmental character of the narrative and its pronounced focus on the miraculous serve as an implicit challenge to the verities of pagan religion. The work's virtually exclusive focus on the figure of Jesus – and only on certain traits of Jesus – means that it is intended to discredit popular conceptions of the gods by showing the superiority of Jesus. The agonism at work here is hardly subtle or theologically sophisticated – in fact, it is only one step up from the taunt, 'My god's better than your god', but evidently the author considered it to be effective with a largely uneducated audience.

Most influential in this regard are Jesus's miracles. They dominate the work from beginning to end, and characterize its understanding of the divine. The unquestioned dominance of the miraculous in the *Paidika* strongly suggests that it was catering to an unsophisticated audience that were drawn to the miraculous, both for its entertainment value, and, more pressingly, for the benefits it might provide. Not only that, but the implicit agonism of the miracles performed by Jesus situated his deeds in a competitive context where the validity of his message confirmed by his marvels. For this reason, the miracle stories were likely the main attraction for the *Paidika*'s audience, and instrumental in securing pagan converts or strengthening the faith of those who had already become converts.

This audience was, in all likelihood, associated with the 'Great Church', the mass of uneducated Christians who relied more upon belief than upon reason, and were far more interested in marvels and entertaining stories than doctrinal niceties. In this respect the *Paidika* fulfilled their requirements admirably, and it is highly probable that the *Paidika* was deliberately written with them in mind.

This audience also helps to explain other emphases in the *Paidika* that employ various narrative techniques designed to make the story palatable to an uneducated audience. These techniques follow naturally from the inherent conflicts in the representation of Jesus as a child deity. One of these is humour. The author plays on paradox, especially when the pre-existent Christ is punished by his fallible human father, Joseph.[1] Here, a Graeco-Roman audience would, in all likelihood, be quick to laugh at the dilemma and – possibly – to reflect on the implications of the incarnation.

The *Paidika*'s focus on Jesus development allows the author to avail himself of another technique, also grounded in paradox, namely the juxtaposition of an impotent child with divine power. The representation of a helpless infant with superhuman abilities is a well-established theme in world literature, and is attractive both because of its inherent contrast and because an audience wants to see what sorts of inventive scenarios the author will construct. Humans never seem to tire of feats featuring superhuman actors. An additional frisson emerges when (for a time at least) the actors are portrayed as acting badly, leading the audience to consider what sort of mayhem the 'heroes' will bring about, and how they will relent and return from 'the dark side'. The *Paidika*'s Jesus does not disappoint, and virtually half of the work is devoted to the actions of the 'bad Jesus'.

A third technique used by the author is related to the 'bad Jesus', and this pertains to the subversive qualities of the *Paidika*. While the adult Jesus is often seen as condemning the status quo, the subversive qualities of the *Paidika* are even more corrosive. Although the 'reformed' Jesus comes to promote strong family values, support the poor and reward his third teacher, it is hard for the hearer to forget that he has flouted all of these institutions earlier. And the reasons for Jesus's condemnations are still not fully resolved by the end of the work. Mary and Joseph still seem unaware of his precise identity and his first two teachers remain ignorant. Those figures in whom social authority resides are discredited by Jesus. Seeing these authorities getting their come-uppance is hugely attractive

---

1. This paradox is well expressed in the 1926 painting by Max Ernst, 'Young Virgin Spanking the Infant Jesus in Front of Three Witnesses' (http://quod.lib.umich.edu/h/hart/x-381549/05d110671). Jesus has lost his halo, but Mary's is still in place.

to a popular audience, who, more often than not, suffer under the thumb of such authorities.

All of these narrative features give the *Paidika* a distinctive character, and helped to guarantee its influence with a popular audience. In fact, the *Paidika*'s author proved far more successful than he intended and guaranteed that the longevity and influence of his work would endure for millennia to come.

BIBLIOGRAPHY

Editions and Translations

Burke, Tony (forthcoming). *The Infancy Gospel in the Syriac Tradition*.
Burke, Tony (2016). 'The Infancy Gospel of Thomas (Syriac)', in Tony Burke and Brent Landau (eds), *New Testament Apocrypha. More Noncanonical Scriptures*, vol. 1, 61–8. Grand Rapids: Eerdmans.
Burke, T. (2010). *Infancy Gospel of Thomas, De infantia Iesu Evangelium Thomae Graecae*. CCSA 17. Turnhout: Brepols.
Cullmann, O. (1991). 'The Infancy Story of Thomas', in E. Hennecke and W. Schneemelcher (eds), *New Testament Apocrypha*, vol. 1: *Gospels and Related Writings*. Rev. edn, 439–53. Louisville: Westminster John Knox.
Delatte, A. (1927). *Anecdota Atheniensia*, vol. 1. Paris: Bibliothèque de la Faculté de Philosophie et Lettres de l'Université de Liège.
Ehrman, B. and Z. Pleše, eds (2011). *The Apocryphal Gospels*. New York: Oxford University Press.
Elliott, J. K. (1993). *The Apocryphal New Testament*. Oxford: Clarendon Press.
Fabricius, J. A. (1703). *Codex Apocryphus Novi Testamenti*. Hamburg: Benjamin Schiller.
Grébaut, S. (1919). 'Les Miracles de Jésus. Texte éthiopien publié et traduit'. *Patrologia Orientalis* 12 (4): 554–652.
Hadavas, C. T. (2014). *The Infancy Gospel of Thomas: An Intermediate Ancient Greek Reader*. CreateSpace.
Hock, R. F. (1995). *The Infancy Gospels of James and Thomas*. The Scholars Bible 2. Santa Rosa: Polebridge.
James, M. R. (1924). *The Apocryphal New Testament*. Oxford: Clarendon Press.
Kaiser, U. (2012). 'Die Kindheitserzählung des Thomas', in C. Markschies and J. Schröter (eds), *Antike christliche Apokryphen in deutscher Übersetzung*. 2 vols, 930–59. AcA I/1-2: Tübingen: Mohr Siebeck.
McNamara, M., J.-D. Kaestli, R. Beyers, D. Ó Laoghaire, P. Ó Fiannachta, B. Ó Cuív, and C. Breatnach, eds (2001). *Apocrypha Hiberniae*, vol. 1. *Evangelia Infantiae*. CCA 13. Turnhout: Brepols.
Meyer, A. (1904). 'Kindheitserzählung des Thomas', in E. Hennecke (ed.), *Handbuch zu den neutestamentlichen Apokryphen*, 132–42. Tübingen: Mohr.
Miller, R. J. (1992). *The Complete Gospels*. Sonoma: Polebridge.
Mingarelli, G. L. (1764). 'Epistola... de apocrypho Thomae evangelio' in *Nuova raccolta di opuscoli scientifici*, Vol. 12: 73–155.
Peeters, P. (1914). *Évangiles apocryphes*. 2 vols. Paris: A. Picard, vol. 2: 307–19.
Rosén, T. (1997). *The Slavonic Translation of the Apocryphal Infancy Gospel of Thomas*. Acta Universitatis Upsaliensis: *Studia Slavica Upsaliensia* 39. Uppsala: Almqvist & Wiksell.
Santos Otero, A. de (1967). *Das Kirchenslavische Evangelium des Thomas*. Patristische Texte und Studien 6. Berlin: de Gruyter.

Santos Otero, A. de. (2003). *Los Evangelios apócrifos: Colección de textos griegos y latinos, version crítica, estudios introductorios y comentarios*. Rev. edn. 276–300. Madrid: Biblioteca de Autores Cristianos.

Schneider, G. (1995). *Evangelia Infantiae Apocrypha. Apocryphe Kindheitsevangelien*. Fontes Christiani 18. Freiburg: Herder.

Thilo, J. C. (1832). Codex apocryphus Novi Testamenti. Vol. 1: 275–315. Leipzig: Vogel.

Tischendorf, C. (1853 [2nd edn 1876] Rp. 1966.). *Evangelia Apocrypha*. Hildesheim: Georg Olms.

Voicu, S. J. (1997). 'Histoire de l'enfance de Jésus,' in F. Bovon and P. Geoltrain (eds), *Écrits apocryphes chrétiens*, vol. 1, 191–204. Paris: Gallimard.

Wright, W. (1865). *Contributions to the Apocryphal Literature of the New Testament*. London: Williams and Norgate.

Articles and Monographs

Aasgaard, R. (2006). 'Children in Antiquity and Early Christianity: Research History and Central Issues'. *Familia* 33: 23–46.

Aasgaard, R. (2009). 'From Boy to Man in Antiquity: Jesus in the Apocryphal *Infancy Gospel of Thomas*'. *Thymos: Journal of Boyhood Studies* 3: 3–20.

Aasgaard, R. (2009a). 'Uncovering Children's Culture in Late Antiquity: The Testimony of the *Infancy Gospel of Thomas*', in Cornelia B. Horn and Robert R. Phenix (eds), *Children in Late Antique Christianity*, 1–27. STAC 58: Tübingen: Mohr Siebeck.

Aasgaard, R. (2010). *The Childhood of Jesus: Decoding the Apocryphal Infancy Gospel of Thomas*. Eugene: Wipf and Stock.

Aasgaard, R. (2010a). 'The Gospel for Early Christian Children: A Re-assessment of the Infancy Gospel of Thomas'. *Studia Patristica* 45: 439–44.

Abraha, T. and D. Assafa (2010). 'Apocryphal Gospels in the Ethiopic Tradition,' in J. Frey and J. Schröter (eds), *Jesus in apokryphen Evangelienüberlieferungen*. WUNT 2.254, 611–53. Tübingen: Mohr Siebeck.

Achtemeier, P. (2008). *Jesus and the Miracle Tradition*. Eugene: Cascade.

Adams, E. (2013). *The Earliest Christian Meeting Places. Almost Exclusively Houses?* LNTS 450. London: Bloomsbury.

Amsler, F. (2011). 'Les Paidika Iesou, un nouveau témoin de la rencontre entre judaïsme et christianisme à Antioch au IVe siècle?' in C. Clivaz, A. Dettwiler, L. Devillers, E. Norelli with B. Bertho (eds), *Infancy Gospels. Stories and Identities*. WUNT 281, 433–58. Tübingen: Mohr Siebeck.

Anderson, G. (2000). *Fairytale in the Ancient World*. London and New York: Routledge.

Anderson, G. (2004). *Sage, Saint, and Sophist. Holy Men and their Associates in the Early Roman Empire*. London and New York: Routledge.

Aune, D. E., ed. (2003), *The Westminster Dictionary of New Testament and Early Christian Literature and Rhetoric*. Louisville and London: Westminster John Knox.

Aune, D. E., ed. (2006). *Apocalypticism, Prophecy and Magic in Early Christianity*. WUNT 199: Tübingen: Mohr Siebeck.

Baars, W. and J. Helderman (1993). 'Neue Materialien zum Text und zur Interpretation des Kindheitsevangeliums des Pseudo-Thomas'. *Oriens christianus* 77: 191–225.

Baars, W. and J. Helderman. (1994). 'Neue Materialien zum Text und zur Interpretation des Kindheitsevangeliums des Pseudo-Thomas (Fortsetzung)'. *Oriens christianus* 78: 1–32.

Bagatti, B. (1976). 'Nota sul Vangelo di Tomasso Israelita'. *Euntes Docete* 29: 482–9.
Bagley, A. (1985). 'Jesus at School'. *The Journal of Psychohistory* 13: 13–31.
Bakke, O. M. (2005). *When Children Became People*. Minneapolis: Fortress.
Balla, P. (2003). *The Child-Parent Relationship in the New Testament and its Environment*. WUNT 155. Tübingen: Mohr Siebeck.
Bauckham, R. (1994). 'The Brothers and Sisters of Jesus: An Epiphanian Response to John Meier'. *CBQ* 56: 686–700.
Bauckham, R. (2000). 'Imaginative Literature', in Philip Esler (ed.), *The Early Christian World*, 791–812. London and New York: Routledge.
Bauer, W. (1967 [1909]). *Das Leben Jesu im Zeitalter der neutestamentliche Apokryphen*. Darmstadt: Wissenschaftliche Buchgesellschaft.
Baumgarten, A. (2014). 'The Rule of the Martian in the Ancient Diaspora: Celsus and His Jew', in Peter J. Tomson and Joshua Schwartz (eds), *Jews and Christians in the First and Second Centuries: How to Write Their History*. CRINT 13, 398–430. Leiden and Boston.
Beaumont, L. (1995). 'Mythological Childhood: A Male Preserve?' *Annual of the British School at Athens* 90: 339–61.
Behr, J. (2013). *Irenaeus of Lyons. Identifying Christianity*. Oxford: Oxford University Press.
Bell, R., J. E. Grubbs and T. Parkin, eds (2013). *The Oxford Handbook of Childhood and Education in the Classical World*. Oxford and New York: Oxford University Press.
Bennema, C. (2002). *The Power of Saving Wisdom. An Investigation of Spirit and Wisdom in Relation to the Soteriology of the Fourth Gospel*. WUNT 2.148. Tübingen: Mohr Siebeck.
Betsworth, S. (2015). *Children in Early Christian Narratives*. LNTS 521. London: Bloomsbury.
Bird, S. E. (1992). *For Enquiring Minds. A Cultural Study of Supermarket Tabloids*. Knoxville: University of Tennessee.
Blackburn, B. (1991). *Theios Anêr and the Markan Miracle Traditions*. WUNT 2.40. Tübingen: Mohr Siebeck.
Boardman, J. et al. (1988). 'Heracles'. *LIMC* 4 (2): 253–70
Bockmuehl, M. (2017). *Ancient Apocryphal Gospels*. Louisville: Westminster John Knox.
Bolyki, J. (1995). 'Miracle Stories in the Acts of John', in Jan N. Bremmer (ed.), *The Apocryphal Acts of John*, 15–35. Kampen: Kok Pharos.
Bousset, W. (1970). *Kyrios Christos*. Nashville and New York: Abingdon.
Bovon, F. (2002). *Luke 1*. Hermeneia: Minneapolis: Fortress.
Bovon, F. (2005). 'Miracles, Magic and Healing in the Apocryphal Acts of the Apostles', in F. Bovon (ed.), *Studies in Early Christianity*, 253–70. Grand Rapids: Baker.
Bovon, F. (2009). 'The Child and the Beast: Fighting Violence in Ancient Christianity', in Glen E. Snyder (ed.), *New Testament and Christian Apocrypha. Collected Studies II*. WUNT 237, 223–45. Tübingen: Mohr Siebeck.
Bovon, F. (2012). 'Beyond the Canonical and the Apocryphal Books, the Presence of a Third Category: The Books Useful for the Soul'. *HTR* 105: 125–37.
Bovon, F. (2013). 'The First Christologies: Exaltation and Incarnation, or From Easter to Christmas', in Luke Drake (ed.), *The Emergence of Christianity. Collected Studies III*. WUNT 319, 17–31. Tübingen: Mohr Siebeck.
Bowersock, G. W. (1994). *Fiction as History. Nero to Julian*. Berkeley: University of California.
Bradley, K. (2013). 'Envoi', in R. Bell, J. E. Grubbs and T. Parkin (eds), *The Oxford Handbook of Childhood and Education in the Classical World*, 644–62. Oxford and New York: Oxford University Press.
Branham, B. (1989). *Unruly Eloquence. Lucian and the Comedy of Traditions*. Cambridge, MA and London: Harvard University Press.

Brown, P. (1971). 'The Rise and Function of the Holy Man in Late Antiquity'. *JRS* 61: 80–101.

Brown, R. E. (1993). *The Birth of the Messiah. A Commentary on the Infancy Narratives in Matthew and Luke*. Rev. edn. New York: Doubleday & Company.

[Chartrand-]Burke, T. (1998). 'Authorship and Identity in the Infancy Gospel of Thomas'. *TJT* 14: 27–43.

[Chartrand-]Burke, T. (2001). 'The Infancy Gospel of Thomas: The Text, Its Origins, and Its Transmission'. Ph.D. University of Toronto, http://www.nlc-bnc.ca/obj/s4/f2/dsk3/ftp05/NQ63782.pdf.

[Chartrand-]Burke, T. (2009). '"Social Viewing" of Children in the Childhood Stories of Jesus', in Cornelia B. Horn and Robert R. Phenix (eds), *Children in Late Antique Christianity*. STAC 58, 29–43. Tübingen: Mohr Siebeck.

[Chartrand-]Burke, T. (2010a). 'Review of Reidar Aasgaard, *The Childhood of Jesus: Decoding the Apocryphal Infancy Gospel of Thomas*'. *JECS* 18: 470–1.

[Chartrand-]Burke, T. (2012). 'Depictions of Children in the Apocryphal Infancy Gospels'. *Studies in Religion/Sciences Religieuses* 41: 388–400.

[Chartrand-]Burke, T. (2013a). 'The Infancy Gospel of Thomas from an Unpublished Syriac Manuscript: Introduction, Text, Translation, and Notes'. *Hugoye: Journal of Syriac Studies* 16 (2): 225–99.

[Chartrand-]Burke, T. (2013b). *Secret Scriptures Revealed. A New Introduction to the Christian Apocrypha*. London: SPCK.

[Chartrand-]Burke, T. (2015a). 'Entering the Mainstream: Twenty-five Years of Research on the Christian Apocrypha', in P. Piovanelli and T. Burke (eds), *Rediscovering the Apocryphal Continent. New Perspectives on Early Christian and Late Antique Apocryphal Texts and Traditions*. WUNT 349, 19–47. Tübingen: Mohr Siebeck.

[Chartrand-]Burke, T., ed. (2015b). *Forbidden Texts on the Western Frontier. The Christian Apocrypha in North American Perspectives*. Eugene: Cascade.

Burke, T. and B. Landau (2016a). 'Introduction', in T. Burke and B. Landau (eds), *New Testament Apocrypha. More Noncanonical Scriptures*, vol 1, viii–xlii. Grand Rapids: Eerdmans.

Burkett, D. (2011). 'Jesus in Luke-Acts', in D. Burkett (ed.), *The Blackwell Companion to Jesus*, 47–63. Oxford: Wiley-Blackwell.

Burridge, R. (1992). *What are the Gospels? A Comparison with Graeco-Roman Biography*. SNTSMS 70. Cambridge: Cambridge University Press.

Burz-Tropper, V. (2013). 'Jesus als Lehrer in apokryphen Evangelien', in Jens Schröter (ed.), *The Apocryphal Gospels within the Context of Early Christian Theology*, 719–35. Leuven, Paris and Walpole: Peeters.

Cameron, A. (1991). *Christianity and the Rhetoric of Empire*. Sather Classical Lectures 55. Berkeley, Los Angeles and Oxford: University of California Press.

Cameron, R., ed. (1982). *The Other Gospels. Non-Canonical Gospel Texts*. Louisville and London: Westminster John Knox.

Carp T. (1980). '"Puer senex" in Roman and Medieval Thought'. *Latomus* 39: 736–9.

Carroll, J. T. (2012). *Luke*. NTL. Louisville: Westminster John Knox.

Cartlidge, D. R. and J. K. Elliott (2001). *Art & the Christian Apocrypha*. London and New York: Routledge.

Casey, M. F. (2007). 'The Fourteenth-Century *Tring Tiles*: A Fresh Look at their Origin and the Hebraic Aspects of the Child Jesus' Actions'. *Peregrinations* 2: 1–53.

Chadwick, H., ed. (1980). *Origen. Contra Celsum*. Cambridge: Cambridge University Press.

Chartrand-Burke, T. (2003). 'The Greek Manuscript Tradition of the *Infancy Gospel of Thomas*'. *Apocrypha* 14: 129–51.

Chartrand-Burke, T. (2008a). 'Completing the Gospel: *The Infancy Gospel of Thomas* as a Supplement to the Gospel of Luke', in L. DiTommaso and L. Turcescu (eds), *The Reception and Interpretation of the Bible in Late Antiquity: Proceedings of the Montreal Colloquium in Honour of Charles Kannengiesser, 11-13 October, 2006*, 101-19. Leiden and Boston: Brill.

Chartrand-Burke, T. (2008b). 'The *Infancy Gospel of Thomas*', in P. Foster (ed.), *The Non-Canonical Gospels*, 126-38. London: T&T Clark.

Clauss, M. (2014). 'Wunder und Kaiserkult', in B. Kollmann and R. Zimmermann (eds), *Hermeneutik der frühchristlichen Wundererzählungen. Geschichtliche, literarische und rezeptionsorientierte Perspektiven.*, WUNT 339, 153-64. Tübingen: Mohr Siebeck.

Clark, G. (1994). 'The Fathers and the Children', in Diana Wood (ed.), *The Church and Childhood*. SCH 31, 1-27. Oxford: Blackwell.

Clay, J. S. (1989). *The Politics of Olympus. Form and Meaning in the Major Homeric Hymns*. Princeton: Princeton University Press.

Clivaz, C., A. Dettwiler, L. Devillers, E. Norelli with B. Bertho, eds (2011). *Infancy Gospels. Stories and Identities*. WUNT 281. Tübingen: Mohr Siebeck.

Conrady, L. (1903). 'Das Thomasevangelium: Ein wissenschaftlicher kritischer Versuch'. *Theologische Studien und Kritiken* 76: 377-459.

Considine, P. (1969). 'The Theme of Divine Wrath in Ancient East Mediterranean Literature'. *Studi Micinei ed Egeo-Anatolica* 8: 85-159.

Cooper, K. (2005). 'Ventriloquism and the Miraculous: Conversion, Preaching, and the Martyr Exemplum in Late Antiquity', in K. Cooper and J. Gregory (eds), *Signs, Wonders, Miracles. Representations of Divine Power in the Life of the Church*. SCH 41, 22-45. Woodbridge: Boydell.

Couch, J. N. (2006). 'Misbehaving God: The Case of the Christ Child in Laud Misc. 108 "Infancy of Jesus Christ"', in B. Wheeler (ed.), *Mindful Spirit in Late Medieval Literature: Essays in Honor of Elizabeth D. Kirk*, 312-43. New York: Palgrave.

Cousland, J. R. C. (2002). *The Crowds in the Gospel of Matthew*. NovTSup 102. Leiden and New York: E. J. Brill.

Cousland, J. R. C. (2015). '*Deus Necans*: Jesus in the *Infancy Gospel of Thomas*', in D. Arbel et al. (eds), *Not Sparing the Child: Human Sacrifice in the Ancient World and Beyond. Studies in Honor of Professor Paul G. Mosca*, 165-89. London and New York: Bloomsbury T&T Clark.

Cousland, J. R. C. (forthcoming). 'Soundings in the Christology of the *Infancy Gospel of Thomas*: The Rewriting of Luke 2:41-52 in *Paidika* 17'.

Cribiore, R. (2001). *Gymnastics of the Mind. Greek Education in Hellenistic and Roman Egypt*. Princeton and Oxford: Princeton University Press.

Cueva, E. P. and S. N. Byrne, eds (2014). *A Companion to the Ancient Novel*. Chichester: Wiley Blackwell.

Cullmann, O. (1991a). 'Infancy Gospels', in E. Hennecke and W. Schneemelcher (eds), *New Testament Apocrypha*, vol. 1: *Gospels and Related Writings*. Rev. edn, 414-69. Louisville: Westminster John Knox.

Currie, S. (1993). *Childhood and Christianity from Paul to the Council of Chalcedon*. Ph.D Dissertation. University of Cambridge.

Curtius, E. R. (2013 [1953]). *European Literature and the Latin Middle Ages*. Bollingen Series 36. Princeton and Oxford: Princeton University Press.

Davies, S. (1980). *The Revolt of the Widows. The Social World of the Apocryphal Acts*. Carbondale and Edwardsville: Southern Illinois University Press.

Davies, S. (2009). *The Infancy Gospels of Jesus. Apocryphal Tales from the Childhoods of Mary and Jesus*. Woodstock: Skylight Paths.

Davis, S. J. (2012). 'Bird Watching in the *Infancy Gospel of Thomas*. From Child's Play to Rituals of Divine Discernment', in S. E. Myers (ed.), *Portraits of Jesus*. WUNT 2.321, 125–53. Tübingen: Mohr Siebeck.

Davis, S. J. (2014). *Christ Child. Cultural Memories of a Young Jesus*. New Haven and London: Yale University Press.

De Jonge, H. (1977–78). 'Sonship, Wisdom, Infancy: Luke 11. 41-51a'. *NTS* 24: 317–54.

Deines, R. (2012). 'Christology between Pre-existence, Incarnation and Messianic Self-Understanding', in M. F. Bird and J. Maston (eds), *Earliest Christian History*. WUNT 2.320, 75–116. Tübingen: Mohr Siebeck.

Den Boeft, J. (2004). 'Miracles Recalling the Apostolic Age' in A. Hilhorst (ed.), *The Apostolic Age in Patristic Thought*. VGSup 70, 51-62. Leiden and Boston: Brill.

Dodds, E. R. (1951). *The Greeks and the Irrational*. Berkeley: University of California Press.

Dornseiff, F. (1925). *Das Alphabet in Mystik und Magie*. Stoicheia 7. 2nd edn. Leipzig and Berlin: B. G. Teubner.

Dover, K. J. (1972). *Aristophanic Comedy*. Berkeley: University of California Press.

Dover, K. J. (1974). *Greek Popular Morality in the Time of Plato and Aristotle*. Oxford: Basil Blackwell.

Dunn, J. D. G. (2003). *Jesus Remembered. Christianity in the Making*, vol. 1. Grand Rapids and Cambridge: Eerdmans.

Dunn, J. D. G. (2015). *Neither Jew nor Greek. A Contested Identity. Christianity in the Making*, vol. 3. Grand Rapids and Cambridge: Eerdmans.

Dzon, M. (2011). 'Boys Will Be Boys: The Physiology of Childhood and the Apocryphal Christ Child in the later Middle Ages'. *Viator* 42: 179–226.

Eastman, D. (2015). 'Cursing in the Infancy Gospel of Thomas'. *VC* 69: 186–208.

Ehrman, E. (2003). *Lost Christianities. The Battles for Scripture and the Faiths We Never Knew*. Oxford and New York: Oxford University Press.

Eidinow, E. (2007). *Oracles, Curses, and Risk Among the Ancient Greeks*. Oxford: Oxford University Press.

Eidinow, E. (2016). 'Popular Theologies. The Gift of Divine Envy' in E. Eidinow (ed.), *Theologies of Ancient Greek Religion*, 205–32. Cambridge: Cambridge University Press.

Elliott, J. K. (2011). 'Ancient Apocryphal Portraits of Jesus', in D. Burkett (ed.), *The Blackwell Companion to Jesus*, 145–59. Oxford: Wiley-Blackwell.

Elliott, J. K. (2013). 'The "apocryphal" New Testament', in J. C. Paget and J. Schaper (eds), *The New Cambridge History of the Bible*, vol. I: *From the Beginnings to 600*, 455–78. Cambridge: Cambridge University Press.

Elliott, J. K. (2015). 'Christian Apocrypha and the Developing Role of Mary', in A. Gregory and C. Tuckett (eds), *The Oxford Handbook of Early Christian Apocrypha*, 269–88. New York and Oxford: Oxford University Press.

Enslin, M. (1951). 'Along Highways and Byways'. *HTR* 44: 67–92.

Erlemann, K. (2013). 'Erweckung eines verunglückten Spielkameraden (Junge auf dem Dach) KThom 9', in R. Zimmermann et al. (eds), *Kompendium der frühchristlichen Wundererzählung*, vol. 1, 843–6. Gütersloh: Gütersloher Verlag.

Eve, E. (2002). *The Jewish Context of Jesus' Miracles*. JSNTSS 231. New York: Sheffield.

Eyben, E. (1991). 'Fathers and Sons', in B. Rawson (ed.), *Marriage, Divorce and Children in Ancient Rome*, 114–43. Oxford: Clarendon Press.

Falls, T. B., tran. (1948), *Saint Justin Martyr*. FC 6. Washington: Catholic University of America Press.

Faulkner, A., ed. (2011). *The Homeric Hymns. Interpretative Essays*. Oxford: University Press.

Felsch, D. (2011). *Die Feste im Johannesevangelium*. WUNT 2.308. Tübingen: Mohr Siebeck.
Felsch, D. (2013). 'Spielender Schöpfer (Erschaffung der Spatzen) KThom 2 (arabK 36.46; Koran Sure 3,49)', in R. Zimmermann et al. (eds), *Kompendium der frühchristlichen Wundererzählung*, vol. 1, 827–31. Gütersloh: Gütersloher Verlag.
Fitzmyer, J. (1991). 'κύριος'. *EDNT* 2: 328–31.
Foster, P. (2006). 'Educating Jesus: The Search for a Plausible Context'. *JSHJ* 4: 7–33.
Foster, P., ed. (2009). *The Apocryphal Gospels. A Very Short Introduction*. Oxford: Oxford University Press.
Foster, P., (2014). 'The Education of Jesus in the Infancy Gospel of Thomas', in P. Doble and J. Kloha (eds), *Texts and Traditions. Essays in Honour of J. Keith Elliott*, 327–47. Leiden and Boston: Brill.
Fowler, R. (2010). 'Gods in Early Greek Historiography', in J. N. Bremmer and A. Erskine (eds), *The Gods of Ancient Greece*, 318–34. Edinburgh: Edinburgh University Press.
Francis, J. A. (1995). *Subversive Virtue. Asceticism and Authority in the Second-Century Pagan World*. University Park: Pennsylvania State University Press.
Frankfurter, D. (1994). 'The Magic of Writing and the Writing of Magic: The Power of the Word in Egyptian and Greek Traditions'. *Helios* 21: 189–221.
Fraser, P. M. and E. Matthews (1987–2010). *A Lexicon of Greek Personal Names*. 6 Vols. Oxford: Clarendon Press.
Frend, W. H. C. (2005), 'The Place of Miracles in the Conversion of the Ancient World to Christianity', in K. Cooper and J. Gregory (eds), *Signs, Wonders, Miracles. Representations of Divine Power in the Life of the Church*. SCH 41, 11–21. Woodbridge: Boydell.
Frey, J. (2011). 'How Could Mark and John Do without Infancy Stories? Jesus' Humanity and His Divine Origins in Mark and John', in C. Clivaz et al. (eds), *Infancy Gospels. Stories and Identities*, 189–215. WUNT 281. Tübingen: Mohr Siebeck.
Frey, J. (2015). 'Texts about Jesus: Non-canonical Gospels and Related Literature', in A. Gregory and C. Tuckett (eds), *The Oxford Handbook of Early Christian Apocrypha*, 13–47. New York and Oxford: Oxford University Press.
Frey, J. and J. Schröter, eds (2010). *Jesus in apokryphen Evangelienüberlieferungen*. WUNT 2.254: Tübingen: Mohr Siebeck.
Frickenschmidt, D. (1997). *Evangelium als Biographie. Die vier Evangelien im Rahmen antiker Erzählkunst*. TANZ 22. Tübingen and Basel: Franke Verlag.
Frilingos, C. (2009). 'No Child Left Behind: Knowledge and Violence in the Infancy Gospel of Thomas'. *JECS* 19: 27–54.
Frilingos, C. (2016). 'Parents Just Don't Understand: Ambiguity in Stories about the Childhood of Jesus'. *HTR*: 109: 33–55.
Gallagher, E. V. (1991). 'Conversion and Salvation in the Apocryphal Acts of the Apostles'. *Second Century* 8: 13–29.
Gamble, H. (1995). *Books and Readers in the Early Church*. New Haven and London: Yale University Press.
Gantz, T. (1993). *Early Greek Myth*. Baltimore and London: Johns Hopkins.
Garitte, G. (1956). 'Le fragment géorgien de l' "Évangile de Thomas."' *RHE* 51: 513–20.
Gaspari, C. (1986). 'Dionysus'. *LIMC* III (1): 420–514.
Gathercole, S. (2015). 'Other Apocryphal Gospels and the Historical Jesus', in A. Gregory and C. Tuckett (eds), *The Oxford Handbook of Early Christian Apocrypha*, 250–68. New York and Oxford: Oxford University Press.

Gero, S. (1971). 'The Infancy Gospel of Thomas. A Study of the Literary and Textual Problems'. *NovT* 13: 46–80.

Gero, S. (1988). 'Apocryphal Gospels: A Survey of Textual and Literary Problems', *ANRW* II 25 (3): 3969–96.

Gitter, S. and A. De Vries (1968). 'Symptomatology, Pathology, and Treatment of Bites by Near Eastern, European, and North African Snakes', in W. Bücherl and E. Buckley (eds), *Venomous Animals and their Venom*, vol. I, 359-401. New York: Academic Press.

Gnilka, C. (1983). 'Greisenalter'. *RAC* 12: cols. 995–1094.

Godley, A. D. (1981). *Herodotus*. 4 vols. LCL. Cambridge, MA: Harvard University Press.

Goggin, T. A., ed. and tran. (1969). *Saint John Chrysostom. Homilies on St. John 1-47*. FTC 33. Washington: Catholic University of America Press.

Goldstein, R. and G. Stroumsa (2007). 'The Greek and Jewish Origins of Docetism'. *Zeitschrift für Antikes Christentum/Journal of Ancient Christianity* 10: 423–41.

Graf, F. (2004). 'Theology, Theodicy, Philosophy: Greece and Rome', in S. I. Johnson (ed.), *Religions of the Ancient World*, 541–5. Cambridge, MA and London: Harvard University Press.

Graham, D. W., ed. (2010). *The Texts of Early Greek Philosophy*. 2 Vols. Cambridge: Cambridge University Press.

Grant, R. M. (1952). *Miracle and Natural Law in Graeco-Roman and Early Christian Thought*. Amsterdam: North Holland Publishing Company.

Gregory, A. and C. Tuckett, eds (2015). *The Oxford Handbook of Early Christian Apocrypha*. New York and Oxford: Oxford University Press.

Griffin, J. (1980). *Homer on Life and Death*. Oxford: Clarendon Press.

Guez, J.-P. (2009). 'To Reason and to Marvel: Images of the Reader in the *Life of Apollonius*', in M. Paschalis, S. Panayotakis and G. Schmeling (eds), *Readers and Writers in the Ancient Novel*. Ancient Narrative Supplementum 12, 241–53. Groningen: Barkhuis and Groningen University Library.

Hägg, T. (2004). *Parthenope*. Copenhagen: University of Copenhagen/Museum Tusculanum.

Hägg, T. (2012). *The Art of Biography in Antiquity*. Cambridge: Cambridge University Press.

Häkkinen, S. (2005). 'Ebionites', in A. Marjanen and P. Luomanen (eds), *A Companion to Second-Century Christian 'Heretics'*. VGSup 76, 247–8. Leiden and Boston: Brill.

Hall, S. G. (2004). 'In the Beginning was the Codex: The Early Church and its Revolutionary Books', in R. N. Swanson (ed.), *The Church and the Book*. SCH 38, 1–10. Woodbridge: Boydell.

Halliwell, S. (2008). *Greek Laughter. A Study of Cultural Psychology from Homer to Early Christianity*. Cambridge: Cambridge University Press.

Hamerton-Kelly (1973). *Pre-existence, Wisdom and the Son of God*. SNTSMS 21. Cambridge: Cambridge University Press.

Hannah, D. (2008). 'The Four-Gospel "Canon" in the *Epistula Apostolorum*'. *JTS* 59: 598–633.

Hansen, W., ed. (1998). *Anthology of Ancient Greek Popular Literature*. Bloomington and Indianapolis: Indiana University Press.

Hanson, R. P. C. (1980). 'The Christian Attitude to Pagan Religions up to the Time of Constantine the Great'. *ANRW* 23 (2): 910–73.

Harris, W. V. (1989). *Ancient Literacy*. Cambridge and London: Harvard University Press.

Hartenstein, J. (2010). 'Das Kindheitsevangelium des Thomas', in WiBeLex (2010) (www.wibilex.de). (http://www.bibelwissenschaft.de/stichwort/51906/)

Hartenstein, J. (2013). 'Hinfuhrung', in R. Zimmermann et al. (eds), *Kompendium der frühchristlichen Wundererzählung*, vol. 1, 781–92. Gütersloh: Gütersloher Verlag.
Hengel, M. (1977). *Crucifixion*. Philadelphia: Fortress.
Hengel, M. (1995). *Studies in Early Christology*. London and New York: T&T Clark.
Hennecke, E. and W. Schneemelcher, eds (1991), *New Testament Apocrypha*. 2 vols. Rev. edn. Louisville: Westminster John Knox.
Hernández de la Fuente, D. (2013). 'Parallels between Dionysus and Christ in Late Antiquity: Miraculous Healings in Nonnus' *Dionysiaca*', in A. Bernabé et al. (eds), *Redefining Dionysus*. MythosEikonPoiesis, vol. 5, 464–87. Berlin: de Gruyter.
Hezser, C. (2001). *Jewish Literacy in Jewish Palestine*. TSAJ 81. Tübingen: Mohr Siebeck.
Hill, C. E. (1999). 'The *Epistula Apostolorum*: An Asian Tract from the Time of Polycarp'. *JECS* 7: 1–53.
Hill, C. E. (2010). *Who Chose the Gospels? Probing the Great Gospel Conspiracy*. Oxford and New York: Oxford University Press.
Hills, J. (1990). *Tradition and Composition in the* Epistula Apostolorum. *HDR* 24. Minneapolis: Fortress.
Holladay, C. (1983). *Fragments from Hellenistic Jewish Authors. Volume 1: Historians*. SBLTT 20. Chico: Scholars Press.
Holzbach, M. C. (2013). 'Ein aufmüpfiger Schüler (Der Knabe Jesus kennt die Buchstaben) KThom 14', in R. Zimmermann et al. (eds), *Kompendium der frühchristlichen Wundererzählung*, vol. 1, 862–8. Gütersloh: Gütersloher Verlag.
Hoornaert, E. (1988). *The Memory of the Christian People*. Maryknoll: Orbis.
Horn, C. B. (2010). 'Apocryphal Gospels in Arabic, or some Complications on the Road to Traditions about Jesus', in J. Frey and J. Schröter (eds), *Jesus in apokryphen Evangelienüberlieferungen*. WUNT 2.254, 583–609. Tübingen: Mohr Siebeck.
Horn, C. B. (2015). 'Depiction of Children and Young People as Literary Motifs in Canonical and Apocryphal Acts', in P. Piovanelli and T. Burke (eds), *Rediscovering the Apocryphal Continent. New Perspectives on Early Christian and Late Antique Apocryphal Texts and Traditions*. WUNT 349, 223–44. Tübingen: Mohr Siebeck.
Horn, Cornelia B. and John W. Martens (2009). *'Let the Little Children Come to Me'. Childhood and Children In Early Christianity*. Washington: Catholic University of America Press.
Horn, C. B. and R. Phenix, Jr. (2010). 'Apocryphal Gospels in Syriac and Related Texts Offering Traditions about Jesus', in J. Frey and J. Schröter (eds), *Jesus in apokryphen Evangelienüberlieferungen*. WUNT 2.254, 527–55. Tübingen: Mohr Siebeck.
Hornschuh, M. (1965). *Studien zur* Epistula Apostolorum. PTS 5. Berlin: de Gruyter.
Horsley, R. (2015). 'The Gospel of Mark in the Interface of Orality and Writing', in A. Weissenrieder and R. B. Coote (eds), *The Interface of Orality and Writing*. BPC 11, 144–65. Eugene: Cascade.
Hurtado, L. (2003). *Lord Jesus Christ. Devotion to Jesus in Earliest Christianity*. Grand Rapids and Cambridge: Eerdmans.
Hurtado, L. (2015). 'Who Read the Early Christian Apocrypha?' in A. Gregory and C. Tuckett (eds), *The Oxford Handbook of Early Christian Apocrypha*, 153–66. New York and Oxford: Oxford University Press.
Hurtado, L. (2016). *Destroyer of the Gods. Early Christian Distinctiveness in the Roman World*. Waco: Baylor University Press.
Instone, S. (2009). *Greek Personal Religion. A Reader*. Oxford: Aris & Phillips.
Johnson, L. T. (2009). *Among the Gentiles. Greco-Roman Religion and Christianity*. New Haven and London: Yale University Press.

Jones, C. P. (2014). *Between Pagan and Christian*. Cambridge and London: Harvard University Press.

Jones, F. S. (1990). 'Ebionites', in E. Ferguson et al. (eds), *Encyclopedia of Early Christianity*, 287–8. New York and London: Garland.

Käsemann, E. (1968). *The Testament of Jesus*. London: SCM.

Kahl, W. (1994). *New Testament Miracle Stories in their Religious-Historical Setting*. Göttingen: Vandenhoeck & Ruprecht.

Kaiser, U. U. (2010). 'Jesus als Kind. Neuere Forschungen zur Jesusüberlieferung in den apokryphen "Kindheitsevangelien"', in J. Frey and J. Schröter (eds), *Jesus in apokryphen Evangelienüberlieferungen*. WUNT 2.254, 253–69. Tübingen: Mohr Siebeck.

Kaiser, U. U. (2011). 'Die sogenannte "Kindheitserzählung des Thomas." Überlegungen zur Darstellung Jesu als Kind, deren Intention und Rezeption', in C. Clivaz, A. Dettwiler, L. Devillers and E. Norelli (eds), *Infancy Gospels. Stories and Identities*. WUNT 281, 459–81. Tübingen: Mohr Siebeck.

Kee, H. C. (1983). *Miracle in the Early Christian World*. New Haven and London: Yale University Press.

Keener, C. (2015). *Acts. An Exegetical Commentary 24:1-28:31*, vol. 4. Grand Rapids: Baker.

Kenney, T. M. and M. Dzon, eds (2012). *The Christ Child in Medieval Culture: Alpha Es Et O!* Toronto: University of Toronto.

Klauck, H.-J. (2003). *Apocryphal Gospels*. London and New York: T&T Clark.

Kleinknecht, H. (1967). 'ὀργή κτλ'. *TDNT* V 382–92.

Klijn, A. F. J. and G. J. Reinink (1973). *Patristic Evidence for Jewish-Christian Sects*. NovTSup 36. Leiden: Brill.

Koch, Dietrich-Alex (1975). *Die Bedeutung der Wundererzählungen für die Christologie des Markusevangeliums*. Berlin and New York: de Gruyter.

Koester, H. (1971). 'One Jesus and Four Primitive Gospels', in James M. Robinson and Helmut Koester (eds), *Trajectories through Early Christianity*, 158–204. Philadelphia: Fortress.

Koester, H. (1992). *Ancient Christian Gospels. Their History and Development*. Philadelphia and London: TPI/SCM.

Konstan, D. and I. Ramelli (2014). 'The Novel and Christian Narrative', in E. P. Cueva and S. N. Byrne (eds), *A Companion to the Ancient Novel*, 180–97. Chichester: Wiley Blackwell.

Konstan, D. and R. Walsh (2016). 'Civic and subversive biography in antiquity', in K. de Temmerman and K. Demoen, (ed.), *Writing Biographies in Greece and Rome: Narrative Technique and Fictionalization*, 26–43. Cambridge University Press.

Koskenniemi, E. (2014). 'Apollonius of Tyana, the Greek Miracle Workers in the Time of Jesus and the New Testament', in B. Kollmann and R. Zimmermann (eds), *Hermeneutik der frühchristlichen Wundererzählungen. Geschichtliche, literarische und rezeptionsorientierte Perspektiven*. WUNT 339, 165–81. Tübingen: Mohr Siebeck.

Krauss, T. J. (1999). '"Uneducated", "Ignorant", or even "Illiterate"? Aspects and Background for an Understanding of ΑΓΡΑΜΜΑΤΟΙ (and ΙΔΙΩΤΑΙ) in Acts 4.13'. *NTS* 45:434–49.

Laager, J. (1957). *Geburt und Kindheit des Gottes in der griechischen Mythologie*. Winterthur: Verlag P. G. Keller.

Lampe, G. W. H. (1965). 'Miracles and Early Christian Apologetic', in C. F. D. Moule (ed.), *Miracles*, 203–18. London: A. R. Mowbray.

Lampe, P. (2001). 'Early Christians in the City of Rome. Topographical and Social Historical Aspects of the First Three Centuries' in J. Zangenberg and M. Labahn (eds.), *Christians as a Religious Minority in a Multicultural City*, 20–32. JSNTSup 243. London and New York: Continuum.

Landesmann, P. (2010). *Die Darstellung 'Der zwölfjährige Jesus unter den Schriftgelehrten' im Wandel der Zeiten*. BIS 101. Leiden and Boston: Brill.

Lane Fox, R. (1986). *Pagans and Christians*. New York: Knopf.

Lapham, F. (2003). *An Introduction to the New Testament Apocrypha*. London and New York: T&T Clark.

Larson, J. (2007). *Ancient Greek Cults. A Guide*. New York and London: Routledge.

Leppin, H. (2007). 'Old Religions Transformed: Religions and Religious Policy from Decius to Constantine', in Jörge Rüpke (ed.), *A Companion to Roman Religion*, 96–108. Malden: Blackwell.

Leyerle, Blake (2013). 'Children and "the Child" in Early Christianity', in R. Bell, J. E. Grubbs and T. Parkin (eds), *Oxford Handbook of Childhood and Education in the Classical World*, 559–79. Oxford and New York: Oxford University Press.

Litwa, D. (2014). *Iesus Deus: The Depiction of Jesus as Mediterranean God*. Minneapolis: Fortress.

Lloyd-Jones, H. (1971). *The Justice of Zeus*. Berkeley: University of California Press.

Lowe, M. (1981). 'Ἰουδαῖοι of the Apocrypha. A Fresh Approach to the Gospels of James, Pseudo-Thomas, Peter and Nicodemus'. *NovT* 23: 56–90.

Luomanen, P. (2007). 'Ebionites and Nazarenes', in M. Jackson-McCabe (ed.), *Jewish Christianity Reconsidered. Rethinking Ancient Groups and Texts*, 81–118. Minneapolis: Fortress.

Luther, S. (2013). 'Nichts ist unmöglich – mit Jesus (Die Streckung des Bretts) KThom 13 (arabK 38f.)', in R. Zimmermann et al. (eds), *Kompendium der frühchristlichen Wundererzählung*, vol. 1, 852–61. Gütersloh: Gütersloher Verlag.

Luther, S. (2014). 'Erdichtete Wahrheit oder bezeugte Fiktion? Realitäts- und Fiktionalitätsindikatoren in frühchristlichen Wundererzählungen – eine Problemanzeige', in B. Kollmann and R. Zimmermann (eds), *Hermeneutik der frühchristlichen Wundererzählungen. Geschichtliche, literarische und rezeptionsorientierte Perspektiven.*, WUNT 339, 345–68. Tübingen: Mohr Siebeck.

MacMullen, R. (1981). *Paganism in the Roman Empire*. New Haven and London: Yale University Press.

MacMullen, R. (1983). 'Two Types of Conversion to Early Christianity'. *Vig. Christ.* 37: 174–92.

MacMullen, R. (1984). *Christianizing the Roman Empire*. New Haven and London: Yale University Press.

MacMullen, R. (1985–6). 'Conversion: A Historian's View'. *JECS* 5: 67–81.

MacMullen, R. (2009). *The Second Church: Popular Christianity A.D. 200-400*. Atlanta: SBL.

Markschies, C. and J. Schröter, eds (2012). *Antike christliche Apokryphen in deutscher Übersetzung*. 2 vols. AcA I/1-2: Tübingen: Mohr Siebeck.

Martin, D. (2007). *Inventing Superstition. From the Hippocratics to the Christians*. Cambridge and London: Harvard University Press.

McCarthy, M. (2009). 'Divine Wrath and Human Anger'. *Theological Studies* 70: 845–74.

McCracken, G. E. (1949). *Arnobius of Sicca. The Case against the Pagans*. ACW 7-8. Cork: Mercier Press.

McNamara, M. (2010). 'Jesus in (Early) Irish Apocryphal Gospel Traditions', in J. Frey and J. Schröter (eds), *Jesus in apokryphen Evangelienüberlieferungen*. WUNT 2.254, 685–739. Tübingen: Mohr Siebeck.
McNeil, B. (1976). 'Jesus and the Alphabet'. *JTS* 27: 126–8.
Meier, J. (1991). *A Marginal Jew. Rethinking the Historical Jesus*. New York: Doubleday.
Meier, J. (1994). *A Marginal Jew. Rethinking the Historical Jesus*, vol. II. New York: Doubleday.
Meier, J. (1997). 'On Retrojecting Later Questions from Later Texts: A Reply to Richard Bauckham'. *CBQ* 59: 511–27.
Meier, J. (1999). 'The Present State of the "Third Quest" for the Historical Jesus. Loss and Gain'. *Biblica* 80: 459–87.
Michel, C. (1924). *Évangiles apocryphes*. Paris: A. Picard, vol. 1: xxiii–xxxii; 161–89.
Miller, R. J. (2003). *Born Divine. The Births of Jesus and Other Sons of God*. Santa Rosa: Polebridge.
Miranda, J. P. (1977). *Die Sendung Jesu im vierten Evangelium*. SBS 87. Stuttgart: Katholisches Bibelwerk.
Mirecki, P. (1992). 'Thomas, Infancy Gospel of'. *ABD* 6: 540–44.
Most, G. W. (2007). *Hesiod. The Shield, Catalogue of Women, Other Fragments*. LCL. Cambridge, MA: Harvard University Press.
Müller, C. D. G. (2012). 'Die *Epistula Apostolorum*', in C. Markschies and J. Schröter (eds), *Antike christliche Apokryphen in deutscher Übersetzung*. 2 vols, AcA I/1-2, 2.1062–92. Tübingen: Mohr Siebeck.
Münch, C. (2013). 'Heimlicher Wohltäter (Die wunderbare Vermehrung der Saat) K Thom 12', in R. Zimmermann et al. (eds), *Kompendium der frühchristlichen Wundererzählung*, vol. 1, 847–51. Gütersloh: Gütersloher Verlag.
Mussies, G. (2008). 'Reflections on the Apocryphal Gospels as Supplements', in Alberdina Houtman et al. (eds), Empsychoi Logoi. *Religious Innovations in Antiquity*, 597–611. Leiden and Boston: Brill.
Narro, Á. (2013). 'L'importance de la foule (Ο ΟΧΛΟΣ) dans L'Évangile de l'enfance de Thomas l'Israélite', in Jens Schröter (ed.), *The Apocryphal Gospels within the Context of Early Christian Theology*, 627–38. Leuven, Paris and Walpole: Peeters.
Nesselrath, H.-G. (1995). 'Myth, Parody, and Comic Plots: The Birth of Gods and Middle Comedy', in G. W. Dobrov (ed.), *Beyond Aristophanes. Transition and Diversity in Greek Comedy*, 1–27. Atlanta: Scholars Press.
Neusner, J. (1964). 'Zacchaeus/Zakkai'. *HTR* 57: 57–9.
Neyrey, J. (1998). *Honor and Shame in the Gospel of Matthew*. Louisville: Westminster John Knox.
Nock, A. D. (1961 [1933]). *Conversion*. Oxford: Oxford University Press.
Nock, A. D. (1972). *Essays on Religion and the Ancient World*. 2 vols. Edited by Zeph Stewart. Cambridge, MA: Cambridge University Press.
Noret, J. (1972). 'Pour une édition de L'Évangile de l'enfance selon Thomas'. *AnBoll* 90: 412.
Opstelten, J. C. (1952). *Sophocles and Greek Pessimism*. Amsterdam: North-Holland.
Paget, J. C. (2010). *Jews, Christians and Jewish Christians in Antiquity*. WUNT 251. Tübingen: Mohr Siebeck.
Parker, R. (1996). 'Gods Cruel and Kind: Tragic and Civil Theology', in C. B. R. Pelling (ed.), *Tragedy and the Historian*, 143–60. Oxford: Oxford University Press.
Parker, R. (2005). *Polytheism and Society at Athens*. Oxford: Oxford University Press.
Parker, R. (2011). *On Greek Religion*. Ithaca and London: Cornell University Press.
Paulissen, L. (2003). 'Jésus à l'école. L'enseignement dans l' *Évangile de l'Enfance selon Thomas*'. *Apocrypha* 14: 153–75.

Paulissen, L. (2004). 'Jésus enfant divin: Processus de reconnaissance dans l' *Évangile de l'Enfance selon Thomas*'. *Revue de Philosophie Ancienne* 22: 17–28.
Pellegrini, S. (2012). 'Das Protevangelium des Jakobus', in C. Markschies and J. Schröter (eds), *Antike christliche Apokryphen in deutscher Übersetzung*. 2 vols, 903–29. AcA I/1-2: Tübingen: Mohr Siebeck.
Pellegrini, S. (2012). 'Kindheitsevangelien', in C. Markschies and J. Schröter (eds), *Antike christliche Apokryphen in deutscher Übersetzung*. 2 vols, 886–902. AcA I/1-2: Tübingen: Mohr Siebeck.
Pelling, C. (1990). 'Childhood and Personality in Greek Literature', in C. Pelling (ed.), *Characterization and Individuality in Greek Literature*, 213–44. Oxford: Clarendon Press.
Penner, T. (2012). '*Res Gestae Divi Christi*: Miracles, Early Christian Heroes, and the Discourse of Power in Acts', in D. F. Watson (ed.), *Miracle Discourse in the New Testament*, 125–73. Atlanta: SBL.
Perkins, P. (2015). 'Christology and Soteriology in Apocryphal Gospels', in A. Gregory and C. Tuckett (eds), *The Oxford Handbook of Early Christian Apocrypha*, 196–212. New York and Oxford: Oxford University Press.
Pervo, R. (1987). *Profit with Delight. The Literary Genre of the Acts of the Apostles*. Philadelphia: Fortress Press.
Pervo, R. (1996). 'The Ancient Novel Becomes Christian' in G. Schmeling (ed.), *The Novel in the Ancient World*, 685–711. Leiden: Brill.
Phillipart, G. (1972). 'Fragments palimpsestes latins du Vindobonensis 563'. *Anal Boll* 90: 391–411.
Piovanelli, P. and T. Burke, eds (2015). *Rediscovering the Apocryphal Continent. New Perspectives on Early Christian and Late Antique Apocryphal Texts and Traditions*. WUNT 349. Tübingen: Mohr Siebeck.
Rebell, W. (1992). *Neutestamentliche Apokryphen und Apostolische Väter*. Kaiser: Munich.
Remus, H. (1983). *Pagan-Christian Conflict over Miracle in the Second Century*. Patristic Monograph Series 10. Cambridge: Philadelphia Patristic Foundation.
Rhee, H. (2005). *Early Christian Literature. Christ and Culture in the Second and Third Centuries*. London and New York: Routledge.
Richardson, N. (2010). *Three Homeric Hymns: To Apollo, Hermes, and Aphrodite*. Cambridge: Cambridge University Press.
Riemer, U. (2006). 'Miracle Stories and Their Narrative Intent in the Context of the Ruler Cult of Classical Antiquity', in M. Labahn and B. J. L. Peerbolte (eds), *Wonders Never Cease*. LNTS 288, 32–47. London and New York: Continuum.
Robbins, V. K. (2005). 'Lukan and Johannine Tradition in the Qu'ran: A Story of (and Program for) *Auslegungsgeschichte* and *Wirkungsgeschichte*', in T. Penner and C. Vander Stichele (eds), *Moving Beyond New Testament Theology? Essays in Conversation with Heikki Räisänen*, 336–68. Helsinki and Göttingen: Finnish Exegetical Society/Vandenhoeck & Ruprecht.
Schäfer, P. (2012). *The Jewish Jesus. How Judaism and Christianity Shaped Each Other*. Princeton and Oxford: Princeton University Press.
Scheingorn, P. (2012). 'Reshapings of the Childhood Miracles of Jesus', in T. M. Kenney and M. Dzon (eds), *The Christ Child in Medieval Culture: Alpha Es Et O!*, 254–92. Toronto: University of Toronto.
Schlichting, Günther (1982). *Ein jüdisches Leben Jesu*. WUNT 24. Tübingen: Mohr Siebeck.
Schmahl, G. (1974). 'Lk 2,41-52 und die Kindheitserzählung des Thomas 19,1-5'. *Bibel und Leben* 15: 249–58.

Schnackenburg, R. (1993). *Jesus in the Gospels. A Biblical Christology*. Louisville: Westminster John Knox.
Schnelle, U. (1992). *Antidocetic Christology in the Gospel of John*. Minneapolis: Fortress.
Schröter, Jens, ed. (2013). *The Apocryphal Gospels within the Context of Early Christian Theology*. Leuven, Paris and Walpole: Peeters.
Scullion, S. (2014). 'Religion and the Gods in Greek Comedy', in M. Fontaine and A. C. Scafuro (eds), *The Oxford Handbook of Greek and Roman Comedy*, 340–55. Oxford: Oxford University Press.
Sels, N. (2010). 'The function of irony in mythical narratives. Hans Blumenberg and Homer's ludicrous gods', in M. J. van Binsbergen and E. Venbrux (eds), *New Perspectives on Myth: Proceedings of the Second Annual Conference of the International Association for Comparative Mythology, Ravenstein (the Netherlands), 19-21 August, 2008*. Haarlem (the Netherlands): Papers in Intercultural Philosophy and Transcontinental Comparative Studies (PIP-TraCS), No. 5: 409–26.
Shinan, A. (1996). 'Synagogues in the Land of Israel. The Literature of the Ancient Synagogue and Synagogue Archaeology', in S. Fine (ed.), *Sacred Realm. The Emergence of the Synagogue in the Ancient World*, 130–52. New York and Oxford: Oxford University Press.
Sider, R. J. (2012) (ed.). *The Early Church on Killing*. Grand Rapids: Baker.
Siebert, G. (1990). 'Hermes'. *LIMC* V.1 285–387 with V.2.
Siker, J. S., ed. (2015). *Jesus, Sin, and Perfection in Early Christianity*. Cambridge and New York: Cambridge University Press.
Skarsaune, O. (2007). 'The Ebionites', in O. Skarsaune and R. Hvalvik (eds), *Jewish Believers in Jesus*, 419–62. Peabody: Hendrikson.
Slusser, M. (1981). 'Docetism: A Historical Definition.' *Second Century*: 163–72.
Snyder, H. G. (2000). *Teachers and Texts in the Ancient World. Philosophers, Jews and Christians*. London and New York: Routledge.
Söder, R. (1969 [1932]). *Die apokryphen Apostelgeschichten und die romanhaft Literatur der Antike*. Stuttgart: Kohlhammer.
Stewart, E. (2015). 'Sending a Boy to do a Man's Job: Hegemonic Masculinity and the "boy" Jesus in the *Infancy Gospel of Thomas*'. *HTS* 71: 1–9.
Strange, W. A. (1996). *Children in the Early Church*. Carlisle: Paternoster.
Strecker, G. (1996). *The Johannine Letters*. Hermeneia. Minneapolis: Fortress.
Stroumsa, G. (2016). *The Scriptural Universe of Ancient Christianity*. Cambridge, MA and London: Harvard University Press.
Stroumsa, G. (2004). 'Christ's Laughter: Docetic Origins Reconsidered.' *JECS* 12: 267–88.
Talbert, C. H. (1980). 'Prophecies of Future Greatness: The Contribution of Greco-Roman Biographies to an Understanding of Luke 1:5-4:15', in J. L. Crenshaw and S. Sandmel (eds), *The Divine Helmsman. Studies on God's Control of Human Events, Presented to Lou H. Silberman*, 129–41. New York: Ktav.
Theissen, G. (1983). *The Miracle Stories of the Early Christian Tradition*. Philadelphia: Fortress Press.
Thomas, C. M. (2004). *The Acts of Peter, Gospel Literature, and the Ancient Novel. Rewriting the Past*. Oxford and New York. Oxford University Press.
Thundy, Z. P. (1989). 'Intertextuality, Buddhism, and the Infancy Gospels', in J. Neusner, E. S. Frerichs and A. J. Levine (eds), *Religious Writings and Religious Systems*. BSR 1, vol. 1, 17–73. Atlanta: Scholars Press.
Thundy, Z. P. (1993). *Buddha and Christ. Nativity Stories and Indian Traditions*. SHR 60. Leiden: Brill.

Tuckett, C. (2015). 'Introduction: What is New Testament Apocrypha?' in A. Gregory and C. Tuckett (eds), *The Oxford Handbook of Early Christian Apocrypha*, 3–12. New York and Oxford: Oxford University Press.
Twelftree, G. (1999). *Jesus. The Miracle Worker*. Downers Grove: Intervarsity Press.
Unger, D. J. and J. J. Dillon, ed. and tran. (1992). *St Irenaeus of Lyons. Against the Heresies Book 1*. ACW 55. New York and Mahwah: Paulist Press.
Upson-Saia, K. (2013). 'Holy Child or Holy Terror? Understanding Jesus' Anger in the Infancy Gospel of Thomas'. *Church History* 82: 1–39.
Van Aarde, A. (2005). 'The infancy Gospel of Thomas: Allegory or myth – Gnostic or Ebionite?' *Verbum et Ecclesia* 26: 826–50.
Van Aarde, A. (2006). 'Ebionite Tendencies in the Jesus Tradition: The *Infancy Gospel of Thomas* Interpreted from the Perspective of Ethnic Identity'. *Neotestamentica* 40: 353–82.
Van Aarde, A. (2013). 'The Ebionite Perspective in the Infancy Gospel of Thomas', in Schröter, Jens (ed.), *The Apocryphal Gospels within the Context of Early Christian Theology*, 611–26, Leuven, Paris and Walpole: Peeters.
Van der Loos, H. (1965). *The Miracles of Jesus*. NovTSup 9. Leiden Brill.
VanderKam, J. C. (2004). *From Joshua to Caiaphas. High Priests after the Exile*. Minneapolis and Assen: Fortress/Van Gorcum.
Vergados, A. (2011). 'The *Homeric Hymn to Hermes*: Humour and Epiphany' in Andrew Faulkner (ed.), *The Homeric Hymns. Interpretative Essays*, 82-104. Oxford: University Press.
Van Oyen, Geert (2011). 'Rereading the Rewriting of the Biblical Traditions in the Infancy Gospel of Thomas (*Paidika*)', in C. Clivaz, A. Dettwiler, L. Devillers, E. Norelli with B. Bertho (eds), *Infancy Gospels. Stories and Identities*. WUNT 281, 482–505. Tübingen: Mohr Siebeck.
Van Oyen, Geert (2013). 'The *Protevangelium Jacobi*: An Apocryphal Gospel?' in Jens Schröter (ed.), *The Apocryphal Gospels within the Context of Early Christian Theology*, 271–304. Leuven, Paris and Walpole: Peeters.
Versnel, H. S. (1999). 'Κόλασαι τοὺς ἡμᾶς τοιούτους ἡδέως βλέποντες "Punish those who Rejoice in Our Misery": On Curses and *Schadenfreude*', in David R. Jordan et al. (eds), *The World of Ancient Magic*. Papers from the Norwegian Institute at Athens 4, 125–62. Bergen: Norwegian Institute at Athens.
Versnel, H. S. (2005). 'Making Sense of Jesus' Death. The Pagan Contribution', in J. Frey and J. Schröter (eds), *Deutungen des Todes Jesu im Neuen Testament*. WUNT 181, 213–94. Tübingen: Mohr Siebeck.
Versnel, H. S. (2011). *Coping with the Gods: Wayward Readings in Greek Theology*. Leiden and Boston: Brill.
Versnel, H. S. (2015). 'Prayer and Curse', in E. Eidinow and J. Kindt (eds), *The Oxford Handbook of Ancient Greek Religion*, 447–61. Oxford: Oxford University Press.
Vielhauer, P. (1975). *Geschichte der urchristlichen Literatur*. Berlin: de Gruyter.
Vitz, E. B. (2001). 'The Apocryphal and the Biblical, the Oral and the Written, in Medieval Legends of Christ's Childhood: The Old French *Evangile de l'Enfance*', in N. M. Reale and R. E. Sternglantz (eds), *Satura. Studies in Medieval Literature in honour of Robert Raymo*, 124–49. Donigton: Shaun Tyas.
Voicu, S. J. (1991). 'Notes sur l'histoire du texte de l'*Histoire de l'enfance de Jésus*'. *Apocrypha* 2: 119–32.
Voicu, S. J. (1997). 'Histoire de l'enfance de Jésus', in F. Bovon and P. Geoltrain (eds), *Écrits apocryphes chrétiens*, vol. 1, 191–204. Paris: Gallimard.

Voicu, S. J. (1998). 'Verso il testo primitivo dei Παιδικὰ τοῦ κυρίου Ἰησοῦ. "Racconti dell'infanzia del Signore Gesù."' *Apocrypha* 9: 7–95.
Voicu, S. J. (2004). 'La tradition latine des *Paidika*'. *Bulletin de l'AELAC* 14: 13–21.
Voicu, S. J. (2011). 'Ways to Survival for the Infancy Apocrypha', in C. Clivaz, A. Dettwiler, L. Devillers, E. Norelli with B. Bertho (eds), *Infancy Gospels. Stories and Identities*. WUNT 281, 401–17. Tübingen: Mohr Siebeck.
Von Bendemann, R. (2013). 'Anhaltende Trockenheit (Die Verfluchung des Sohnes des Annas) KThom 3 (arabK 46f.)', in R. Zimmermann et al. (eds), *Kompendium der frühchristlichen Wundererzählung*, vol. 1, 832–42. Gütersloh: Gütersloher Verlag.
Von Wahlde, U. C. (2015). *Gnosticism, Docetism, and the Judaisms of the First Century. The Search for the Wider Context of the Johannine Literature and Why It Matters*. LNTS 517. London: Bloomsbury.
Voorwinde, Stephen (2005). *Jesus' Emotions in the Fourth Gospel. Human or Divine?* LNTS 284. London and New York: T&T Clark.
Weinreich, O. (1909 Rp. 1969). *Antike Heilungswunder*. Berlin: de Gruyter.
West, M. L. (1997). *The East Face of Helicon*. Oxford: Clarendon Press.
West, M. L. (2003). *Greek Epic Fragments*. LCL. Cambridge, MA: Harvard University Press.
Westermann, C. (1984). *Genesis 1-11*. Minneapolis: Augsburg.
Whitenton, M. R. (2015). 'The Moral Character Development of the Boy Jesus in the *Infancy Gospel of Thomas*'. *JSNT* 38: 219–40.
Wiedemann, T. (1989). *Adults and Children in the Roman Empire*. London: Routledge.
Williams, F., ed. and tran. (2013). *The Panarion of Epiphanius of Salamis, Books II and III. De Fide*. NHMS 79. 2nd edn. Leiden and Boston: Brill.
Williams, M.A. (1999). *'Rethinking Gnosticism': An Argument for Dismantling a Dubious Category*. Princeton: Princeton University Press.
Wilson, R. M. (1978). 'Apokryphen II'. *TRE* 3: 316–62.
Wilson, S. G. (1995). *Related Strangers. Jews and Christians 70-170 C.E.* Minneapolis: Fortress.
Winter, B. W. (2001). *After Paul Left Corinth. The Influence of Secular Ethics and Social Change*. Grand Rapids and Cambridge: Eerdmans.
Worth, R. H. (2003). *Alternative Lives of Jesus: Noncanonical Accounts through the Early Middle Ages*. Jefferson and London: McFarland & Company.
Wright, W. (1923). *Julian*. Vol. 3. LCL. Cambridge, MA: Harvard University Press.
Zimmermann, R. et al., eds (2013). *Kompendium der frühchristlichen Wundererzählung*, vol. 1. Gütersloh: Gütersloher Verlag.

SUBJECT INDEX

Abraham 79
Acts, Apocryphal. *See* Apocryphal Acts
Adam 84
Aeschylus 35
agonism 88, 111–15, 118–19
Alexandria 12, 51
Ananias 25, 27
Annas 2, 38, 88–9, 105
Annas's son 19, 38, 51, 53, 69, 71, 85, 88–9, 94
Antioch 12
Antiope 36
Aphrodite 36, 43
Apocrypha, Christian 1, 7, 8, 17, 23, 87
Apocryphal Acts 25, 81 n.30, 107–8, 114, 118
apocryphal gospels 4, 20
Apollo 37, 40–1, 43–4
Apollonius of Tyana 114
apologists 35
Apostles 132, 87 n.40, 111, 114
aretology 83
Artemis 36
Artapanus of Alexandria 25–6
ascetics 28
Asia Minor 12
Athenaeus 91

baptism 31, 99
Barnabas 112
Basilides 99
Battus 40
Bethlehem 2, 20, 39
biography/*bios* 14–18, 20, 55–7, 64, 66
Buddhist traditions 12, 33, 98

Caiaphas 89
Callisto 36
Cerinthus 99–100
Celsus 31, 45–6, 93, 109–10, 115 n.45. *See also* Origen

Chrysostom, John 11–12, 21, 67
Christians 20, 31, 45, 47, 98, 106–7, 109–13, 119
Christology 23, 59, 71, 75–103, 117
Clement of Alexandria 35–6
converts to Christianity 14, 106–7, 109, 111 n.25, 112–13, 119
Corinth 89
Corinthians 45
Croesus 36–7
crowds 64, 70, 81–3, 105, 114
crucifixion 45, 99
Cyril of Alexandria 70 n.90
Cypria 35

daimones 20, 112
Danaë 36
date (of *Paidika*) 5, 7–12, 13, 19
demiurge 97–8
Dionysus 37, 40, 42, 46, 76, 118
disciples 25–7, 84 n.46, 93, 113
divine justice 34
Docetism 46 n.110, 97–9, 100, 102

Ebionism 97, 100–1
Egypt 6, 12, 18, 33, 93, 98
Edessa 12
Elijah 25–6, 86
Elisha 25–6, 84–5, 87, 89–90
Elymas 25, 27, 90, 114
Epiphanius of Salamis 11–12, 100
Euripides 35–8, 91
Eusebius 93
exorcism 89 n.68, 103

fiction 18–20

Galen 109–10
Gnosticism 3, 10, 14, 19 n.108, 21, 32, 55, 57, 96–8, 102, 116

Subject Index

Gospels, canonical   vii–viii, 1, 7, 12, 15–18, 21, 24, 26–8, 44, 46–7, 53, 56, 58, 60, 63, 70, 73, 76, 82, 84, 86, 88, 95–6, 98, 102–6, 115, 117–18

Hanina ben Dosa   87, 93
Hasidim   25
Hebrew language   33
Hellenistic era   20
Herakles   42, 75–6
Hermes   29, 39–44, 46, 112, 118
Herodotus   36–7
Hesiod   35, 40
Hindu traditions   33
Hippolytus   36
Hippolytus of Rome   100
Holy Spirit   27, 93
Homer   34–5, 39, 40, 43, 112–13
Homeric Hymns   29, 39, 40–4
Honi the Circle-Drawer   25–6
Hubris   37–9, 42, 46, 89
humour   43–5, 119

Infancy Gospels   15–16, 18
infancy narratives (Christian)   39
infancy narratives (pagan)   39–43
Io   36
Irenaeus   8–12, 21, 60, 67, 89 n.68, 99–100
Israel   84, 101, 106
Israelites   13, 101, 105

James (brother of Jesus)   3, 11, 13–14, 18, 51, 69, 70–1, 92–4, 96, 100
Jeremiah Apocryphon   87
Jerusalem   6, 13, 17, 50, 65, 101
Jewish holy men   25–8, 46
Jewish people   61, 64, 76, 81, 83
Jewish traditions   25, 31, 101, 102, 105–8, 113, 116
John the Baptist   11
Joseph   1–3, 8–9, 27, 44, 49–51, 53, 58–9, 61, 69, 76–9, 82, 87, 89, 99–101, 115–16, 119
Julian   35

Koran   32

lepers   84
Leto   37

Linus   42
Lucian   20, 43, 102, 110

magic/magicians   32, 46, 52, 86, 92 n.85, 93–4, 96, 112–14, 115 n.45
Malta   93
Marcosians   8–10, 91, 97–8
Mary   1, 3, 9, 50, 51, 58, 77, 80, 83, 86, 99, 101, 119
Messiah   27, 102
monophysitism   99
Moses   15, 25–6, 85–6

Nag Hammadi   vii, 3
Nazareth   2, 20, 49, 90
nemesis   37–9, 46
Nestorius   70
New Testament   1 n.1–2, 17, 25, 27, 44, 75, 76, 94
Nicodemus   79
Niobe   37
novels   14, 107

Olympian gods   39–47, 76, 113
Origen   31, 46, 93, 100, 110, 112

Palestine   12
parabiblical texts   16, 26
parevangelical texts   16, 24, 33, 56, 98
Passover   105
Paul   25, 27, 45, 90, 92, 93, 101, 107, 112, 114
Pentheus   37, 38
Peter   25, 27, 114
Phaedra   36
Pharaoh   25
Pharisees   2, 53, 77, 82, 83, 85, 105, 107
pneumatology   103
Prometheus   35
Protevangelium of James   7, 18, 49, 106–8

realia   50, 105
resurrection of Jesus   15, 46, 77
Romulus   15

Sapphira   25, 27
Sabbath   2, 19, 52–3, 84–6, 88, 101, 105–6, 109

Satan   38, 93 n.93
Septuagint (LXX)   16, 26, 76, 84 n.44–6, 93, 103, 106–7
Simon of Cyrene   99
Simon Magus   114
Suetonius   15
Syria   12, 13, 28
Syrian ascetics. *See* ascetics

thaumaturgy. *See* magic
theology in the *Paidika*   25, 29–30, 47, 71, 73, 96, 102–3, 108, 119
Theseus   15
Thomas   vii–ix, 2, 3, 12–14, 107
Trinity   92, 110

Vienna   4 n.9, 5, 31 n.46
virgin birth   99

wrath (of God)   27, 30

Xenophanes   34, 35
Xerxes   37

Yahweh   26, 37, 98, 106

Zeno   2–3, 11, 31, 33, 44, 51, 53, 61, 67, 69, 71, 94–5, 107, 114
Zeus   35–36, 40–4, 112–113
Zacchaeus   2, 58–63, 67–69, 73, 79, 82, 90–2, 95, 97, 100, 114

INDEX OF MODERN AUTHORS

Aasgaard, R.   viii, ix, 5 n.15, 6, 8 n.43, 12, 13 n.78, 26 n.15–16, 28–29, 32, 44 n.105, 50 n.6,8,10, 59, 70–1, 88 n.65
Amsler, F.   9 n.48, 10 n.55, 31, 49, 101
Achtemeier, P.   7, 20

Baars, W.   12, 97–8
Bauer, W.   96
Betsworth, S.   14, 29 n.34, 54 n.25, 70–1
Bovon, F.   81, 94
Bowersock, G.   20, 107 n.13
Burke, T.   viii–ix, 1, 3–6, 10, 13–15, 19, 25–9, 50 n.4, 54–8, 60 n.55, 63, 70 n.17, 78, 87–8, 91 n.81, 97, 102

Chartrand-Burke, T.   25–6, 64
Clark, G.   66–7
Cullman, O.   14 n.83, 24, 60, 96, 106 n.6

Davis, S. J.   ix, 16–18, 32, 50 n.6, 54 n.25, 58, 88, 89 n.70, 90 n.74–5
Deines, R.   71
Dornseiff, F.   98

Eastman, D.   25 n.14, 27–8, 88, 89 n.69
Ehrman, B.   3, 4, 13 n.79
Enslin, M.   65–6
Erlemann, K.   59, 94

Fabricius, J. A.   v
Foster, P.   50, 69 n.86
Frey, J.   99

Gero, S.   4, 10 n.55, 11 n.61

Halliwell, S.   44
Helderman, J.   12, 97–8
Hengel, M.   45
Hock, R. F.   84 n.43–6

Horsley, R.   108
Hurtado, L.   52

Johnson, L. T.   72, 76
Jones, F. S.   101

Käsemann, E.   80
Kaiser, U. U.   32, 66, 102–3
Klauck, H.-J.   11 n.60, 97 n.104
Kleinknecht, H.   37
Koester, H.   19

Landesmann, P.   vii n.6
Lane Fox, R.   112–13
Leyerle, B.   54 n.24, 60
Litwa, D.   ix, 30 n.40, 33–4, 39, 41 n.92, 57 n.44, 75
Luther, S.   87

MacMullen, R.   108 n.18, 109 n.20–1, 112–13
Meier, J.   19–20, 94
Miller, R. J.   32, 69 n.87

Narro, Á.   83
Nock, A. D.   20, 75, 90 n.73, 113–14

Paulissen, L.   64 n.67–8, 67 n.82, 91–2
Pelling, C.   56
Pleše, Z.   3, 4

Santos Otero, A. de   97
Schneider, G.   24
Schmahl, G.   78
Schnackenburg, R.   79
Sider, R. J.   60–1
Siker, J. S.   59
Strecker, G.   99

Tischendorf, C.   vii n.1, 4–6, 82 n.33–4, 83 n.40

Upson-Saia, K. ix, 30–2

Van Aarde, A. 14 n.85, 32, 100–2
Van Oyen, Geert 4, 6, 7 n.40, 17, 26 n.15, 78 n.13, 80 n.26

Voicu, S. J. viii n.13, 4, 6 n.27, 7 n.38, 8 n.42–3, 11, 68 n.84, 100

Whitenton, M. R. 66, 89 n.67
Wilson, R. M. 98

INDEX OF ANCIENT AUTHORS

OLD TESTAMENT

Genesis   31, 52, 71, 84, 86, 93, 103
1.9 (LXX)   84 n.44
1.9-10   84
1.10   98
1.20-25   84
2.2-3   86
2.7 (LXX)   84 n.46, 93 n.87
19.11   90 n.72

Exodus
15.22-5   84
20.11   86
31.17   86

Leviticus
Chs. 11-16   84

1 Samuel
2.26   65 n.70

1 Kings   26
18.40   25
21.17-29   25

2 Kings   26
1   25
1.9-12   25
2.19-22   84 n.43
2.23-4   25, 89
2.21   85 (*bis*)
4.38-41   87
4.42-4   87
5.20-27   25
6.1-7   87
6.15-23   90
6.18   25

Job
34.14-15   93

Psalms
33.9   90
104.29-30   93

Proverbs
30.4   86

NEW TESTAMENT

Matthew   18 n.102, 19, 26, 83 n.41, 49, 88 101
2.19-23   49
5.17-20   101
5.21-22   27
8.2-3   84 n.43
10.11-15   25
10.35-7   115
10.38-9   115
11.25   27
12.1-8   85 n.49
12.9-14   85 n.49
12.46-50   115
14.33   31, 53, 95
21.15-16   27
21.18-19   25, 26
21.18-22   87
21.19   88, 95
Ch. 23   115
28.17   95
5.17-20   101

Mark   15
1.44   84
2.23-8   85 n.49
3.4   70
3.5   58 n.48
10.14   58 n.48
11.12-14   88
11.12-22   25-6, 88
12.9-14   85 n.49

Index of Ancient Authors

Luke	7, 12, 15–18, 26–7, 33, 49, 51, 62–6, 76–8, 87, 95, 101, 105, 109, 117–18	5.21	86
		6.32	79 n.19
		6.33	79 n.19, 93
2.21-22	65 n.73	6.41	79 n.19
2.40	65, 77	6.42	79 n.19
2.41-52	7, 15–17, 50, 65, 76–8, 102, 105, 118	6.50	79 n.19
		6.51	79 n.19
2.42	17, 65	6.58	79 n.19
2.47	77	7.15	80
2.49	77	7.19-24	85 n.49
2.52	65, 77	7.21	80
3.2	88	7.27	90 n.71
3.9	88 n.65	7.34-6	90 n.71
3.23	17, 65	8.14	90 n.71
6.1-5	85 n.49	8.23	79 (bis)
6.6-11	85 n.49	8.56-8	78
6.9	70	9	85
7.11-17	63, 82 n.33	9.6	85
9.5	25	9.11	85
9.51-6	26	9.14	85
9.56	70	9.14-16	85 n.49
10.10-12	25	9.15	85
10.13-15	25	9.16	85
12.52-3	115	9.29	90 n.71
13.10-17	85 n.49	11.1-46	82 n.33
13.32	115	11.35	44
14.1-6	85 n.49	12.47	70
17.14	84	18:13-24	38, 88
18.35-43	63	18.19	38 n.79
24.27	77	18:22-3	38
24.32	77	18:24	88
24.45	77	20.22	93
24.52 (v.l.)	95 n.97		
		Acts	18, 26–7, 88, 114
John	11, 12, 16, 46, 62–3, 71–2, 76, 78–81, 85–6, 90, 99, 102–3, 118	4.6	88
		4.12-14	109 n.21
1.2	79	5.1-11	25
1.14	58	5.4,9	27
1.46	90	9.36-42	82 n.33
2.11	80	13.6-11	25, 90
3.3	79 n.19	13.9	27
3.7	79 n.19	13.11	27
3.13	79 n.19	14.8-18	112
3.15	81	15.21	106 n.8
3.27	79 n.19	19.11	79 n.19
3.31	79 (bis)	19.13	89 n.68
5.17	53	20.9-12	82 n.33
5.17-19	86	28.3-6	93

Romans
9.21   85 n.50

1 Corinthians   111
1.23-24   45
13.1   76, 92, 101
13.11   92

NEW TESTAMENT APOCRYPHA

Acts of John   99 n.119

Arabic Infancy Gospel   viii, 5, 8 n.45

Acts of Thomas
3   8 n.44
17   8 n.44
79   14 n.82

Epistula Apostolorum
4   8–10

Gospel of Pseudo-Matthew   18, 106
31.2   8 n.45
38.1   8 n.45

Gospel of Thomas   vii–ix, 3, 13–14, 97
4   14 n.82
9   14 n.82
40   88 n.65
77   14 n.82

Infancy Gospel of Thomas
Superscript   15 n.91, 18
Chapter 1
1   2, 20, 107
Chapter 2   2, 11
1   17, 50, 52, 57, 65, 84 (*bis*)
1-3   23
2   50, 57, 84–5
2-4   1, 105
3   85 (*bis*), 105
4   84, 85 n.51
5   82, 105
Chapter 3   1, 2, 11
1   85, 105 (*bis*)
1-3   88
2   53
3   38, 57

3.3-4.1   23, 57
Chapter 4   1, 2, 11
1   39, 41 n.92, 51, 57, 64, 82 (*bis*), 95
1-2   89
2   27, 82, 115
Chapter 5   2, 11
1   39, 57, 61
1-2   58
1-3   61, 115
2   44
3   53 (*bis*)
Chapter 6   2, 4 n.8, 10, 77
1   10
2   60
3   10, 58
4   59, 61 (*bis*), 76, 78, 101 (*bis*)
4-8   80
5   53, 57 n.42, 64, 82
6   64, 76, 78, 84 n.46, 115
7   50 n.10, 105
7-8   81
8   58, 60, 68, 100
9   8, 58, 68
15   33
Chapter 7   2
1-4   53, 61
2   79 (*bis*), 84 n.44, 92, 95
3   14 n.82, 44, 92, 95
4   68, 106
Chapter 8   2
1   59, 62 (*bis*), 67, 69, 79 (*bis*)
1-2   68, 94(*bis*)
2   24, 58 (*bis*), 68 (*bis*), 69, 81
Chapter 9   3, 59
1   50 (*bis*), 51(*bis*), 57(*bis*)
1-3   11, 94 (*bis*)
3   31, 95, 102, 106
Chapter 10   1, 3, 11, 86
1   65
1-2   51, 80 (*bis*)
2   51, 58, 80, 82, 95, 106
Chapter 11   1, 3, 11, 14 n.82, 87
1-2   53
Chapter 12   1, 3, 11, 87
1   8, 65

1-2	51, 106	Slavonic	5
2	51, 82, 87 (*bis*)	(Old) Irish	5, 17 n.101, 31 n.45, 94 n.95
Chapter 13	1, 3, 10, 58		
1-2	8, 9, 10	Syriac	v–vii, 5–7, 13, 15 n.91, 17 n.101, 18 n.104, 28, 69 n.87, 91 n.81, 97, 100
2	10, 53, 68		
3	115		
Chapter 14	3	**Protevangelium of James**	7, 18, 106–108
1-3	58		
2	33, 53, 64, 82, 105, 106	22	49
4	24, 68, 81, 94 (*bis*)		
Chapter 15	3	**Pseudo-Matthew**	
1-2	11, 13, 51	31.2	8
2	69, 70, 93 n.87	38.1	8
Chapter 16	3, 14 n.82		
1	11, 70	GRAECO-ROMAN AUTHORS	
1-2	69, 95	**Aeschylus**	
1-3	94 (*bis*)	*Prometheus Bound*	
3	64, 68, 70, 81–3, 95, 107	233-8	35
Chapter 17	3, 17, 63–5, 77		
1	17 (*bis*), 65	**Alcaeus**	
2	77	Frag. 308	40 n.89
3	77, 96, 101, 115		
4	82–3, 106, 107	**Antoninus Liberalis**	
5	68, 77, 106	23	40 n.89&90
Chapter 18	5, 6 n.32, 11, 82 n.33		
		(Pseudo-) Apollodorus	
Greek recensions		*Bibliotheca*	37 n.74, 40 n.89, 42 n.96&98
Ga	4-5, 11, 49 n.2, 58 n.49, 70 n.89, 80 n.24, 95, 100, 103 n.135, 105 n.1		
		2.1.3	36 n.67
Gb	4 n.9, 6, 13, 95	2.4.1-2	36 n.67
Gd	6 n.27, 13, 18, 58 n.49, 70 n.89, 80 n.24, 95, 102 n.133, 103 n.135, 105 n.1, 106 n.5	2.4.9	42 n.98
		2.8.2	36 n.67
		3.5.2	42 n.96
		3.5.5	36 n.67
(Egyptian Prologue)	5–6, 13, 18	3.10.2	40 n.89
Gs	vi, 2, 4, 6, 8–9, 15, 17 n.101, 18 n.4, 50, 58 n.49, 66, 79 n.18, 80, 82–3, 89, 91 n.81, 94, 95, 99 n.117, 105 n.1	**Apuleius**	
		Florida 19	94 n.92
		Athenaeus	
		Deipnosophistae	
Versions of the *Paidika*		10.454b-f	91
Aramaic	33		
Armenian	5	**Cypria**	
Ethiopic	5, 7 n.38	Frag. 1	35 n.66
Georgian	5		
Greek	v–vi, 3–7, 33, 49	**Diodorus Siculus**	
Latin	vi, 4–7, 13	3.67.2	42 n.98

Euripides
Bacchae 37-8
1346-9 37
Frag. 382 91
Helen
38-41 35
Hippolytus
48-50 36
1420-22 36
Orestes
1639-42 35

Herodotus
Histories 36-7, 46
1.32 36 n.70
1.86 36 n.71
4.40 36 n.70
7.10 36 n.70
7.46 36 n.70

Hesiod
Frag.
204.95-104 35 n.66

Homer 34-5, 39, 40, 43, 112-13
Iliad 35, 36, 42-3
1.518-23 43
5.318-430 43
5.426 43
5.814-898 43
6.130-40 42 n.97
8.18-28 113
14.315-28 43
Odyssey
8.266-366 43
10.306 112

Homeric Hymns 39-42
Hymn to Hermes 4 29, 39-44
13-18 40
46 41 n.92
296-7 44
389-90 44
405-6 44
Hymn to Hermes 18 39 n.85
Hymn to Dionysius 1 39 n.85
Hymn to Dionysius 7 39 n.85, 39-42
3 39 n.85
3-4 42
Hymn to Apollo 3 40
Hymn to Demeter 2 40

Horace
Carmen Saeculare
1.10.9-10 40 n.89

Hyginus
Astronomica
2.17 42 n.96
Fabulae
7 36 n.67
134 42 n.96
145 36 n.67
177 36 n.67

Julian
Against the Galilaeans
44A 35

Juvenal
Satires 13.93 90 n.72

Lucian 43
De Morte Peregrini
11-13 110
13 45 n.108
16 110
Fugitivi
19 67 n.80
Philopseudes
5 111 n.26
Vera Historia 20

Nonnus
Dionysiaca 46

Ovid 37
Metamorphoses
1.588-746 36 n.67
2.477-507 36 n.67
2.679-707 40 n.89
2.685-707 40 n.90
3.582-691 42 n.96

Philostratus
Imagines 1.26 40 n.89
Vita Apollonii 4.45 94 n.92

Pliny the Elder
Natural History
Book 20   93 n.85

Plutarch   15, 34–5, 66
De Superstitione
170 D-E   34-35

Porphyry
Christ.
Frag. 67   109

Quintilian
Institutes   50 n.10

Scholiast on the *Iliad*
15.256   40 n.89

Strabo
Geography
1.2.8   111–12

Tacitus
Histories
5.1-5   109 n.19

Valerius Maximus
Memorabilia
1.1.17   90 n.72

Xenophanes
Frag. 17   35 n.66

JEWISH AND LATE ANTIQUE WRITINGS
Apocryphon of Jeremiah 87

Artapanus of Alexandria
Frag. 3   25 n.12, 26

Josephus
Against Apion
2.175   106 n.12
Jewish Antiquities
14.22-24   25 n.12

Koran
3.49   32
5.110   32

Mishnah
Miqwa'ot
5.6   84 n.48
Niddah
5.6   50 n.3
Shabbat
7.2   38 n.80

Talmud
b.Berakhot
20.3   93 n.90
y.Berakhot
2.4   31 n.46
5.1   93 n.90
b.Sanhedrin
107b   32

Toledoth Jesu   31–2
15, 34-35   32

CHURCH FATHERS

Arnobius of Sicca
Adversus nationes
II.70   76 n.4

Augustine
City of God
22.8   111

Clement of Alexandria
Protrepticus
31   35–6

Cyril of Alexandria
Epistle 23   70 n.90

Epiphanius of Salamis
Panarion
51.20.2-3   11–12

Irenaeus
Adversus Haereses
1.20.1   8–12, 21
1.26.1   99 (bis)
2.21.4   60
2.32.4-5   89 n.68
3.11.8   1 n.2

Jerome
Commentarii in Joel
2.28   109

John Chrysostom,
Homily 17 on St. John   11–12, 21
Homily 4.4 on Colossians   67

Justin Martyr
Dialogue with Trypho
88.8   8
First Apology
15.7   109
16.4   109
66.3   111
67.3   111

Maximus the Confessor
Life of the Virgin
62   21

Minucius Felix
Octavius 19.15   112 n.29

Origen   31, 46, 93, 100, 110, 112
Celsus
1.9   110, 112 n.29
1.18   112 n.29
1.46   112 n.32
1.67   45–6
1.68   93
1.71   115 n.45, 112 n.32
2.55   94 n.92

2.49   112 n.32
2.63   46
2.70   46
2.76   31
3.26   94 n.92
3.32-3   94 n.92
3.44   109
3.49   109
3.55   109–10
3.75   109–10
5.15   112 n.29
5.19   112 n.29
5.29   112 n.29
5.59-60   109 n.20

Tertullian
Apologeticus
46.9   110
De praescriptione haereticorum
7   110
De testimonio animae
1   108 n.17
Adversus Praxean
3   1

GREEK PAPYRI
Greek Magical Papyri
PDM xiv. 563-74   92 n.85
PGM VII 193-6   92 n.85
PGM XVIIb 1–23   94 n.91
PGM XXVIII a-c   92 n.85
PGM CXII   92 n.85
PGM CXIII   92 n.85
Oxyrhynchus Papyri
1.119   51 n.15